THE LEGAL METHODOLOGY OF HAI GAON

Program in Judaic Studies
Brown University
BROWN JUDAIC STUDIES
Edited by
Jacob Neusner,
Wendell S. Dietrich, Ernest S. Frerichs,
Calvin Goldscheider, Alan Zuckerman

Project Editors (Project)

David Blumenthal, Emory University (Approaches to Medieval Judaism)
William Brinner (Studies in Judaism and Islam)
Ernest S. Frerichs, Brown University (Dissertations and Monographs)
Lenn Evan Goodman, University of Hawaii (Studies in Medieval Judaism) (Studies in
Judaism and Islam)
William Scott Green, University of Rochester (Approaches to Ancient Judaism)
Ivan Marcus, Jewish Theological Seminary of America
(Texts and Studies in Medieval Judaism)
Marc L. Raphael, Ohio State University (Approaches to Judaism in Modern Times)
Norbert Samuelson, Temple University (Jewish Philosophy)
Jonathan Z. Smith, University of Chicago (Studia Philonica)

Number 66
THE LEGAL METHODOLOGY OF HAI GAON

by
Tsvi Groner

THE LEGAL METHODOLOGY OF HAI GAON

by
Tsvi Groner

Scholars Press
Chico, California

THE LEGAL METHODOLOGY OF HAI GAON

by
Tsvi Groner

© 1985
Brown University

Library of Congress Cataloging in Publication Data

Groner, Tsvi.
  The legal methodology of Hai Gaon.

  (Brown Judaic studies ; no. 66)
  Bibliography: p.
  Includes index.
  1. Hai ben Sherira, 939–1038. 2. Geonic literature—History
and criticism. 3. Jewish law—Interpretation and construction.
I. Title. II. Series.
BM501.5.H35G76 1984   296.1'8   84–5566
ISBN 0-89130-748-6

Printed in the United States of America
on acid-free paper

For My Dear Parents

Who unselfishly enabled me to dwell in the tents of Torah.

CONTENTS

PREFACE

This is a study of the legal methodology of Hai ben Sherira (hereafter RHG = Rav Hai Gaon) (939-1038), Gaon of Pumbedita (1004-1038), who later Rabbis and scholars called "the last of the *geonim* in chronology, but the first in eminence." It is based primarily on Rav Hai Gaon's responsa. Responsa—rather than legal monographs — form the logical basis for our study because they most clearly and accurately reflect RHG's practical legal methodology. Responsa are normally meant to resolve a specific problem in a given situation which demands an immediate and succinct resolution. There are many sources from which the responder can draw his response. He may choose to draw from earlier legal literature, from existing codes, from precedence, from custom, intuition, common sense, etc. Use of any one source or a combination would be legitimate, and the responder might not even be consistent — using different sources in different responsa. This versatility might be especially true of the *geonim*, who did not have the benefit (or the hindrance) of a tradition of responsa literature to draw upon as did the later medieval Rabbis. With such a wide range of possibilities to choose from, the responder's personal methodology determined the source from which he would ulti- mately and effectively draw his response, and what that response would be. Hence, a study of these responsa, together with their sources, and how the response evolved from those sources, provides the most accurate means of reconstructing the responder's methodology.

Legal monographs alone, we have found, do not always give a totally accurate picture of their author's legal methodology. They do not address themselves to specific problems rising out of actual situations. The early legal monographs are mainly summations, reorganizations and explanations of the laws found scattered in the Talmud regarding a particular topic. Since they center on the Talmudic decision rather than revolving around any specific legal problems requiring a methodological solution, the author is not called upon to demonstrate the full spectrum of his methodology as he would have were he resolving actual problems.

In the case of Hai Gaon there are additional considerations for choosing responsa as the basis of methodological study: A large number of his responsa are extant (some fifteen hundred identifiable items containing whole responsa, fragments of or citations from responsa). Many of these are in their original language or form. RHG's monographs, on the other hand, significant as they might be for the history of post-Talmudic legal literature, are, for the most part, no longer extant (except for a few fragments and citations). The only two major works which we still have, exist in translation and somewhat abridged form. The responsa therefore, comprise a representative selection.

Even the later *geonim* did not yet have a truly developed tradition to aid them in replying to a questioner's question. We have already suggested this as a reason why their own personal bent, their own sensitivity as to how a religious leader should do this—i.e., their individual methodology—played such a central role in the penning of their responsa. The "responsa tradition" was first established by the *geonim* and, RHG's responsa in particular—so numerous and so often cited by ensuing generations—became the prototype for Jewish legal responsa literature. A study of his responsa, then, bears witness to the earliest development of interstitial Jewish law.

Geonic literature and institutions are intertwined with Talmudic ones, as we shall observe on many occasions. Throughout this study we shall watch Talmudic cases come alive and take on added dimension, serving RHG as points of departure for actual cases that he had to resolve hundreds of years after the completion of the Babylonian Talmud.

Many of RHG's responsa are known to us from collections of geonic responsa. Many others are known from the works of medieval Jewish scholars. Those scholars—particularly residents of the communities which had historical ties with the Babylonian Academies—repeatedly cited the *geonim*. Because of the esteem in which they held the *geonim* (Hai Gaon in particular), they exercised extreme care in order to insure accuracy in their citations and attributions. A number of them still held copies of the original responsa. Even those who did not, had the benefit of living traditions because of their relative proximity in time and location to the *geonim* and to the receivers of the responsa.

Fortunately for us, the medieval sages often recorded their discussions and interpretations of the words of the *geonim*, and these discussions are an excellent guide to the entire geonic period and a reliable source of material. We were also aided by the comments and notes of the editors of all the texts cited in the study or listed in the bibliography, as well as by the other studies cited and listed.*

This study had its inception as a Ph.D. dissertation at the Hebrew University under the supervision of Prof. S. Abramson from whom I learned much, as I did from all my teachers, colleagues (may I mention especially, Prof. Daniel Sperber), and students. My thanks to Haifa University, its publication committee, Plaut Foundation, and Wise chair, and to the Max Richter Foundation, for their aid. Mrs. Doris Kiel helped make this work more lucid than it might have otherwise been. Special thanks to Prof. Jacob Neusner, editor of this series, for his patience and encouragement. The dedication to my dear parents in only a token of my appreciation.

T.G.

---

*Regarding the remarks in the preface which are of a scholarly nature, see e.g.: *Hamaor*, *Gittin*, p. 74; RABD *Pessahim*, p. 15, n. b; RAMBAN, *Milhamot*, *Ketubot*, p. 21 a, *Gittin*, p. 30 b; J Mann, *Texts and Studies* 1, p. 631, p. 109, n. 2; S. Abramson, *Kelalei* . . . p. 13-14; H. Malter, *Saadia* . . . . , p. 278; S. Assaf, *Tequfat* . . . , pp. 217-19; *Tarbiz*, 16, p. 76; *Kirjath Sepher*, 26, p. 72 f.

ABBREVIATIONS AND ACRONYMS[*]

AZ	(Tractate) Abodah Zarah
AZA	Tractate Abodah Zarah, Ms. Jewish Theological Seminary, New York, 1957
b.	ben, ibn ("son of")
BB	(Tractate) Baba Batra
BBA	S. Abramson, Talmud Babli, Tractate Baba Batra
BEMERKAZIM	S. Abramson, Bemerkazim Ubitfuzot Bitqufat Hageonim
Ber.	(Tractate) Berakot
BGR	BiurHaGra, see Sulḥan Àruḳ
BHG	R. Simeon Qayara
BHM	Hamaor to the RIF
Bib. or Bibliog.	Bibliography
BM	(Tractate) Baba Mezia
BQ	(Tractate) Baba Qama
BT	Babylonian Talmud
BY	Beit Joseph (See Turim)
CP	Caftor Wa-pherach
DCA	A Digest of Commentaries on the Tractates . . . Aghmati
Deut.	Deuteronomy
DGK	Der Gaonaische Kommentar zur Mishnaordnung Teharoth
DRG	Die Rechtsgutachten der Geonim (BIB IA5).
ed. pr.	First Edition
EHE	Even Haezer section of Sulḥan Àruḳ
Einleitung	J. Muller, Einleitung in Die Responsen der Babylonischen Geonen
EJ	Encyclopedia Judaica
ET	Encyclopedia Talmudica
f. or ff.	following

---

[*] See also the acronyms in the register of names (persons 2). Standard abbreviations have not been included.

Geonica	V. 2 of Geonica, Genizah Studies by L. Ginzberg (Bib. IA13).
GKT	Der Gaonäische Kommentar zur Ordnung Tohoroth
GNK	Ginze Kedem
GNS	Genizah Studies 2, by L. Ginzberg (Bib. IA19)
GRA	Gaonic Responsa ed. S. Assaf Jerusalem, 1928 (Bib. IA18)
HG	Halachoth Gedoloth of Simeon Qayara, 5308 Venice or 5635 Warsaw ed.
HGB	Halachoth Gedoloth, 1888 Berlin ed.
HGHM	Hagahot Maimoniot
HGN	Hemda Genuzah (Bib. IA6)
Hildesheimer	E.E. Hildescheimer, Die Komposition...
HOM or HOSM	Hosen Mispat section of Sulhan Aruk
HP	Halachot Pesuqot
HS	Hilkot Shehitah
HSG	Halichische Schriften der Geonim (Bib. IA9)
IGRSG	Iggereth Rav Sherira Gaon
INYANOT	S. Abramson, Inyanot Besifrut Hageonim
Itim	Sepher Ha-Ittim
JJLG	Jahrbuch der Judische - Literarischen Gesellschaft (Frankfurt A.M.)
JQR	Jewish Quarterly Review
KELALEI	S. Abramson, Kelalei Hatalmud Bedivrei HaRamban
Ket.	(tractate) Ketubot.
KGE	Kurze Geonäische Entscheidungen (Bib. IA1)
KRS	Kirjath Sefer
LYCK	Geonic Responsa (Bib. IA7)
M	Mishnah, Misnah
Meg.	Megillah, scroll and Tractate
MGA	Magen Avraham. See Sulhan Aruk
MGWJ	Monatsschrift für Geschichte und Wissenschaft des Jüdentums
MH	Geonic Responsa, S. Assaf. Jerusalem 5687 (Bib. IA16).
Misifrut	Gaonica, 1933 (Bib. IA20)
MM	Magid Misneh

Mordecai	Pisqei Rav Mordekai
MPS	Mispetei Sebuot
MQ	(Tractate) Moed Qatan
MQM	Mekach Umemkar
Ms., mss.	manuscript(s)
MT	Mishneh Torah (Yad Hahazaqah)
n.	note
no.	number
NS	New Series
Num.	Numerei
o.b.m.	of blessed memory
OG	Otzar Ha Geonim (Thesaurus of the Geonic Responsa) (Bib. IA22)
OH	Orah Hayim, section of Sulhan Aruk
OHM	Otzar Hilluf Minhagim
ORH	Orchoth Chajim
OZ	Or Zarua
Pes.	(Tractate) Pesahim
pl.	Plural
Qid.	(Tractate) Qiddusin
R.	Rabbi
RABAD	Hasagot Harabad
RABIAH	Sefer Rabiah, R. Eliezer ben Joel ha Levi
RAN	Rabbi Nissim ben Reuben Gerondi
RDG	Responser der Geonim – A. Harkavy (Bib. IA10)
re	in regard to
REJ	Revue des Etudes Juives
RESPONSA	J. Mann, The Responsa of the Babylonian Geonim as a source of Jewish History.
RGA	Responsa Gaonica, ed. S. Assaf. Jerusalem, 1942. (Bib. IA21)
RH	(Tractate) Rosh Hashanah
RHG	Rav Hai Gaon
RIF	Halachot of R. Yitzhak Alfasi

RLOW	Responsen der Lehrer des Ostens und Westens (Bib. IA11)
RNG	S. Abramson, R. Nissim Gaon Libelli Quinque.
RSBG	Rabban Simeon ben Gamaliel
RSdG	Rav Saadya Gaon
RSG	Rav Serira Gaon
R. Yeruham	Toldot Adam Wehavah, Rav Yeruham b. Mesulam
SA	Sulhan Àruk
Sab.	(Tractate) Sabat
SAK	Siftei Kohen
	See Sulhan Àruk
SAN	(Tractate) Sanhedrin
SBHA (SBH)	Shibolei Haleket (R. Zidekiah b. Abraham Harofe)
SMA	Sefer Meirat Àynayim
	see Sulhan Àruk
s.n.	parallel reference are noted there
SRA	Seder R. Amram Gaon
SRSG	Siddur R. Saadiah Gaon
SS	Saarei Simhah
ST	Shaare Teshubah
	(Bib. IA4)
STA	Seder Tannaim ve Amoraim
STMQ	Sitah Mequbezet
SUA	S(h)ulhan Àruk
s.v.	sub voce ("under the word," see "under")
SZ	Saarei Zedeq (Bib. 1A3)
TAZ	Turei Zahav
	see Sulhan Àruk
Tequfat	S. Assaf, Tequfat Hageonim Wesifruta
The Jews	J. Mann, The Jews in Egypt and in Palestine Under the Fatimid Caliphs.
TMI	Temim Deim
TOSR	S. Lieberman, Tosefet Risonim.

TRY	Talmidei R. Jonah
T and S	J. Mann, Texts and Studies in Jewish History and Literature, V.I.
TTA	A. Hyman, Toldoth Tannaim ve'Amoraim
TTV	A. Hyman, Toldoth Tannaim ve'Amoraim
v.	"see" (vide)
V.	Volume
VL	R. Rabbinovicz, Variae Lectiones
Yeb.	(Tractate) Yebamot
YOD	Yoreh Deḥh
	Section of Sulḥan Ȧruk

KEY TO TRANSLITERATIONS

P	פ , ף	)	א
F	פ , ף	B	בּ
Ẓ	צ , ץ	B	ב
Q	ק	G	ג
R	ר	D	ד
Ṣ, (Sh)#	שׁ	H	ה
S	שׂ	V, W*	ו
Ṭ	טּ	Z	ז
T	ת	Ḥ	ח
		T	ט
		Y, J	י
		Ḳ	כ , ך
		K	כ , ך
		L	ל
		M	מ , ם
		N	נ , ן
		S	ס
		(	ע

---

*The letter "vav" (ו) as connecting preposition is W, and as consonant V.

#The letter "shin" (ש) is sometimes transliterated as Ṣ, and sometimes Sh in cases where the word is commonly used in English, e.g. Shofar, Mishnah, kosher, etc.

INTRODUCTION

Anyone even faintly familiar with Jewish law and practice of the past millennium appreciates that it is largely derived from the Babylonian Talmud (BT). Few stop to ask what brought this about; from what point in history has it been so? Who considers the question: How did the supremacy of the Babylonian Talmud evolve? The extraordinary feat of its compilation certainly did not generate force enough to accomplish this. Intrinsically it is neither a legal codex nor a handbook of Jewish custom and practice, but rather a compilation of oral-law material studied in the amoraic academies. Only the Rabbis, scholars, codifiers, judges and religious leaders of later years turned it into the principal source for Jewish legal and religious development. Our question, then, is "when and how did this come about?"

For an answer we must look to the *geonim* (sing. *gaon*) and the geonic period. *Gaon,* when used as a technical term—and that is how we shall use it—is the title that was given to the heads of the two leading Babylonian (Iraqi) Talmudic academies (Sura and Pumbedita) from the end of the sixth century until the middle of the eleventh (the geonic era). The Palestinian academy heads also used the title. Only later was the title used honorifically for other important Rabbis, but even then, within the academies the title was reserved for the academy heads. More recently in Jewish history—and down to our day—the title became so widespread that it lost its meaning.

The title *gaon* is derived from the full name of the academies, *Yeshivat Gaon Ya^cakob,* which in turn is taken from a verse in Psalms (47, 4), "He shall choose . . . the pride [*gaon*] of Jacob whom he loved." Jacob, is, of course, synonymous with Israel. *Gaon,* in the verse, can be alternately translated "glory" or "excellence." So, the *gaon* is the excellency of all of Israel. Originally, the full appellation was, "head of the *Gaon Ya^cakob* academy." Eventually it was shortened to just *gaon* (this is the proper historical explanation, popular legend regarding the derivation of the term not withstanding).

The *geonim* were indeed the pride, the glory, and the excellencies of Israel throughout the geonic era. They were the acknowledged religious leaders, spiritual guides, legal authorities, mentors and instructors not only of the Babylonian communities, but of all the Jewish communities within the Babylonian sphere of influence during this period. This meant spiritual leadership of almost all the major

1

Jewish communities of the time—from Spain and parts of Asia minor down through the Maghreb (Morocco, Algeria and Tunisia of today), the majority of the Egyptian congregation, through Iraq itself, and out to Persia and the surroundings. In the eyes of members of any of these communities, that group included all the Jewish communities that really mattered. Actually it meant all of the "Spanish" and "Oriental" (eastern) communities which were not in the Palestinian sphere of influence.

The *yeshivot* of the *geonim* were the centers of learning of the Jewish world and the seminal points of its legal and literary creativity. The aspiring young scholars of Iraq made their way to the academies' study halls, where they were joined by the most promising talent from all the communities connected with the academies, even the most distant ones. The cream of Jewish youth came because of their conviction that they could never reach the pinnacle of understanding the Torah, the spectrum of Jewish knowledge, without coming under the personal tutelage of the heads of the Babylonian academies. The most illustrious scholars and eminent communal leaders would send their own sons to study at the geonic academies thereby enhancing the prestige and the erudition of the young men, and simultaneously cementing the bonds which linked the outlying communities with the academies. So great was the reputation of the geonic academies and so significant the instruction received there, that even communities outside the Babylonian sphere of influence sent their students there. During the gaonate of Hai and his father, Serira, their Pumbedita academy accommodated the sons of the heads of the Jewish communities of Italy, Sicily, Asia Minor, France and even Palestine itself, in addition to the usual flow from Spain, North Africa, and Egypt (see S. Assaf, *Tequfat Hageonim Wesifrutah* [henceforth Tequfat] p. 43).

Students who had attended the academies would normally maintain some communication with them throughout their lives. Ample opportunity was offered for this. Those who became judges were usually appointed by or came under the jurisdiction of one or the other of the academies. The academies' courts also heard cases too difficult for local judges to handle, served as a court of appeals, and took on cases in which one of the contestants insisted on appearing before it rather than before the local judge. If a former student served as Rabbi of a congregation, he would often refer his difficult questions to the *geonim* or other scholars in the academy for their advice and opinion before acting. Laymen, too, were given sufficient opportunity to maintain ties with their alma mater. Twice a year, during the months of Adar (the month preceding Passover, the spring festival) and Elul (the final month of the year, in the autumn), the academies conducted *kalah** months. During these months the activities of the academies were designed more for the public at large, than for the matriculated students, whose interests were catered to during the rest of the year. Anyone wishing to attend could spend the full month or any portion of it at the academy. The syllabus during these months was one of the tractates of the Babylonian Talmud. At the close of each *kalah* month, notification was given of the tractate to be studied at the next *kalah*, giving the participants ample opportunity for preparation. During the *kalah* the regular staff and senior students of the academy lectured and led discussions on different levels about the prescribed tractate and topics related to it. Thus each participant found his proper framework, whether he was a layman with minimum Talmudic knowledge or an accomplished scholar coming to renew his connection with the academy.

The *kalah* months served their purpose well enough for those who lived close to the academies and had the time to participate. But what of those unable to participate because of distance or some other reason? How were they meant to communicate with the academy? And what is a "nearby" scholar meant to do if he wishes to solicit the advice and opinion of the academy, but lives too far to just "drop in," and the *kalah* months are still far off? In these cases communication was maintained by what historical perspective regards as the major literary institution and most significant contribution of the geonic era: geonic responsa—written questions and replies. Petitioners would usually accumulate a few queries which they wanted to ask the *geonim*, and send them on to the academy in one missive. Nearby communities did not normally have difficulties in finding a way to transmit the questions to the geonim as there were usually enough travelers willing to submit the queries personally. Hence, these communities could send only a few at a time, and could send them directly. The more distant congregations were apt to gather a larger number of questions together, and send them off to the nearest official representative of the academy. He, in turn, would forward them to the academy together with other official communications, whenever he

---

*The etymology of *kalah* (beauty, bride, rules, general, paragon, principle, etc.) is still undecided. See, most recently, our note in ALEI SEFER 8, p. 21, n. 79.

might find a caravan traveling in that direction. Contributions, both to the *geonim* and to the academies would, as a rule, be sent together with the questions.

Questions arriving in a group would be answered as a group, in the same order. The *geonim* took great pains to get the responsa off as quickly as possible, returning them to the questioners through the same channels in which they arrived, and in the language asked, Judeo-Arabic, or geonic aramaic, the more distant congregations receiving their responsa via the representatives of the academy (see our article in ALEI SEFER, 2). Thousands of such responsa are known to us.

What topics did these questions and responsa cover? Many were requests for advice on temporal issues, particularly communal organization and affairs. Others dealt with various facets of religious life and activity. Some solicited exegesis of books of the Bible or specific verses, others commentary and explanation of some talmudic text—a difficult tractate, *sugya*, passage, or word—or of early rabbinic material. Doctrinal issues— philosophy, beliefs and opinions of Judaism—were also dealt with. The majority of the questions, however, sought the *gaon's* decision in matters of *halakah*—Jewish law which embraces every aspect of individual, public, and communal life. Among the thousands of known geonic responsa we find questions and replies dealing with the following topics, inter alia: prayer and benedictions, Sabbath and Festivals, ritual slaughter of animals, prohibited and permitted foodstuffs, burial and mourning, marriage, divorce, dowry *(ketubah)*, locus and interest, purchases, sales and rentals, inheritance, wages and salaries, business transactions, court procedures, judges, witnesses, election and appointment of communal officials, etc.

The tone of the questions and their panegyrical exordia leave little doubt as to an absolute acceptance of the *gaon's* authority. It is apparent that all parties felt bound by whatever solution the *geonim* would advise. When we view the large number of questions addressed to the *geonim,* coming from so many different communities and covering such a wide range of topics, and recall that in each case the *gaon's* word was law, we begin to perceive the weight of geonic influence and authority. The picture emerges of profound leadership acknowledged throughout the Jewish communities. This point was by no means lost on the *geonim* themselves. They had a clear understanding of their position, hegemony, and authority (even stylistically, they used the *pluralis majestis).*

What was the source of this authority? The *geonim* regarded the Talmudic sages,

the Babylonian *amoraim*, as the supreme authority universally acknowledged throughout
Jewry.   As they considered themselves direct successors of those sages, their own
authority was a direct derivative. Historically we find much to support this approach.
An accurate chronological account of the period will reveal that the *amoraim* were in
fact followed by a group of little known sages called the *saboraim*, who gave final
literary form to the Babylonian Talmud.   Their original contributions are not usually
deemed significant by scholars (see Julius Kaplan, *The Redaction of the Babylonian
Talmud*, New York, 1933, chapters 21, 22, 25).   Hence, it is not surprising that their
periods are often thought of as an extension of the amoraic era. Therefore the *geonim*
can be considered direct successors of the Babylonian *amoraim* not only spiritually but
historically as well.

The succession had a physical–geographical dimension as well.   The geonic
community dwelt in the same area as the amoraic one, an area not given to rapid
change.   Overall conditions were therefore very similar.   Even after the academies
moved from Sura and Pumbedita to Baghdad—to be near the nerve center of caliphate
activity—they still retained the names and customs of Sura and Pumbedita. Change of
locale was insignificant. The amoraic academies, too, had left Sura and Pumbedita when
occasion demanded and nonetheless retained their original names and customs.   The
major institutions of the Babylonian Jewish communities during the geonic era were a
carry over from amoraic times (compare David Goodblatt, *Rabbinic Institution in
Sasanian Babylonia*, Leiden, 1975).   The functions of the Exilarch, academy heads, and
communal judges, were structured as they had always been. The *kalah* months which
involved the whole community in the affairs of the academy were a throwback to
talmudic days. For this reason, the *geonim* felt that their status as academy heads was
substantially no different from that of the *amoraim*. If the *amoraim* were undisputed and
uncontested authorities, then so were they.

Demarcation lines between eras sometimes appear more distinct from a historical
perspective than they did at the time of the events. At other times a second glance at
such lines reveals arbitrary, even muddled, markings of some earlier historian. In either
case we cannot fault a contemporary figure for lacking sensitivity to the transition from
his era to another. It is in this light that we should judge the *geonim* when they
sometimes regard the whole span from the third to the eleventh centuries as one

continuous time unit, resulting in their reserving privileges for themselves, that we might think the *amoraim* alone were entitled to.

The blurring of distinction between two eras exists even in the *Epistle of R. Serira Gaon*—that classic of medieval Jewish historiography, which served as the basis for much later historical research. Historians normally begin an account of the geonic era with R. Hanan of Asqiya in 589. This practice is based on a passage in the *Epistle* (pp. 99-100): "And these are the *geonim* who were in our city of Pumbedita after those events, towards the end of the Persian empire from the [Seleucidean] year 900 [589 C. E.]: Master R. Hanan of Asqiya and after him. . . ." Nevertheless, RSG does not hesitate to apply the appellation *gaon* to earlier academy heads. Thus, R. Joseph remained *gaon* in the academy a number of years (*Epistle*, p. 99), "And afterwards there was R. Ribai of Rub from our academy and there are those that say he was a *gaon*" (ibid.). Now, RSG is not saying that R. Ribai was a *gaon* in the narrow technical sense of the word. What this passage means is simply that there was a tradition—which RSG was unable to confirm—that this noted *sabora* was also the head of the Pumbedita academy (i.e., *gaon*, v. Lewin, n. 7). Thus we find no basis for the view that RSG is intimating here that some sages thought that the geonic era commenced with R. Ribai (compare EJ 7, 315). If the mere use of the term "*gaon*" were a correct indication, we would have to begin with R. Joseph (supra) and even with R. Asi of whom RSG writes, "During all these years after R. Papa, R. Asi was *gaon* in Sura" (*Epistle*, p. 90). Obviously then, as far as RSG is concerned, *gaon* is simply the appellation of the head of the academy. He makes no distinctions between the amoraic, saboraic, or geonic epochs. In fact it is highly doubtful whether he really means to designate R. Hanan as the first *gaon*. What he rather seems to state is that R. Hanan was the Pumbedita academy's first head after it reopened in its ancestral home following the Persian persecution. We are thus unable to find a clear statement in the *Epistle* which points out a demarcation line between the saboraic and geonic eras.

We draw the same conclusion from the verb RSG uses to mean "serve as academy head": *MLK* (literally, "reigned"). He applies it equally to what we consider all three periods (amoraic, saboraic, geonic), which again, implies that RSG does not distinguish one from the other. The same holds true for RSG's descriptions of Babylonian (Jewish) socio-religious institutions. They are not typically descriptive of any one period, but convey the impression that they are intentionally applicable to the whole period from the time of the institution's inception right down to RSG's time, with few exceptions. Such, for example, is his portrait of *Rigla Sabbath*, when the Exilarch would lecture at Sura, or similarly the Exilarch's official residence and authority (see ibid., pp. 90–92). Indeed the whole narrative of the *Epistle* is one continuous flow from Talmudic times through the saboraic era on to the geonic period right up until RSG's own day, with no change of style, mood, or terminology. In this continuum of development, it is difficult and perhaps methodologically wrong, to pinpoint a transition between the three periods on a chronological level. Perhaps we should best consider the *amoraim*, *saboraim*, and *geonim* from a literary rather than chronological point of view.

These references in the *Epistle* illustrate most vividly how the *geonim* viewed themselves as a link in the chain of tradition and authority emanating from the *amoraim*. They undertook their role without tension, conflict, or strife, feeling no need for self assertion. Their position and authority—in their eyes—derived directly from that of the *amoraim*. This was not merely delusive self-appraisal. The correspondence between the communities and the *geonim*, the many epistles exchanged on such a variety of issues, the requests for advice and decisions on divergent topics, the readiness to accept geonic decree as binding law, the voluntary contributions forwarded to maintain the living standard of the *geonim* and the academies, all indicate that Jewish communities within the Babylonian sphere of influence held the *geonim* in greater esteem than perhaps even the *geonim* themselves realized.

For this esteem the *geonim* were indebted to the Babylonian *amoraim* and their creation—the Babylonian Talmud (as we have explained)—and the debt was repaid in full. Thus, we are now closer to an answer to our opening question: What caused the supremacy of the Babylonian Talmud? We have already suggested that the most significant contributing factor was the responsa, so let us examine further their composition. The majority of the questions were requests for authoritative decisions on points of day-to-day Jewish law *(halakah)*. The *gaon* was expected to provide a distinct and authoritative response. Now, by its very nature a responsum of this sort differs from an academic discourse or from a legal code. It differs in that it deals with only one question, one which it must resolve immediately and succinctly. The respondent cannot hide behind literary niceties. The solution must be practical and in keeping with the mainstream of legal thought, custom, and practice. As the basis of his decision the respondent may use intuition, literary sources, prevalent custom, tradition, precedent, analogies, or any other resource, guided by his own legal philosophy and methodology. Whatever his choice of source, it is construed as a sign of what he deems significant, and it is assumed that he will base his decision on the most authoritative resource available. The communities were sensitive to all of this and, receiving a large number of responsa and being cognizant of the sources themselves, were able to discern the ultimate authorities upon which the respondents based their adjudication.

In the case of the geonic responsa which were these ultimate authorities? The *geonim* mostly based their rulings on the Babylonian Talmud. No matter what the question, the *geonim* would turn for guidance and direction to it. Could a solution be gleaned from among its numerous and lengthy discussions? In some geonic responsa detailed discourses explain how the decision was arrived at out of the Talmud. In addition to the responsa, the *geonim* based all their legal works chiefly on the Babylonian Talmud. The texts either followed the Talmud chapter by chapter or comprised rearrangements of its legal discussions. By setting up the Babylonian Talmud as their ultimate source in their responsa and other legal works, and driving the point home through the sheer numerical volume of the responsa, the *geonim* established the Babylonian Talmud as the primary authority for rulings on points of Jewish law *(halakah)* among all the communities which came under their influence.

The central position accorded the Babylonian Talmud was not confined just to literary activity. During the *kalah* months in the academy—the main periods of mass education—the lectures, discussions and instruction all revolved around one of the tractates of the Babylonian Talmud. Throughout the academic year, when the geonic academies catered to the aspiring young scholars of Babylonia (Iraq) and the entire Jewish world, again the syllabus was the Babylonian Talmud, its exegesis and traditions. Consequently, all those trained in the geonic academies were imbued with the spirit of the Babylonian Talmud and regarded it as the basis for study and instruction. This spirit and regard were subsequently disseminated among the communities in whose midst those academy graduates dwelt, whether in an official religious capacity or as lay leaders.

The influence of the *geonim* was not bound by space nor time. Their responsa, legal treatises, and talmudic exegesis became prototypes which Jewish savants utilized throughout the ages. Later Rabbis, scholars, judges, and codifiers perpetuated the geonic tradition maintaining the Babylonian Talmud as the main basis of legal decisions and instruction, even in geographical areas like Europe which were not initially under geonic domination or influence. Thus, the Babylonian Talmud was established as the supreme authority in matters of Jewish law, practice, and tradition by the unique interaction of forces between the *geonim* and the Talmud itself, abetted by the profound influence they exerted on their own and succeeding generations.

Theoretically, had the *geonim* chosen some other source—literary or other—as the basis for their responsa, codes and instruction in the academy, that source might have achieved the status currently enjoyed by the Babylonian Talmud. But in reality this could never have occurred. It was inevitable that the *geonim*, who were steeped in Babylonian tradition and saw themselves as an extension of the Babylonian *amoraim*, should choose the Babylonian Talmud as their central source of reference. Realistically, no other possibility existed. Thus, we arrive at the phenomenon of a mutual, self-renewing conferment of status. On the one hand, the *geonim* derived their authority from being a continuation of the Babylonian *amoraim* and their Talmud. On the other hand, these very same *geonim* firmly and finally established that it be the Babylonian Talmud which would occupy the central position in Jewish religious and legal instruction and learning. And it was their literary activity which determined that future development of Jewish law and practice should derive principally from that same Babylonian Talmud.

RAV HAI GAON

His Life and Literary Heritage

Rav Hai[1] Gaon [hereafter RHG] (939-1038)[2] was the son of a *gaon* (Serira), the grandson of a *gaon* (Haninah), and the great-grandson of a *gaon* (Judah), all of the Pumbedita Academy. Although the prominence of certain Babylonian families in the academies led to a number of father-son combinations in the geonate, [3] RHG is the only known case of a fourth generation *gaon*. RSG and RHG descended from an exilarchic family which gave up its exilarchic claims and functions because of the unethical behavior of the exilarchs, and preferred to serve as academy heads (IGRSG 92-93). They claimed Davidic ancestry. RHG's seal had in it the figure of a lion, corresponding to the figure of the lion on the standard of the tribe of Judah and of Judean kings. This seal was to indicate Hai's descent from the royal house of David.[4]

With such a lineage RHG was early steeped in the tradition of the Babylonian academies. Indeed, from a relatively young age he was groomed for the post he was destined to attain, particularly by aiding his father in correspondence, literary activity, and especially by helping with the instruction of the students.[5] The culmination of his training was his appointment—by his father—*Av-Bet-Din* (head of the court), second in the hierarchy of the Academy, in 985. He eventually succeeded his father to the geonate in 1004, two years before RSG's death.[6]

RHG was instrumental in helping his father raise the Academy from the disorganization and decline in which he found it, and reestablishing its central position as the major seat of learning and authority in the Jewish world (v. T and S, 87-88). For the most part, the rebuilding was accomplished by the time RHG ascended to the geonate, so that he had no really serious problems to grapple with during his reign (except for an occasional financial or political crisis, v. e.g., T and S, 90; 115). The rivalry with the sister academy at Sura had also been resolved during RSG's tenure by RHG's marriage to the daughter of the eminent *gaon* of Sura, R. Samuel b. Hofni.[7] In contrast with earlier *geonim* and more difficult times, we find no serious complaints from RHG during his geonate about any long-term financial difficulties, nor are there any hints of problems with the outlying communities (with the possible occasional exception of Spain) regarding authority, communication or cooperation. On the contrary, the picture we get is one of status and authority. Hence he was able to devote his efforts to the needs of the Academy, to the disemmination of law and learning both in the Academy and in writing and to fostering close relationships with Jewish communities near and far.

These efforts bore fruit. From the seat of his Academy in Baghdad,[8] RHG maintained close and warm relationships with all the important Jewish communities and their leaders—lay and spiritual. For most of them, RHG was the undisputed religious leader and authority. First and foremost among these was, naturally, the whole of his own Babylonian (Iraqi) community (v. e.g., Mann, RESPONSA [13] f.], which traditionally accepted the Academy head as its spiritual leader. The most special of the relationships with the communities outside of Iraq was with that of the Maghreb, particularly with the circle of the Academy of R. Jacob b. Nissim and R. Nissim b. Jacob in Kairouan.[9] There were also close relationships with the Babylonian orientated community in Egypt (Fustat) and its spiritual leaders, Shmarya b. Elhanan, Elhanan b. Shmarya, and Sahlan b. Abraham.[10] RHG even managed to maintain cordial relations with the community in Palestine. At least one of its leaders acknowleged the supremacy of Hai's Academy, by sending his son to study there.[11]

The Pumbedita Academy in Baghdad attained great heights during RHG's reign, and drew multitudes of students from all over Iraq, from the communities under the cultural influence of the Babylonian academies, and even from communities outside of it. In the latter, the heads of the community would set the tone by sending their sons to study under Hai, in recognition of the academic excellence of his Academy. We find mention of students from such places as Iraq, North Africa, Egypt, Spain, Byzantium, Italy, Sicily and Palestine.[12] As noted poetically by Samuel HaNagid (cit., n. 2), the great attention R. Hai heaped upon the students was somewhat of a substitution for the son he did not leave.

The ultimate measure of influence and authority RHG achieved in his lifetime is the vast number of responsa he sent to questions posed to him—by Rabbis, by leaders, and individuals from all walks of life—from the divergent communities: Iraq, North Africa, Egypt, Spain, Persia, the Arabian Gulf, Italy, and the Byzantine Empire. The questions covered a wide range of topics: all aspects of Jewish religious and "civil" law (e.g., Sabbath, holidays, prayer and benedictions, ritual slaughter, prohibited foodstuffs, usury, purchase and sale, rentals, marriage and divorce, dowry, etc.); requests for commentaries and explanations of Talmudic and Biblical passages; advice on communal appointments and administration. The degree of his authority is underscored by the willingness of the questioners—*a priori*—to accept his decisions on all these matters. RHG's share of the identified geonic responsa is out of any proportion to the length of his geonate. Some fourteen hundred responsa, about a third of all the identifiable geonic responsa, can be attributed to RHG, or to RHG and RSG jointly. These responsa are found in all the important collections of geonic responsa (see the bibliography) in print or in manuscript. Whole responsa of RHG or segments thereof are cited profusely, with great admiration and respect, by the leading medieval authors who had access to geonic material and traditions (e.g., RH, RNG, RIF, Ibn Ghayat (SS), Itim, Ittur, RMBN, R. Zachariah Aghmati, etc.). A detailed study of these responsa forms the bulk of the present work.

RHG's second most important literary activity (after his responsa) was the composition of monographs on specific legal topics, in the footsteps of the great Sura *geonim*, R. Saàdya,[13] and Hai's father-in-law, R. Samuel b. Hofni. Like them, he wrote the monographs in Arabic. They were composed before he assumed the geonate, and became popular immediately (RHG himself was asked detailed questions about minute points in them);[14] another sure sign of RHG's status in the Jewish world.

The most important and famous of RHG's monographs is his TREATISE ON PURCHASE AND SALE ("*Aṣara w'al Bua^c*." Hebrew: "*Ha Meqaḥ we Ha Memkar*" [hereafter MQM]). In its sixty chapters RHG attempts to cover every aspect of the topic (e.g., what items may be sold; by whom; on what days; how is a sale consummated, etc). Already in RHG's lifetime MQM became very popular. It was translated into Hebrew some forty years after his death by R. Isaac b. Reuben of Barcelona. This translation provides the text for the published version of MQM (ed. pr. Venice, 5362). There exists in manuscript another translation, abridged but more literal. Great chunks of the Arabic original were found in the Cairo Genizah (see Abramson, cited n. 14). To this day MQM is considered the finest work on the topic of sales, and is still referred to by codifiers, responders, and commentators when discussing relevant points. It is a classic in the genre of legal monographs.

His second important monograph—composed before MQM—is *KITAB AL AIMEN* (Hebrew: *Mispetei Sebuot*), the Treatise on Oaths (hereafter MPS). In this work RHG strives to arrange and explain in detail all the Talmudic law and much of the geonic tradition and custom regarding oaths taken in a courtroom. He divides the work into two sections: oaths of the respondent and oaths of the claimant. MPS encompasses both Mosaic and Rabbinic oaths. This work too, gained immediate popularity and RHG was queried about what he wrote in it. An anonymous Hebrew translation—perhaps translated during RHG's lifetime—was published in Venice in 5362. Large segments of the Arabic original are extant in Genizah fragments. The work is cited extensively by later Rabbis.

His other published work is a treatise on court documents (SEFER HAṢTAROT) published from manuscripts by S. Assaf (as a supplement to TARBIZ, 1, Jerusalem, 5690). The original work contained the texts of 28 documents, prefaced by brief descriptions, with connecting statements.

We now give a list of other monographs of RHG no longer extant. Citations from some were found in medieval works, an occasional fragment was rescued in The Genizah, some are known just from mention in medieval literature or in ancient book lists.

A. MANNERS OF THE JUDGES (Adab al Qada. Hebrew: "Musar Hadayanim")— Customs, procedures, and manners of judges, and laws relevant to court administration and procedure. The work contained at least fourteen chapters. Judging from the number of citations and fragments, it was quite well known in medieval times.[15]

B. ABBUTTERS' RIGHTS (Kitab a Ṣufàh)—Cited a number of times by medieval authors and in book lists.[16]

C. A TREATISE ON THE LAWS OF RITUAL SLAUGHTER (Hilḳot Sheḥitah) which also included laws of terefah. It is mentioned only once in Rabbinic literature, but it is mentioned by a Karaite author too, and in a book list.[17]

D. MATTERS PERMITTED AND PROHIBITED (Inyanim be Issur Ve Heter)—The paucity of citations makes it impossible to draw a clear picture as to the breadth of the work.[18]

E. "Laws of Phylacteries"—Seems not to be a full fledged work, but rather a short essay on just certain aspects of the laws of phylacteries. Fragments were published in GNK 3 and 4.

RHG's most significant non-legal work is Al-Hawi, a Biblical-Talmudic dictionary. Fragments have been published and yet others await publication. See S. Abramson,

LESHONENU 41, p. 108 f.

RHG (alone or in collaboration with RSG) composed commentaries of various sorts on a number of Talmudic tractates (sometimes only to specific words, *sugyot*, or chapters). Most were in response to requests, or were arrangements of what had originally been responses to requests. Among the tractates to which (at least partial) commentaries have reached us, are: Berakot,[19] Shabbat,[20] Hagigah,[21] Avoda Zara,[22] Baba Batra,[23] and Ḥullin (an explanation of words).[24]

RHG also left a considerable poetic legacy. *Sämmtliche Gedichte Rab Hai Gaon . . . der gelehrten J. Reifmann, J. M. Senders*, was published in Lemberg, 5649. A partial collection with a detailed introduction summarizing the material was published by H. Brody in *Studies of the Research Institute for Hebrew Poetry*, vol. 3, p. 3 f. A supplement to RHG's poetic collection was published by E. Fleischer in SINAI 67, p. 180–198. Most recently, Y. Hasidah published *RESHUYOT LEPARSHIOT HATORAH* attributed to RHG (Jerusalem, 1976). See his Introduction, especially p. 5.

Epistles of RHG have been published in various forums, especially by J. Mann (T and S, THE JEWS, and RESPONSA), S. Abramson (*BEMERKAZIM* and TARBIZ 31) and B. M. Lewin (supplements to IGRSG). See also OG Qiddushin 419.

We have surveyed RHG's rich literary output, much of which has reached us, and we have noted that even the contemporary scholar can learn much from it. Even the works which are no longer extant are quite well attested to and documented. We were also able to paint a fairly detailed portrait of his activity as head of the Academy and as religious leader of the Jewish communities. In contrast, we have very little biographical information on his long life except for the most basic data. At first glance this might be said to be ironic; but at further glance perhaps not, since the Jewish people have always identified their religious and spiritual leaders with their literary work and spiritual-religious-communal activities; their private lives never were of great interest. So, too, regarding RHG; to his people, his historical essence was his works, and they, together with accounts of the grandeur of the Academy, have largely been preserved. About the man, all we can say, in broad terms, is that he seems to have been well versed in the general knowledge befitting a scholar of his time.[25] We will pay little attention to the various legends and popular traditions regarding his life and death—though the tradition regarding his eternal resting place in "Sinai" may contain a historical element.[26]

RHG was the last of the "grand" *geonim,* who reigned in splendor. He was highly esteemed not only by his contemporaries—who turned to him with their questions and problems, accepting his decisions and responsa as decisive and authoritative—but also by the great medieval Rabbis who cited these responsa regularly and had their Rabbinic thought molded by them. His influence on these later Rabbis can readily be seen throughout the present work, in the numerous citations of RHG responsa from the works of these medieval Rabbis, and especially in the many discussions and decisions which they based on those cited passages. We know that RHG attained a ripe age and served for many years as Gaon in the Academy. He was thus able to mold the geonate in his own style and exert a profound far-reaching influence on his younger contemporaries and on ensuing generations.

SOURCES OF AUTHORITY

Tradition and Practice

The quasi-regal status of the geonim was derived from the traditional chain of authority of Israel as we have described. Hai, last of these majestic dignitaries, "reciprocated", as it were, by establishing the chain of tradition as the ultimate authority in questions of law and religious practice. Just as the "Community of Israel" traditionally sought religious and spiritual leadership in the Babylonian academies for almost a millennium, so did the last great head of those academies—Hai—recognize the tradition of that community as ultimately authoritative in matters of religious practice.[1] For he realized that any such practice is undoubtedly deeply rooted in the unbroken chain of tradition of Jewish oral law.[2]

An example of his invoking this tradition as an authority is found in his exposition on the universally accepted order and number of the notes sounded when blowing the *shofar* on the New Year Festival. RHG was asked by the disciples of R. Jacob b. Nissim of Kairouan (OG RH 117) to clarify his stand regarding the various Amoraic innovations recorded in the Babylonian Talmud (RH 33b f.), and what—in his mind—was the accepted practice before those innovations. The Gaon replies (ibid., pp. 61-2):

> That practice by which we fulfill our obligation and the will of our creator is established and certain in our hands. That which we do is a legacy which has been deposited, transmitted,[3] and received in tradition from fathers to sons, for continuous generations in Israel from the days of the prophets unto the present time. Namely, that we blow (the *shofar*) while sitting, according to custom and then—while standing during the order of the Benedictions[4]—we again blow three notes three times. This is the current law, and it is simple and widespread throughout all of Israel. Since this is the established common practice in our hands, and the law transmitted to Moses on Sinai is that the obligation is thus fulfilled, all difficulties therein have vanished.

The ideological justification for citing tradition as the absolute authority and best proof of the veracity of practice is found a few lines further on in the responsum:

> How do we know at all that we are commanded to blow [the *shofar*] on this day? Moreover, regarding the essence of the written law, how

are we to know that it is indeed the Mosaic law, that which he [Moses] wrote through Divine Revelation, if not through the mouths of the Community of Israel. Behold then, it is these very same mouths which testify as to the veracity of the Mosaic Law, which testify equally that by our actions we fulfilled our obligations and that thus has it been transmitted[3] to them by tradition from the mouths of the prophets, as Law transmitted to Moses in Sinai. Indeed it is the words of the multitude which stand to prove the authenticity of each mishnah and every Gemara. Greater than any other proof is to go out among the people and see how they act, "go out and see the custom of the folk" [Ber. 45a, s.n. in matters of ritual]. Herein lies the essence and the authority. Only afterwards do we examine all that has been discussed in the Mishnah or Gemara about this issue. All conclusions derived from them which are compatible with how we are minded are perfectly fine, but if there is anything which is not quite in keeping with our understanding—and cannot be clearly proven—it cannot uproot the roots. It is incumbent that we look upon that root not on account of any specific need concerning the performance of the commandment. Behold that root furnishes itself with the greatest proof of its authenticity, the fact that it has been perpetuated, just as a law transmitted to Moses in Sinai.

This responsum, then, contains RHG's credo as to the ultimate source of authority and the guideline for ruling.

Despite the significance RHG attaches to the tradition of the community, he hardly ever refers to it in his responsa, probably because customs which were the common practice of all Israel, were not normally challenged or questioned, hence were not brought before the Gaon for judgment or opinion. It was rather the fine point, the exception for which no clear ruling existed, which required the Gaon's arbitration. Nevertheless we do find two responsa in which RHG clearly invoked the tradition of the community as an authority.

A. RHG was asked (ṢZ 4, 3, 55) to rule in the case of a man who gave a gift to someone and then wished to have it nullified, seemingly having had regrets. The donor attempted to fall back on technical points. His main claim was that the witnesses who witnessed the "gift" did not bear testimony that the gift was made in public. RHG examined the pertinent Talmudic passage (BB 40b):

> R. Judah said: A deed of gift drawn up in secret is not enforceable.
> [What is meant by a deed of gift drawn up in secret? R. Joseph said:

If the donor said to the witnesses, 'Go and write it in some hidden place.' Others report that what R. Joseph said was: If the donor did not say to the witnesses, 'Find a place in the street or, in some public place and write it there.' What difference does it make which version we adopt?—It makes a difference where the donor simply told the witnesses to write, without specifying where].

"They closed their discussion thus," continued RHG, "What is the rule where the donor does not specify [the place of writing]?—Rabina said we do not suspect [that the donor meant it to be written secretly]; R. Ashi said that we do suspect. The law is that we do suspect" (ibid., 41a).[5] "Certainly," argued RHG, "there is nothing here that tells us that, where the donor does not specify, it is not enforceable. All it tells us is that we suspect, which means we have to scrutinize each case very carefully and consider whether the gift should be nullified, if there be some reason to put it aside." What is normally the outcome of this scrutiny? RHG finds the answer in common practice: "It is well known and rather valid common daily practice that a father, when making a gift of his possessions to his son, does so using either the terminology of an explicit gift or some other terminology." The point RHG is making is this. It is quite clear from daily practice that even though the donor does not use the "gift written in public" formula, nevertheless, if the intent is clear then the gift is valid. Here, too, since at the time of presentation, there was full intent to present a gift, the formula used is not crucial, and the donor's later regrets inconsequential. The governing principle is, therefore, if something is common practice, it can be relied upon as an authoritative and legally correct precedent.

B.   Another ruling relying on common practice. Samuel stated: "The scroll of Esther does not impart uncleanliness to the hands" (Meg. 7a). RHG was asked whether the law is according to Samuel (OG Meg. 36). Samuel's statement clearly implies that in his view the scroll of Esther does not originate in divine inspiration and should not be considered among the Holy Scripture.[6] RHG's conclusive argument that the law cannot possibly be according to Samuel is that "all of Israel number it [the scroll] among the Holy Scriptures." Here too the reasoning behind this ruling is that common practice and tradition of the entire community must be correct and authoritative.

Let us not be fooled by the dearth of quotations from RHG citing tradition as the source for his ruling. It does not at all detract from our contention that he places the tradition and practice of all of Israel at the center of his legal philosophy, as he himself so eloquently stated in OG RH 117 (cited above). The reason for the dearth of quotations is simple. Community practice and common knowledge tend to eliminate controversial issues which require the intervention of gaonic authority. Customs accepted by all communities, having been transmitted from father to son, are beyond contention and questioning. Since they are common practice no one contests them. Hence, only in the few rare cases where some doubt arose (e.g., *shofar*-blowing and the scroll of Esther), or where the opportunity presented itself to use common practice as proof (e.g., gifts), only then did RHG avail himself of the opportunity and state his view in clear terms. In essence, tradition and common practice are the most basic and elementary and therefore usually the ultimate supreme authority for the whole halachic framework.

The Babylonian Talmud

Only after having mentioned—be it ever so briefly—the most basic of RHG's legal sources, the tradition of Israel, can we proceed to that literary work which quantitatively serves as the major source for RHG's decisions and rulings, the Babylonian Talmud. We have already explained the unique mutual relationship between the *geonim* and the Babylonian Talmud (BT). On the one hand, the *geonim* derived their authority as the successors of the revered Babylonian *Amoraim*. On the other hand, it was they who carved an exalted niche for the Talmud and its compilers, the *Amoraim*, through their responsa and other literary works. This held true of Hai no less than of the other *geonim* and perhaps more so. Being the fourth successive descendant of his lineage to have attained the geaonate, his reputation, stature, and authority as keeper of the realm were great. As scion of the family succession he was unusually proud and sensitive to the past attainments of Academy heads. Hence he was consistently looking to the Babylonian Talmud for solutions to any point of law requiring resolution which arose (i.e., was not universally acknowledged). He took the clear and unyielding stand in a number of responsa, that whenever it is possible to decide an issue by having recourse to BT, he would invariably do so, and seek no further. Only when it was impossible to come to a clear decision based solely on BT would he then have recourse to other sources. Before we go on to clarify how RHG ruled when basing himself on BT, let us for a moment, consider responsa from which we learn that BT is indeed RHG's exclusive source whenever possible.

RHG was addressed by a community which had some of its Passover Eve *Seder* rites challenged by student newcomers (OG Pes. 355). The community wrote that they were accustomed to imbibe five cups of wine instead of the usual four (v. ibid., 351 f.), and omit the customary benediction after the *Hallel* but instead recite Psalm 136 over the fifth cup and conclude with the benediction. After the fifth cup they prohibited any further drinking of wine. The newcomers claimed that two benedictions should be recited, one after the regular *Hallel* over the fourth cup and one after Psalm 136 (called the Great *Hallel*) over the fifth cup. Moreover, they permitted drinking wine even after imbibing the fifth cup.

RHG deals with the issues one by one. Regarding the first he claims: "The Talmud does not spell out what benediction is recited after the fifth cup[7] by one who prefers to recite the Great *Hallel* over a fifth cup." Since the Talmud says nothing explicit he resorts to deciding between the custom of the questioners and their adversaries *ex silencio Talmudis*: "Since the Talmudic Rabbis did not say to recite two benedictions," the custom of the questioners seems the more plausible and tenable. Quite clearly then, RHG offers his own judgment only because "the Talmud did not spell it out" and "its Rabbis did not say." Had there been anything explicit in the Talmud, it would have been binding and the discussion would have been closed right there.

Regarding the second point—whether one may drink after the fifth cup—RHG again takes up the same line of reasoning: "We have not found a prohibition in the Gemara." It is only regarding eating, claims Hai, that "we [the Gemara] say we must not eat anything once we have recited the grace after meals." Nevertheless, he points out that his own custom, going back to early tradition, does in fact agree with the questioners. Here too, only after establishing that there is nothing straightforward in the Talmud, does RHG invoke his own custom to support the questioner's stand. He leaves no room for doubt that had there been a Talmudic ruling, it alone would have been binding.

His remarks about a son who summoned his father to court are in the same vein. RSG and RHG were asked whether a son could force a father to take an oath (RDG 206). They reply: "We have found no evidence to annul the claim of the son so that the father should not have to take an oath." They proceed to relate how courts normally act in such cases. What they are saying is that they are relating the custom of the courts because they found no evidence in the Talmud on which to base an independent decision. Had there been such evidence, their decision would clearly have been based on that evidence alone.

On another occasion RHG was asked to decide between conflicting opinions as to how properly to shake the *lulab* on *Sukkot*. He opens his remarks with the statement: "No clear cut solution is found in the Talmud on this matter" (OG Sukkah 104). He proceeds to cite Talmudic sources (Sukkah 37b-38a) and shows why they are inconclusive. Only then does he turn to an alternative source, the practice of the elders. Here too, it is quite clear that had any of the Talmudic passages provided conclusive proof for one of the views, he would have unhesitatingly declared it decisive.

We close this chapter with a statement which is an obvious exaggeration, certainly not to be taken literally, but which is indicative of the emphasis RHG places on basing his decisions on the Babylonian Talmud and especially on explicit Talmudic rulings. RSG and RHG were asked about a widower "who remarried and then died leaving a widow, and sons from both wives. The widow has collected the dowry and is still alive. Are the sons of the first wife entitled to *Ktubat Bnin Dikrin*?" [dowry of male offspring][8] (OG Ket 706). Their response: "This matter is not explicit in the Gemara and one does not rule on something not explicit." They proceed to state that there are no known precedents in the Academies for granting sons this claim while a widow is alive.

In truth Hai and Ṣerira often rule on matters not explicit in the Talmud as we shall see in subsequent chapters. As a matter of fact most of those chapters will be devoted to explaining RHG's methodology precisely in cases not explicit in the Talmud. Even in this responsum they make their view clear when they state that there is no precedence for granting the sons' claim during the life of the widow. What then are we to make of the comment about not ruling on something not explicit? What they really wish to convey here comprises two crucial points in their methodology of adjudication. The first is that when a decision is explicit in BT, it requires no further consideration, but is taken as it is. The other is that whenever there is no single accepted tradition in all of Israel, we should try to make BT the basis of our decisions whenever possible. In the responsum in question, RSG and RHG cited Academy precedent only because the Talmud did not touch on that particular point at all. Had it done so, it would have undoubtedly been the source for their decision—explicit or not. BT, even when not explicit, remains their single major source. In the following chapters we shall show just what methodology RHG invokes in adjudication when utilizing the Talmud as a source, both when the decision is explicit in the Talmud, and when it is not—and we shall explain what is meant by an explicit decision.

EXPLICIT TALMUDIC RULINGS

Rulings of the Talmud, Gemara, sugya

Whenever possible RHG bases his decisions on what is explicit in the Talmud. What he means by "explicit" is a distinct ruling or decision on a matter discussed. BT is mostly a compendium of academic syllabi and debates, and a record of discussions which took place in the various amoraic academies, edited into literary form. Since BT is primarily not a legal code we cannot expect to find final legal decisions or rulings in the course of, or following, every Talmudic discussion. In fact such rulings are the exception and in many cases not amoraic at all. Hence, RHG directs attention to those exceptional (although not necessarily rare) instances where there is a definitive ruling or decision. He considers these decisions "matters explicit in the Gemara," and views them as absolutely binding on all post-Talmudic adjudication. It does not concern RHG—nor shall it concern us in this framework—if those explicit decisions found in the Talmud are indeed amoraic or if they are post-amoraic (saboraic or early gaonic) interpolations. Their presence in the Gaon's Talmud is what makes them binding.

RHG's strong feeling on this issue is apparent from a responsum he wrote with atypical acerbity to someone who dared to question a Talmudic ruling, even while acquiescing to it. The full text of the responsum has been preserved by R. Judah of Barcelona (OG Ket. 97). The question asked is why the Talmud decides against R. Tahlifa son of Maraba (Ket. 8a). RHG's diatribe begins: "We do not know what you asked. Since it is expressly stated in the Gemara that the law does not follow him, may we say why does the law follow X and does not follow Y? If so, then [regarding] any law decided in the Gemara according to one of the adversaries, someone "can always arise and say, 'What is the reason?' " His unequivocal stand is therefore, that any explicit Talmudic decision is to be accepted without the least question.

Having seen RHG's express view that he feels obliged to decide issues on the basis of explicit Talmudic rulings whenever possible, and that such rulings cannot be questioned, we proceed to cite examples of such legal decisions from among his responsa. This will be our method throughout. We will reveal RHG's halachic methodology, by first uncovering the guiding principles of adjudication to which he had recourse. Whenever possible we will expressly quote RHG himself, to prove that he adopted the principle. Then we will note other clear mention of the principle. Having proven that the principle is in fact part of his legal methodology, we shall endeavor to point out decisions based on that principle even though RHG does not always specifically mention the principle and at times hardly even alludes to it. Finally we will introduce decisions and rulings which, in our estimation, are also guided by that same principle even though there is absolutely no hint of it in RHG's words.

Regarding the principle of deciding according to explicit Talmudic rulings, then, we have already covered the first stage—express citations from RHG where he invokes such a principle. Here now are decisions of RHG based on explicit Talmudic rulings, in which cases RHG alludes to the principle by associating his own ruling with the relevant Talmudic *sugya*. Although he does not state that the Gemara's rulings serve as the source of his decisions, reference to the *sugya* will show that RHG's decisions follow, literally, explicit Talmudic rulings.

A. RHG was asked if witnesses to a sale or gift, who will be signing the bill of sale (or gift), are required first to ascertain the identity of the seller or donor through testimony (Misifrut, 139a). He replies that there is no need for proper testimony and a mere intimation is sufficient. In the course of his responsum he refers to a number of passages from Yeb. especially 39b, where the ruling is explicit even in the stringent matter of haliza. RHG carries the explicit ruling one step further. How much more so, he reasons, should we rule accordingly, in simple matters like sale and gifts.

B. In a question preserved in Eskol I, 215-16 RHG was asked whether the prohibition of satnez applied only if the linen and wool were hackled, spun, and woven, or even if only one, either hackled, or spun, or woven. He replies that this is explained in the Gemara and cites the discussion (Nidah 61b). He rules that the Mosaic prohibition applies only if they are hackled, spun and woven, but the Rabbis decreed that one of them alone is enough to prohibit. This view that R. Hai expounds is that which is held in the course of the discussion by Mar Zutra who was opposed by R. Asi. R. Hai does not state why he rules according to Mar Zutra, but there can be little doubt that the reason is that towards the end of the discussion the Gemara states explicitly, "the law is in agreement with Mar Zutra."

C. RHG maintains that any court procedure requires three judges. Furthermore judicial procedures of a court composed of two judges is declared invalid (RDG 181). He claims this despite his own admission that regarding the minimum number before whom a husband may cancel his agency for delivering a bill of divorce to his wife, "The law follows him who claims that two suffice [R. Nahman - Gittin 32b] as we say at the end of the *sugya* [ibid., 34a], 'the law follows Nahman and the law follows Nahman.'" The Gaon's argument is that this case is an exception. Despite the general rule requiring three, in this case the Talmud explicitly ruled that the law follows R. Nahman, and we are bound by that explicit ruling.

D.   In discussing division of property among heirs or former partners, in RDG 38 and 55, RHG establishes as a governing rule, the law laid down by R. Joseph, that if the property to be divided consists of two fields adjoining one channel, dependent on one dyke for irrigation (i.e., of equal value), and one of the partners has adjacent land, we grant him his share adjacent to the land he already holds (BB 12b). RHG accepts this guidline although there are *amoraim* who disagree with R. Joseph (i.e., Rabah, demanding even greater consideration and Abaye, claiming no special consideration). Though RHG neither hints at the reason for accepting R. Joseph's view, nor cites it in the responsum, we are virtually certain he has in mind the explicit Talmudic ruling, "the law follows Rav Joseph."

E.   We have already seen (above, p. 18) that RHG accepts as law the ruling of BB 41a, "the law is that we do suspect," and decides accordingly in questions of gifts. Here too, undoubtedly the reason he deems the ruling so binding, and takes painstaking care to abide by it and determine its precise meaning, is because it was an explicit ruling.

So much for responsa in which RHG at least quotes or refers to the Talmudic passages he had in mind as the basis for his rulings. When scrutinizing them we were able to observe that they contained explicit rulings. In many other responsa RHG does not even hint at the Talmudic passage he had in mind. Nonetheless, it appears to us that the next group of decisions are also based on explicit Talmudic rulings.

A.   RDG 326 (!) deals with a series of disputes between tenant and landlord. RHG rules that in disputes regarding the lease (e.g., its term) the landlord is favored. This seems to be based on the explicit Talmudic ruling, "The law is in accordance with R. Nahman and he ruled that the land is in the presumptive possession of its owner" (BM 110a).

B.   "Our Rabbi Hai said: 'When there is no wine and it is necessary to recite the *qiduṣ* over a loaf, we first recite the benediction over the bread and afterwards [the benediction of the sanctification] of the day. Certainly, because the loaf provides the occasion for reciting the *qiduş*, and the *qiduş* is recited over the loaf only where there is no wine' " (OG Ber. 333). The argument of the loaf providing the occasion for reciting the *qiduş* is, in reality, a paraphrase of the argument of the School of Hillel regarding the order of the benedictions in every *qiduş*. Contrary to the School of Shamai, the School of Hillel maintains that the benediction on the wine precedes, "Because the wine provides the occasion for reciting the *qiduş*" (T Ber. 5, 25, quoted in Ber. 51b). The *baraita* itself concludes: "The law is as laid down by the School of Hillel." RHG no doubt believes that this Talmudic ruling—that the law is as laid down by the School of Hillel—is not only binding unto itself, but, coming after the argumentation, suggests acceptance of the argument as well, which consequently also becomes binding. It remains for RHG only to draw an analogy from wine to bread.

We learn from the above that an explicit Talmudic ruling in favor of a particular amora or amoraic stand or opinion does not merely elicit acceptance of that particular stand, but also entails acceptance by RHG of the reasoning behind it as well. We may proceed one step further. If one whose view is explicitly upheld by the Talmud, has made certain fine legal distinctions, and unique interpretations of earlier Talmudic sources in the course of a discussion—in order to make the view tenable--then the explicit Talmudic ruling in favor of that view automatically carries with it RHG's acceptance of those distinctions and interpretations as well.

For example, there is a Talmudic dispute as to whether a transgressor who "eats carrion to provoke" is a credible witness. Abaye holds, "no." Rava says, "yes" (San. 27a). The Gemara explicitly rules in favor of Abaye. In the course of the discussion their respective views cause them to differ regarding the interpretation of a *baraita* which states that those who have trespassed by false oaths cannot serve as witnesses. Abaye interprets the *baraita* as referring both to a vain oath and one concerning money matters, while Rava claims that the *baraita* refers only to oaths concerning money matters. Now, in OG San. 463, we read that RHG disqualifies as witnesses those who have trespassed by false oaths concerning money matters and by vain oaths. RHG obviously felt bound by the Talmud's explicit ruling in favor of Abaye. Moreover, he felt equally bound by Abaye's interpretations which resulted from that view, the view which was confirmed eventually by the Gemara.

This approach is by no means unique to RHG. It is typical of the *geonim*, and is perhaps most clearly stated in an anonymous geonic responsum (RSG?): "That *amora* whom the law follows, all interpretations, solutions, thrusts and replies made according to his view in order to make it tenable, are accepted and stand authoritative" (RGA, p. 63, and see below p. 111).

All the examples we have given to show how RHG followed explicit Talmudic rulings were cases in which the Talmud used terminology clearly denoting such a ruling. The terms used were "*wehalaka*" (Hebrew), "*wehilkata*" (Aramaic)—"and the law is" or "*ain halaka*" (Hebrew), "*leit hilkata*" (Aramaic) "The law is not." These are shining examples of Talmudic rulings. But, RHG also interprets far less distinctive terminology as authoritative Talmudic rulings, binding on him and on all post-Talmudic Jewry. For example, RSG and RHG were asked the precise meaning of "*qolanit*" (a scolding woman" —"a screamer"), who, according to R. Tarfon (M Ket. 7, 6) can be put away without her *ketubah* (OG Ket. 553). The query was: Does the law follow the interpretation found in a *baraita* (Ket. 72b)? The *geonim* take the conflicting view, that of Samuel (ibid.). They write: "We conclude[1] that the *clearest* [explanation] of *qolanit* is like Samuel." This is actually a paraphrase of the pertinent Talmudic discussion which concludes: "Clearly we must revert to the original explanation" [that given in the name of Samuel] (ibid.). Undoubtedly, RSG and RHG viewed this terminology, too, as a Talmudic ruling binding on them.

RHG is so sensitive to whatever might be taken as a Talmudic ruling, that even when the Talmud's stand is non-decisive he instructs that it be followed. For example, BT Pesahim 115a discusses whether *mazot* and *maror* should be wrapped together and eaten as a sandwich during the Passover Eve Seder, as Hillel said, or whether they are to be eaten separately, as the Rabbis held. The Gemara concludes: "Now that the law was not stated either as Hillel or as the Rabbis; one recites 'Who hast commanded us concerning the eating of unleavened bread' and eats; then he recites the blessing, 'concerning the eating of bitter herbs,' and eats; and then he eats unleavened bread and *maror*[2] together without a blessing." In a responsum dealing with a different aspect of eating *mazot* (RGA, pp. 44-5), RHG sees fit to close with this Talmudic instruction, even though it is obviously advice given only because they were unable to arrive at a clear-cut decision.

Nevertheless, since it is the Talmud's stand in resolving a matter in dispute, RHG accepts it as authoritative, just as he does other Talmudic rulings.

Rulings of Specific Individual Amoraim

So far we have given examples of RHG's reliance on explicit rulings of the Talmud itself—the Gemara, the *sugya*. All that we have said holds true equally when the rulings are attributed to specific individual *amoraim* and are uncontested. Why should it matter? If the ruling was stated by the Gemara without reservation, it was generally accepted as conclusive. Here then are examples of explicit rulings of individual *amoraim* which RHG accepts as authoritative and incorporates into his responsa (listed according to *amoraim*).

A. R. Yoḥanan. RHG was asked if a repentant sinner may serve as cantor for the congregation (OG Taanith 57). He rules that all the repentant are welcomed back to the fold. He singles out his source as the statement to that effect by R. Joshua b. Qarḥa and R. Simeon in the course of a tanaic dispute and the explicit ruling by R. Yoḥanan in their favor (AZ 7a).

B. Samuel. "R. Baruk of Greece o.b.m. wrote in the name of R. Hai Gaon that an Israelite may rent an inn, a shop, or a courtyard [in which the Sabbath will not be observed] to a gentile, or a boat in which the gentile sails on the Sabbath. All these are permitted even in the land of Israel—because the law has already been resolved according to R. Jose—and so much more so in other lands" (OZ II 1d). The principle behind the decision is that the rental is permitted because it will become well known that it is a gentile using the property on the Sabbath and not a Jew (cf. below, p. 32). R. Jose referred to this in M AZ 1, 8: "R. Jose says: In the Land of Israel houses may be hired to them but not fields ... while outside the Land, either may be sold to them." "The law has already been resolved according to R. Jose," in RHG's view, undoubtedly because he feels bound by what "Samuel says: 'The law follows R. Jose' " (AZ 21a). RHG thus ultimately rules according to Samuel's explicit decision.

C. R. Huna. RHG was asked to resolve an intricate controversy between an orphaned first-born and his brothers. An unmarried sister died before reaching maturity. The sum which would normally have been set aside for her outfit, as it was set aside to outfit the surviving sisters, consequently reverted to the estate. The firstborn, claimed that he is entitled to the firstborn's double portion[3] of this too, since the sister would have had the legal status of a potential creditor, and the sum in fact remained a part of the estate. The brothers countered that since their sister was entitled to the outfit money, it is as if they are all inheriting her share after her decease (OG Ket. 513). RHG accepts the claim of the firstborn. He then proceeds to clarify the status of such a sister basing his position on the discussion in Ket. 68b: "Even if she had not died but was not maintained by them and did not protest she would have lost her outfit. As our Rabbis taught: The daughters [of a man who left an estate and is survived by sons] whether they had attained their adolescence before they married or whether they married before they had attained their adolescence, lost their right to maintenance but not to their allowance for a marriage outfit; so Rabbi ... [R. Simeon b. Elazar differs] and R. Nahman stated: Huna told me, the law is in agreement with Rabbi. Rava raised an objection against R. Nahman ... This is no difficulty: The one is a case where she protested; the other, where she did not protest. "You learn from this," concludes RHG, "that she has a claim only during this period, and if she died before this she is not entitled to anything. Hence the sum never left the estate and the firstborn receives a double portion of everything." RHG manifestly based his decision on the explicit ruling of R. Huna in favor of Rabbi with the qualification: "And did not protest." Likewise in the Gemara a contradiction between M—seen by the Gemara as representing Rabbi's view—and Rabbi's express view in the baraita is resolved by this qualification.

D.   Rava.   "Rav Hai was asked about Rava's statement, '[The law is:] Leaven in its time, etc., whether mixed with its own kind or with a different kind, is forbidden even when there is a minute quantity, in accordance with Rav; when not in its own time, whether mixed with its own kind or with a different kind, it is permitted in accordance with R. Simeon' [Pesaḥim 30a] ... and he answered that it is quite clear ... that the discussion ends according to the final ruling, and the final ruling upon which their discussion is based is ... 'Rava said: The law is 'Leaven in its time, etc.'" (OG Pes. 57). RHG openly states here that it is the explicit ruling by the *amora*, Rava, which is to be seen as final and authoritative.

E.   Rava.   "Rava said: The law is in accordance with the views of Reiṣ Laqiṣ in the following three rulings ... another is his ruling in connection with the following mishnah. If a man distributed his property verbally and gave to one [son] more and to the others less, or if he assigned to the firstborn a share equal to that of his brothers,[3] his arrangements are valid. If, however, he said 'as an inheritance' his instructions are disregarded. If he wrote either at the beginning or at the end or the middle 'as a gift' his instructions are valid. And in connection with this Reis Laqis stated: [Where the expression 'inheritance' was used together with that of 'gift' in the case of two persons and two fields] No possession is [ever] acquired unless [the testator] had said, "Let X and Y inherit this and that particular field, which I have assigned to them as a gift, so that they may inherit them" (Yeb. 36a-b, s.n.). In discussing this case, RHG stated: "As we say, the law follows Reis Laqis in these three, and this is one of them" (DCA 290a). So, Rava's explicit ruling became, to RHG, an incontrovertible matter of fact—"as we say" (see n. 1).

F.   Rava.   Once more we find (RDG 79, end) that RHG has recourse to this explicit ruling of Rava (cited above, example E) but he hardly even alludes to it. He states that "R. Yoḥanan is consistent in holding that 'acquisition of usufruct is like the acquisition of the capital' (BB 136b, Ṣabat 135b s.n.) but the law does not follow him. R. Hai does not explain why the law does not follow R. Yoḥanan. The explanation undoubtedly is that this is one of those three cases in which Rava explicitly ruled in favor of Reis Laqis.

So we see that RHG does not always tell us that he is invoking the principle of deciding according to an explicit amoraic ruling. There are a number of such cases where some sleuthing uncovers that this was indeed the guiding principle in his decision. Here are two examples of his using this principle without clearly referring to it.

A.   "It is established that the law follows R. Johanan b. Beroqa" (DCA 290a, cited above). The reference is to M BB 8, 5.

> If a man said, 'Such a man shall inherit from me,' and he has a daughter; or 'My daughter shall inherit from me' and he has a son he has said nothing, for he has laid down a condition contrary to what is written in the Law. R. Johanan b. Beroqa says: If he said this of one that is qualified to inherit from him, his words remain valid, but of one that was not qualified to inherit from him his words do not remain valid.

How is it "established?" Undoubtedly, in RHG's eyes, through explicit rulings, in favor of R. Johanan b. Beroqa, by Rabbi, Samuel, and Rava (BB 130a-b).

B.   "And that which we learned in the Mishnah: If two brothers were married to two sisters one of age and the other a minor and the husband of her that was of age died and she awaits levirate marriage with the husband of the minor. R. Eliezer holds: The minor is instructed to exercise right of refusal against her husband, and he contracts levirate marriage with her that was of age who awaits him, and such is the law" (OG Yeb. 552). The mishnah referred to is Yeb. 13, 7, which Hai quotes loosely, interjecting his own statements. More interesting is, how does he know that the law is like R. Eliezer (whose view is disputed in the Mishnah). It seems certain here too he is alluding to an explicit amoraic ruling—that of Samuel (with R. Eliezer concurring): "The law follows R. Eliezer" (Yeb. 110a).

These are three more examples where explicit rulings of R. Yoḥanan serve as the basis of RHG's decisions even though he does not mention them.

A. RDG 38 (also RLOW 133-36) is composed of an intricate—and historically fascinating —set of queries posed to RHG, regarding a family which was exiled from Tlemcen to Asir, whose sons eventually returned to Tlemcen, to reclaim the family property and divide it up. The last issue discussed is the right of the youngest son to remnants of his deceased mother's jewelry, which were at one time put in trust in the hands of a guarantor as part of a general agreement with him. The latter does not deny the rights of the son, but claims he no longer possesses the jewels. He is willing to take an oath to that effect, pay their money value and leave the agreement intact. The son argues that since the guarantor is not handing over the actual jewels, it is a breach of the agreement which consequently becomes void. The conflict had already been brought before local scholars who disagreed. One wished to draw a parallel to a well known Talmudic case: "If a man says to his wife, 'Lo this is thy bill of divorce on condition that you give me my robe,' and the robe was lost, we rule that he meant this particular robe and nothing else [and she is not divorced]. R. Simeon b. Gamaliel says: Let her give him its money value [and the divorce thus becomes valid]." (M Gittin 7, 5 according to the interpretation of BT in Gittin 74b). RHG agrees that our case is parallel to that of the robe. The condition was that the remnants themselves be returned. Now, if we are to follow the view of RSBG we can accept their money value instead. However, according to the first view in M, if the condition is not fulfilled to the letter, the whole agreement dissolves. RHG goes along with the local scholar that the law does not follow RSBG. Hence, in our case too, the whole agreement dissolves. Wherefrom do they know to rule against

RSBG? Undoubtedly from an explicit ruling by R. Yoḥanan that this case is one of the exceptions where RSBG's opinion—as found in the Mishnah—is rejected (Gittin 75a, s.n.).

B.   "He [Hai] was asked if there are circumstances under which an Israelite may rent to a gentile an inn, a large heating oven, and a public bath on a yearly basis" (HSG ii 57, par. 5).   The problem is that labor will be done on the Sabbath (cf. above, p. 28).   RHG permits renting an inn but forbids renting the oven or the bath.   His criterion is the reasoned view of Ben Batira regarding sales, which RHG extends to rentals.[4] Ben Batira permits the sale of a horse to gentiles because "it is only put to a kind of a work which does not involve the bringing of a sin-offering" (AZ 16a and T AZ 2, 3).   Equally, argues RHG, an inn is used to accommodate guests and their livestock, work which does not involve the bringing of a sin-offering.   That is not the case with a bath or oven.   "And," says he, "the law follows Ben Batira."   How does he know that the law follows Ben Batira and not his disputant, Rabbi?   Once again, we venture to suggest that he based this on the explicit ruling by R. Yoḥanan: "The law is with Ben Batira" (AZ 16a).

C.   Writing about the *amidah*, of the additional New Year's service RHG relates and explains the practice of the academies:[5]

> When the assembly prays as a congregation [ḥeber ir] each individual recites only seven benedictions during the silent *amidah* . . . and when the reader assumes the pulpit he recites nine benedictions[6] and thus they all fulfill their obligation [of reciting nine benedictions]. And so the Rabbis state this matter as we learned in the Mishnah, "Like the reader is bound [to say the *amidah*] so is each person bound. Raban Gamaliel says: The reader fulfills the obligation of the many" [M RH 4, 9] . . . Raban Gameliel holds that each individual recites seven benedictions and the reader alone recites Sovereignty, Remembrance and *Shofar* [the additional benedictions] and fulfills the obligation for the many and the law was decided in favor of Raban Gamaliel (OG RH 127).

Again the question arises: Where is it mentioned that the law was decided in favor of Raban Gamaliel?   The answer is that RHG was no doubt alluding to RH 34b: "R. Johanan says the law follows Raban Gamaliel."   An explicit amoraic ruling, becomes, for Hai, conclusive.

Decisions With No Reference to the Source.

We have shown that explicit decisions of *amoraim* serve RHG as a basis for decisions. In the responsa discussed heretofore, RHG states that the law follows one sage or another. With a little effort we were able to show that the basis of his statement in each case was an explicit Talmudic ruling. Having established RHG's use of this principle, we posit that in the following cases too, explicit amoraic rulings served as the basis of his decisions even though he did not allude to them—not even to state that the law is like X or Y. In all the following cases he gives no source nor reason for his decision. We shall complete the reference by showing which amoraic rulings served as his sources.

A.   RHG entertained the claim of a daughter that her father's widow sold a considerable parcel of land from his estate at one time (obviously receiving in return more than her daily needs). The daughter claimed that the sale should be invalidated. The widow admitted the facts, but countered that it was a one-time sale to cover the costs of her maintenance over an extended period. RHG rules that if the sale was to cover what was her due in the past, then the sale is not valid (unless a court had granted her advance dispensation to first pay for her own needs and only later sell property to defray costs). On the other hand, if the sale is meant to cover her future needs, it is valid, "and she may sell [land to suffice her] for six months and the buyer provides her maintenance once every thirty days" (RDG 40). This formula is not original, but appears verbatim in BT, near the end of the discussion cited in part by RHG in this same responsum. "Ameimar said: The law is that [a widow] sell [sufficient land to suffice her] for six months and the buyer provide her maintenance [in installments] once every thirty days" (Ket. 97a). Use of the same words cannot be coincidental. It implies that Ameimar's explicit ruling is the basis for RHG's.

B.   "Rav Hai said: Whoever heard a distant tiding [i.e., learned of the death of a relative for whom he is normally obliged to observe the seven day and thirty day formal mourning periods] after thirty days, observes the formal mourning period for only one day" (OG Maschkin 79). This ruling corresponds to the view of R. Aqiba: "On distant tidings formal mourning obtains for only one day ... 'distant' tidings are [belated tidings] after thirty [days]" (MQ 20a). The sages disagree with Aqiba, and require the usual formal mourning period even in these cases. Here too, RHG subtly hints R. Aqiba's view is the basis for his decision by incorporating Àqiba's terminology into his own responsum. The true question regarding RHG's legal methodology is: Why does he follow R. Àqiba's view when the sages disagree?[7] The answer is undoubtedly because of R. Yoḥanan's explicit ruling[8]: "Although R. Àqiba is lenient ... the halakah is in accordance with R. Àqiba" (MQ 20a).

C. "Rabbi Ṣerira and our Rabbi Hai Gon o.b.m. wrote [cited OG Ket. 148] ... There are two types of ṣtuqi [a child of unknown fatherhood], one ... if the mother says that she conceived of a legitimate Jew, then the child is forbidden in marriage. But the ṣtuqi of Abba Saul [M Qid. 4, 2] is ... when the mother says the child is by a particular [named] legitimate Jew." In such a case the child is "permitted [in marriage] even to a priestly [family] ... like Raban Gamaliel "(who holds that in such a case the mother may be believed, M Ket. 1, 9). What the geonim fail to explain is why they lean toward the highly disputed view of Abba Saul (and R. Gamaliel). Here too, we submit that the source is explicit amoraic rulings in favor of R. Gamaliel (by Samuel Qid. 74a) and in favor of Abba Saul (by Rava, ibid.).

In the cases just considered, Hai hinted in some way at the relevant Talmudic discussion in the intricacies of which we were able to find an explicit amoraic ruling which provided the key to understanding his decision. In the following examples there is not even one hint at the pertinent sugya in the entire responsum. Nevertheless, we feel that they, too, are based on explicit Talmudic rulings, but less obviously. A bit of explanation and clarification in each case should elucidate the connection between the Gaon's decision and a specific Talmudic ruling.

A. A father died leaving a piece of land to two sons. The canal which carried all the necessary water had run in a fixed channel for generations. The sons divided the land into two parts, each agreeing to take one part without alteration. After living peacefully for a few years, the two brothers clashed, and one plugged up the waterway in his half of the property so that the water would not reach his brother. He justified his action with the Talmudic dictum, "If brothers divide [property which they have inherited] neither has the right of way against the other, nor the right of 'windows' against the other, nor the right of 'ladders' against the other, nor the right of a water course [to carry water from the river to his own field through the other's] against the other." This tradition is offered by R. Nahman in the name of Samuel (BB 7b, 65a), with Rav disagreeing. Rav

Hai rules that if years have passed and ḥazaqa of use has been established by the brother, without the owner-brother registering a complaint, he has no right now to deprive his brother of the water. Had he immediately registered his complaint and stated that he is only allowing his brother use of the canal out of goodwill, but that no legal claim is established, then he could, at any future time, deprive the brother of use of the water (RDG 41). On principle then, RHG concurs with the claimant who invoked Samuel's dictum, even though he does not mention Samuel, nor his view, nor indeed the whole Talmudic discussion in the responsum. The reason behind the decision in accordance with Samuel is undoubtedly an explicit ruling found at the end of the aforementioned sugya: R. Nahman, wishing to know the authority of the tradition he transmitted, asked R. Huna (the student of Rav): "Does the law follow our opinion or yours?" He replied: "The law follows your view since you have continued access to the gate of the Exilarch where the judges are in session."

B.   RSG and RHG were asked by R. Jacob b. Nissim of Kairouan to resolve a very intricate and interesting case. A man ran afoul of the authorities and feared that even if he were to escape from the city, they would take revenge on his wife. He therefore did what seems to have been fairly common practice in such cases. He went through the motions of divorcing his wife and transferring property to her in lieu of dowry, in order to avoid the attempts of the authorities to confiscate his property. He wrote the bill of divorce. One of the witnesses to the divorce admitted that the husband had told him that he really had no intention of divorcing his wife; that this manipulation was only to keep the authorities from troubling her; and that the husband did not deem the divorce valid. The husband said the same to his wife. The wife subsequently died, followed by the husband. The heirs of both sides laid claim to the considerable inheritance and dowry. The validity of the divorce became the substantive judicial issue. The heirs of the woman claimed: The divorce was valid, the property became hers and "we are her heirs." Those of the husband countered: The divorce was never valid, so all the woman's property as well as the husband's belongs to us; according to Jewish law a husband is the heir of his wife, but not a wife of her husband.

RSG and RHG deal with the validity of the divorce from many aspects (OG Ket. 203). One of their central arguments to invalidate the divorce is that, if the writ of divorce was not presented to the wife in the presence of two valid witnesses, the divorce is void.[9] This is in keeping with the view of R. Eleazar that "it is the witnesses to the delivery of the writ of divorce that effect the legal separation" (Gittin 9b, s.n.),[10] as opposed to R. Meir who holds that "the witnesses who sign [the writ of divorce] effect the final legal separation." They no doubt rule in divorce cases in favor of R. Eleazar because *amoraim* explicitly ruled in his favor in divorce cases (Gittin 86b).

C.   A widow sold immovable goods from her late husband's estate for her maintenance. The orphan (heir) claimed that the sale was unnecessary and was executed without permission. RHG ruled that if the heir could prove that this were indeed so, the widow's sale would be void, the property be returned to the heir, the widow should return the money to the purchaser and he in turn should claim from the heir any expenses he incurred through investments made in the property (RDG 39). Nowhere in the responsum is there a hint at why declaring the sale unnecessary carries in its wake the sequence of events demanded by R. Hai. We suggest the following reconstruction of his reasoning: Since the widow in reality had no right to sell property, the property was in fact not hers to sell. Hence what she was doing was tantamount to selling something which really did not belong to her.   Accordingly, the case should be judged by the Talmudic rules governing the case of "one who sells a field to his fellow and it turns out not to be his own" (BM 14b). That case gave rise to a dispute between Rav and Samuel. "Rav says: He [the buyer] is entitled to [the return of] the money which he paid for the field [and to] compensation for the improvement [which he made in the field].   While Samuel says: He is entitled to the money [he paid] but not to [compensation for the] improvement." In our responsum RHG seems to establish Rav's view as his basis. Hence, the widow returns the money ("he is entitled to the money") and the heir returns the investment ("[compensation for] the improvement"). The only missing link is why does RHG follow Rav's view rather than Samuel's. Once again our solution is that there is an explicit ruling by Rava following Rav. "Said Rava: The law [in regard to the above controversy] is that he [the buyer] is entitled to the purchase price as well as to [the value of] the improvement" (BM 15b).

A first glance was insufficient to determine the basis of RHG's judgment in this responsum. More careful analysis was required to show that the ultimate basis was an explicit amoraic ruling. There are undoubtedly other responsa for which explicit amoraic rulings lie behind Hai's decisions, but we may have missed them. Even so, we have seen enough examples to convince us of Hai's extensive use of explicit amoraic rulings as the basis for decisions. In fact, the principle of deciding according to explicit amoraic rulings is basic to his methodology of decision-making, and we think there are rarely exceptions. To strengthen this claim let us examine some responsa in which he seems at first to disregard the principle, but more careful scrutiny reveals that they, too, follow the rule.

Exceptions

A.   A widow who knew that she had to take an oath in order to receive her ketubah (see M Ket. 9, 7; Gittin 4, 3) did so on her own initiative and in an unauthorized fashion. Without the prior knowledge of the court or heirs, she stood up in the synagogue anterior, where she could be heard, and took an oath that she had not yet received any payment, hoping that this action would suffice to receive the ketubah. RHG wrote of this action: "It is our view that this oath cannot be considered to replace that which she is obligated to take in court in order to receive payment of her ketubah . . . moreover she is required to hold the Torah scroll in her hands at the time of the oath" (RLOW 3). He seems to be giving two reasons for invalidating the oath: 1) Out of court. 2) Absence of Torah scroll. The second point interests us here, because it seems to run against an explicit amoraic ruling that, post-factum, the holding of any sacred object while taking an oath is valid. "For Rava said: A judge who adjures by 'the Lord God of Heaven [without handing a sacred object to the person taking the oath] is counted as having erred in the ruling of a mishnah, and must repeat [the ceremony correctly]. And R. Papa said: A judge who adjures with phylacteries is counted as having erred in the ruling of a mishnah, and must repeat [the ceremony]. The law is in accordance with the view of Rava, and the law is not in accordance with the view of R. Papa. The law is in accordance with the view of Rava, for he did not hold any [sacred] object in his hand; but the law is not in accordance with the view of R. Papa, for he held a [sacred] object in his hand" (Sebuot 38b). The Talmud, then, explicitly rules that holding any sacred object validates the oath. Why should RHG expressly demand the holding of a Torah scroll in apparent contradiction?

Stranger yet, elsewhere RHG does codify according to this explicit decision, as expected. "Our Rabbis . . . debar a judge who gives an oath . . . without the holding of a sacred object, as they said, 'Rava said: A judge . . . etc.' " (MPS, p. 11). In another directive, too, RHG obviously follows this explicit ruling." There are places which have the adjuror grasp a sacred object rather than the one taking the oath. However, these places are not scrupulous [in keeping the] law" (OG Gittin 167). We deduce: If the one taking an oath grasps a sacred object, not necessarily a Torah scroll, that is acceptable.

In light of the difficulty and apparent contradiction posed by RLOW 3, a careful assessment and accurate account of RHG's view in this matter is in order. Hai holds that ideally whoever takes an oath should grasp a Torah scroll. He spells this out clearly in MPS (p. 106): "The Mosaic oath requires that the one taking the oath grasp a Torah scroll in his hands." This is based on a statement in BT (loc. cit.): "The oath must be administered with a Torah scroll." *Post factum,* the Talmud does validate oaths taken when other sacred objects were held. RHG, of course, feels bound by this indulgence. Hence, RHG is pointing out here that he will not condone the debarment of a judge for anything less severe than not holding a sacred object while administering an oath. Equally, he will not designate a community "unscrupulous" unless they actually validate non-valid oaths. If they at least have the person taking the oath grasp a sacred object, he will not condemn the procedure.

Bearing this distinction in mind should help us understand the strange formulation of a joint responsum of RSG and RHG explaining the technicalities of oaths administered in their court: "We compel whomever is obliged to take a Mosaic oath to grasp a sacred object in his hands as we say, 'The oath must be administered with a Torah scroll' " (OG San. 623). Now, if they cite the pericope requiring a Torah scroll as the basis for their practice, why do they require a sacred object? The explanation must be that although the Torah scroll is the *desideratum,* a sacred object is the minimum that may be tolerated—*post factum*—in fulfillment of the legal requirement.

In the light of all this, let us return to RLOW 3. RHG rules that the widow's oath was invalid because an oath should be administered in court. Then ("moreover" etc.), he proceeds to describe what she ought to have done. To begin with, she should certainly have held a Torah scroll. This does not mean that had she grasped some other sacred object the oath would have been invalidated. On the contrary, had grasping some other sacred object been the only blemish in her oath, RHG would undoubtedly have validated it, in concurrence with the explicit Talmudic ruling, and consistent with what he wrote in MPS 11 and OG Gittin 167. Our final analysis must therefore be that RHG does not decide against an explicit Talmudic ruling, but is rather totally in accordance with it.

B.   Here is another decision which is deceptive at first glance. BT cites a baraita: "Where a person appears in court [literally—'who comes to be judged'] with a deed and with [evidence] of undisturbed possession [ḥazaqa] judgment is given on the basis of the deed; [these are] the words of Rabbi. Simeon b. Gamaliel said: [Judgment is given] on [the basis of his] undisturbed possession" (BB 169b). The explicit amoraic ruling is found further on: "R. Giddal said in the name of Rav, *the halakah* in this case is in accordance with the statement of R. Simeon b. Gamaliel and even Rabbi disagreed only in respect of *lebarer* [to require further evidence to prove the plea]" (BB 170a). Ittur, in discussing the case, transmits the following tradition: "Rav Hai Gaon said that we may draw no conclusions [by analogy] from this case—in which the law is *lebarer* [to require further evidence to prove the plea]—to any other case with the exception of the case of him who claims: 'I repaid to you in the presence of X and Y'" [ibid.] (Ittur ii, 19c, see below, p. 72). Rav Hai, then, holds that in the case of a claimant who appears in court with a deed and undisturbed possession, the ruling is to require further evidence to prove the plea—like Rabbi. This decision seemingly contradicts R. Giddal's explicit ruling in the name of Rav.

In truth, RHG's ruling is consistent with the explicit ruling of R. Giddal in the name of Rav. The apparent inconsistency is due to Rav Hai's reading. Both his reliance on Rav's ruling and his variant reading stand out clearly at the end of chapter forty of MQM, where we read: "We also learned: Where a person appears in court with a deed . . . RSBG says: [Judgment is given] on [the basis of his] undisturbed possession also (!) . . . and R. Giddal said in the name of Rav the *halakah* in this case is in accordance with the statement of Rabbi" (!) "and even Rabbi disagreed only in respect of *lebarer* [to require further evidence to prove the plea]." We therefore conclude that not only is this case not an exception, but that both MQM and the Ittur's tradition are examples of RHG's practice of deciding according to explicit amoraic rulings.

C.   OG Ket. 203 (discussed above, p. 35) closes with a statement rather more difficult to explain. RSG and RHG consider the possibility that the bill of divorce was, after all, handed to the wife in the presence of two valid witnesses (see n. 9), who confirmed their presence by signing the bill. However, it was precisely one of those witnesses who, together with another party, had made it general knowledge, through valid formal testimony, that it was the husband's intent that the whole matter be fictitious, and that he carried it out just to avoid confiscation and harassment by the authorities. Does this oral testimony invalidate the signed, sealed, and delivered bill of divorce? To complicate matters, the second witness who signed on the bill of divorce did not know that the divorce was not genuine.

RSG and RHG end their responsum: "Although the one witness does not say so [that it was fictitious], this one [the one that says it was fictitious] comes to uproot his testimony, and the other remains alone just like that [case] of 'one witness [who] says [that there was] a condition, and one witness [who] says [that there was] no condition' [Ket. 19b] and the law follows R. Papa. And this is the law." The full discussion in Ket. is:

> If one witness says that there was a condition, and one witness says [that there was] no condition, R. Papa said: They both testify to a valid document and only one says that there was a condition, and the one witness has no value where there are two witnesses. R. Huna the son of R. Joshua demurred to this: If so, even if they both say [that there was a condition] [their words should] also [have no value]! But we say [that] they come to uproot their testimony, and this one also comes to uproot his testimony. And the law is according to R. Huna the son of R. Joshua. (MPS, p. 66.)

RSG and RHG seem to be opposing the explicit Talmudic ruling in favor of R. Huna the son of R. Joshua. In this case we know of no extant variant readings. In fact we have clear evidence that RHG's reading was no different from ours, because in MPS he quotes the ruling precisely as it appears in our Talmud. Moreover, he claims that the law is in accordance with that ruling. This is what he writes:

> If one [witness] testifies that a loan or gift is absolute, and one [witness] testifies that it is conditional, even if they are the witnesses whose signatures appeared in the bill, and the bill makes no mention of a condition, and only these witnesses can validate the bill, the law demands that we act according to the witness who testifies that it is conditional, or that we invalidate the bill altogether, as they said, "If one witness . . . to uproot his testimony. And the law follows R. Huna the son of R. Joshua."

Anything equal or similar to this is decided by the same law. Since RSG and RHG compare their case to this Talmudic case, we should have anticipated a decision in favor of R. Huna b. Joshua, invalidating the whole bill of divorce.

Given the ruling in MPS and taking into account all the examples considered heretofore in which RHG invariably ruled consistently with explicit amoraic rulings without a single exception (even when it meant contradicting some other principles of adjudication),[8] common sense will show that there is no exception in this case either. Hence, we suggest an emendation at the close of the responsum to read: "and the law follows R. Huna b. R. Joshua." It appears almost certain that R. Papa is cited because a scribe confused the two disputants. Our emendation is not a stop-gap to solve our difficulty. It is demanded by the context of the responsum. If we examine the responsum's penultimate line, we see that RSG and RHG argue that even though one witness does not testify to the fictitious nature of the divorce his testimony has no value since the other "comes to uproot his testimony just like that of 'one witness says' . . ." Now, the argument of one coming "to uproot his testimony" is precisely the contention of R. Huna b. R. Joshua against R. Papa. Obviously then RSG and RHG mean to rule in his favor, and only due to a scribal error was R. Papa written instead. The responsum should really read just like MPS and the Talmud, and is actually another example of RHG's principle always to rule according to an explicit amoraic decision.

This principle is so deeply ingrained in RHG's legal methodology, that it is unthinkable that he would decide contrary to an explicit Talmudic ruling without an explanation, all the more reason to believe that the cases we have considered are not exceptions. The following shows how apologetic he is when he veers from such a ruling ever so slightly: "The afternoon prayer [may be said] until sunset. R. Judah says until midway through the afternoon. The evening prayer has no set time" [It may be recited at any time after the terminal time of the afternoon prayer, whenever that be, depending on which of the two views is accepted] (M Ber. 4, 1). The Talmud notes that some *amoraim* conducted themselves according to the sages (to whom the Talmud attributed the former view mentioned in the Mishnah) and some according to R. Judah. It concludes that there is no clear ruling and therefore one may act as he chooses (Ber. 27a).

R. Hai said:

> The law was not decided neither according to R. Judah nor according to the sages as we say: "Seeing then that it has not been stated definitely that the law follows the one and not that the law follows

the other[12] if one follows the one he is right, and if one follows the
other he is right" [ibid.]. And this is the conclusion. Even though the
discussion is followed by an explicit ruling, namely, "if one follows the
one he is right, and if one follows the other he is right," nevertheless,
since R. Huna and the other Rabbis did not pray the evening prayer till
night [ibid.] following the view of the sages in M . . . it's best to act in
common with the more than one. Nonetheless if one does so [in
accordance with R. Judah] he is right [OG Ber. 173).

Here then, is a case where there is an explicit Talmudic ruling to allow freedom of
action. RHG accepts this freedom of action granted him and suggests following the
majority. Nevertheless, we sense his uneasiness that by leaning towards one view, he
went against the letter of the Talmudic ruling to allow each individual freedom of
action. Hence, the unusual apologetic tone ("even though the discussion" etc.), and the
immediate supplement of a release clause ("nonetheless, if one" etc.) so rare for one
whose decisions are usually couched in absolute and authoritative terms. From this we
may conclude—regarding the apparent exceptions considered above—that were he ever to
oppose an explicit Talmudic ruling, he would take pains to justify or explain his stand.

Only once did we find RHG holding like a *tana* in spite of an explicit amoraic
decision in favor of his adversary: "Our master Rav Hai said that if no cup [of wine] can
be found [for *Habdala*], when one sees fire and benefits from its light he should recite
the benediction 'who createst the lights of fire'" (ibid., 344). There is a tanaic dispute
whether one should recite this benediction as soon as he sees fire on the termination of
the Sabbath, or recite this and other benedictions for the termination of the Sabbath, in
order, over the cup [of wine]. R. Yoḥanan explicitly rules in favor of R. Judah who holds
that they should be recited in order over the cup (Pes. 54a). Why then did RHG instruct
that we recite the benediction without a cup? Was he contradicting R. Yoḥanan's
explicit ruling?

Perhaps not. Normally (where wine was available) he followed R. Yoḥanan's ruling
which he deemed authoritative and binding as he did all explicit Talmudic rulings. RHG
may have concluded that the tanaic dispute refers only to a situation where there is an
opportunity of having a cup of wine. If there is no such opportunity—as in the case we
are examining—RHG may have felt that even R. Judah would have agreed that one may
scatter the benedictions. Such a line of reasoning is followed by GRA in explaining the

ruling that if the fast of the ninth of Ab falls on Saturday night one recites the benediction on fire as soon as he sees fire (SUA OH 556, 1). GRA refers to BT (loc. cit.) and comments: "In such a case [where there is no opportunity to drink wine] all [including R. Judah] agree [to this practice]." Perhaps this was Hai's view as well. If so, the explicit ruling has no bearing on this case.

Alternatively, Hai may have believed that the tanaic dispute extended to this case. He may have felt that where instructing according to R. Judah meant foregoing the benediction over fire, it was best—but only as an exception—to disregard the ruling in favor of R. Judah and agree with the opposing view in order to preserve the practice of reciting the benediction on the termination of the Sabbath. In such a case—and in such cases only—where the alternative was disagreeable, did RHG ignore an explicit Talmudic ruling.

4

PRINCIPLES OF ADJUDICATION I

Origin and Application

Principles of adjudication are almost as old as divergent opinions among the Rabbis, and can be found throughout the Talmudic literature. As early as the ancient Mishnah of Eduyot—composed in JABNEH according to Rabbinic tradition—there lies the principle that "The *halakah* may be only according to the opinion of the majority . . . the opinion of the individual against that of the majority . . . does not prevail." (M EDUYOTH 1, 5-6). Early *amoraim*, in turn, formulated principles governing tanaic disputes, e.g., Samuel and R. Yohanan regarding laws of mourning (Erubin 46a) and R. Yohanan again (ibid., 46b) regarding the disputes between the leading *tanaim* of the post-persecution period (i.e., R. Judah, R. Jose, R. Meir, R. Simeon b. Yohai). In this latter pericope the principles of *amoraim* of the middle amoraic period are also cited.

Principles of adjudication governing amoraic material are scattered throughout the Gemara. Many of them are anonymous. Since they deal with later amoraic material too, a large number are conceivably saboraic, or at least from the end of the amoraic period.

Although the tradition that legal authorities formulate principles of adjudication was carried forward by *tanaim, amoraim, saboraim,* and early *geonim,* the first known compilation of principles and rules into a proper literary form is *Seder Tannaim ve Amoraim,* part of which is dated late ninth century (see S. Abramson, "Min Hapereq . . .," Sinai 88, p. 193 f. [and now in Bar Ilan University's just published E. Z. Melamed Jubilee Volume, pp. 215-247]). Beyond that, many such principles and rules are strewn throughout the geonic responsa, legal monographs, and introductory and general works the *geonim* wrote relating to the Talmudic literature (see "Tequfat," p. 223 f.). The latter type of literary activity reached its peak with R. Samuel b. Hofni's encyclopedic *INTRODUCTION TO THE TALMUD* (see Abramson in SINAI, cit. sup.).

Many of these geonic principles were actually adaptations and reformulations of the old Talmudic principles. Some were part of an oral tradition (Talmudic or saboraic). Others yet were innovations of various *geonim.* In this study we shall deal with all the principles invoked by RHG regardless of whether they were original or not.

In post-Geonic times among *rišonim* and *aharonim,* the principles became standard

44

support for all *posqim*. They assumed their proper role and position in the sea of later Rabbinic legal literature.

The most basic of all principles governing RHG's decisions, as we have seen, is following an explicit Talmudic ruling. Deciding cases in accordance with Talmudic ruling certainly implies acceptance of Talmudic authority and we have also seen that RHG tries to make BT the basis for his decisions whenever possible (above, p. 19). Cases clearly based on explicit rulings are easy fare for the post-Talmudic respondent, judge, or codifier. What happens, however, when a complicated Talmudic discussion ends without an explicit ruling? Are there principles of adjudication which guide RHG? If so, does he really follow them or does he, in fact, decide arbitrarily? How strictly does he adhere to them, and how does he resolve conflicts between principles or between principles and explicit decisions?

The most relevant declaration of RHG on these issues is found in a joint responsum with RSG to R. Jacob b. Nissim of Kairouan, who had raised similar questions.

> You asked: Those traditions which the Rabbis neglected in the Gemara and never resolved, should we deduce the law from principles governing Mishnah, or how are we to act?
>
> We most certainly do deduce the law [from the principles]. That is the ruling and we take action accordingly. If there is a dispute we seize upon the principles: [In disputes between] R. Meir and R. Judah the law is like R. Judah. Where an opinion is opposed to the majority the law is like the majority. And all the other principles which the Rabbis gathered. Because, if there were something [irregular] the Rabbis would have been specific. And where the principles were not law, the Rabbis were specific. Just as we find *mishnayot* in Kelim and elsewhere from which the law could have been deduced, about which the Rabbis were specific, as we say in Yebamot [43a], "Because of 'a comb for flax whose teeth have been removed,' the law is not like that," even though it is an anonymous mishnah.[1] (RDG 241.)

Although the question, and hence the responsum deals with principles governing *mishnayot*, all that was applied to mishnah holds true equally for principles governing Gemara, as we shall see in the course of our study.

What do we learn from this responsum?

1. That there are principles of adjudication, at least some of which were gathered by the Rabbis.

2. That those principles are authoritative and binding, and are meant to be invoked routinely in legal practice.

3. That if there is an instance in which these principles are not to be applied, we can expect the Talmudic Rabbis to say so.

4. That explicit Talmudic rulings take precedence over all the other principles. If there is a conflict between one of the other principles and an explicit decision, the other principle is not considered and we follow the explicit decision.

These four points can all be deduced from the Talmudic discussion cited (in the responsum) which revolves around the force of the principle: The law follows an anonymous mishnah. R. Nahum asks how this principle can be deemed authoritative, "Surely we learned an anonymous mishnah, 'A comb for flax whose teeth have been removed and of which two remained is unclean. And [if] one [remained, it is] clean' etc. . . . (M Kelim 13, 8. See Neusner, *Purities* II, 27-28] and it is established that the law is not like that mishnah [although it is anonymous]. He [R. Abahu] replied to him: 'With the exception of this, for both R. Yohanan and Reis Laqis, stated: This is not an [authoritative] mishnah' ".

From this discussion we can deduce:

1. That there are principles (e.g., the law is like an anonymous mishnah).

2. That usually they are binding (R. Abahu: This is an exception).

3. That exceptions are pointed out ("R. Yohanan and Reis Laqis stated").

4. That explicit rulings take precedence (all agree that the law is not like M. Kelim, in accordance with R. Yohanan and Reis Laqis).

The reasoning of the Talmud and the *geonim* in turn, for giving precedence to explicit rulings, seems to be that the principles were never intended for cases where there are explicit Talmudic rulings. The Rabbis—earlier and later—who compiled the principles did so to afford adjudication where there was no explicit ruling. It was their desire that we adhere to their rulings, where they exist, rather than to their principles. This is why we opened our study with what really is the most basic of principles: an explicit ruling should be followed. We now can better understand RHG's sharp reaction to anyone challenging an explicit ruling (OG Ket. 97, cited above, p. 23).

The idea that where there are explicit rulings, we are never meant to refer to the principles, was suggested by the Talmud in reply to an *amora's* skeptical query about the principles (Erubin 46b-47a). Principles of adjudication, attributed to Palestinian *amoraim* were introduced in the *sugya*. The Babylonian R. Mesarsya was skeptical about their authority. The Gemara wished to clarify the cause for his skepticism. Over and over again cases are cited in which there was a ruling in favor of R. Simeon when the disputant was R. Judah, suggesting that this led R. Mesarsya to believe that the principle "[In disputes between] R. Judah and R. Simeon the law is like R. Judah" was not authoritative. Again and again the Gemara rejects these suggestions, contending: "But what difficulty is this? When it was stated [well] it was stated." Rashi explains clearly: "Wherever it was stated explicitly that the law is like R. Simeon, [well] it was stated. And for what [cases] did we formulate the principle: In a dispute between R. Judah and R. Simeon the law is like R. Judah? It was for where it was not stated that the law is like the one or the other" (s.v. *heika*). In other words, where there is an explicit ruling we rely on it and do not even consider the principles. But where there exist no explicit rulings, the principles are authoritative. So was the approach in amoraic times, and such was geonic and rabbinic practice.

Some of the explicit Talmudic rulings which we have shown were sources of Hai's decisions, in fact conflict with accepted principles of adjudication. We shall come to more examples in the course of the study.

To close our discussion of this aspect of the theme, we wish to examine just one decision of Hai's—a decision which seems to contradict three principles of adjudication. The only explanation we can offer for the decision is that he was relying on an explicit Talmudic ruling, even though that ruling lies buried somewhere in the middle of a protracted Talmudic discussion. The topic under discussion is the prescribed area of the windpipe within which one must slaughter. Any game cut outside of the prescribed area renders the slaughter invalid (Hullin 18a-b). RHG rules in favor of R. Hanina b. Antigones whose opinion is the most lenient, i.e., allows the widest prescribed area (HS 95a and 98b). There is, to be sure, an explicit Talmudic ruling that the law follows R. Hanina b. Antigones (Hullin 19a). However, this ruling is followed by a lengthy discussion revolving around two views which disagree with R. Hanina—that of the Rabbis and that of R. Jose b. R. Judah (M Hullin 1, 3). We might just as well have thought that the ruling in favor of R. Hanina was *en passant*, while the wording of the rest of the *sugya* suggests three accepted principles of adjudication (which we will discuss at length later) all of which point in the direction of deciding against R. Hanina:

1.   The law follows the majority (the Rabbis).

2.   If a Talmudic discussion clearly revolves around one of the opinions in a dispute, that is the accepted decision.

3.   We should favor an opinion arrived at toward the end of a *sugya.*

If RHG nevertheless decides in favor of R. Hanina b. Antigones, we can only explain it as a statement of his view that an explicit Talmudic decision—no matter where it appears in the *sugya*—takes precedence over any one principle or several principles of adjudication and is binding on all judges and codifiers.

When there is no explicit ruling, RHG bases his decisions on Talmudic material or the Talmudic *sugya* by invoking those "other principles which the Rabbis gathered." The "Rabbis" covered a long time span, including the *tanaim* and *amoraim* themselves who established Talmudic principles, the *saboraim* who formulated many of the principles presently found in the Gemara, and the post-Talmudic Rabbis including RHG's predecessors, teachers, and contemporaries, who widened the bases of existing principles and added new ones. RHG himself, in a creative mold, innovated principles to serve him in the judicial and decision-making processes.

We turn now to a systematic methodological study of those principles. Initially we will follow the general guidelines of RDG 241 and then branch out to study other principles governing the tanaic and amoraic pericopae. We will note all clear Talmudic sources. We will follow the simple format of the previous chapter, that is giving a citation which shows RHG's explicit adherence to the principle, then gathering the responsa where he hinted at its use, and finally suggesting other responsa in which he seems to rely on the principle although he may not adduce to it at all.

Derivation from Undisputed Mishnayot, Beraitot, Statements, and Sugyot

From the procedural manifesto in RDG 241 (above p. 45) we learn that laws transmitted in undisputed *mishnayot,* although neglected by the Gemara, serve RSG and RHG as bases for legal action. A simple example is the concluding statement of RHG's responsum concerning bathing in hot water on the Sabbath or Festivals: "Water heated on a Festival is forbidden for washing but permitted for drinking" (Eskol i, 8). This is taken verbatim from M Shabbat 3, 4.

From RHG's responsa a clear picture emerges of how he extends this rule to other tanaic sources as well. For example, Terumot (49, 4, 6) cites two responsa of RHG whose solutions revolve around the same legal issues. The first is the case of a debtor who sent merchandise to his creditor with the request to sell it for him and send him the money. The creditor sold the merchandise but instead of sending back the profit, he seized the money in payment for the debt. Was he within his rights? The second is from a person who claimed that someone owed him money, and he happened to be holding a loan or a pledge from that person. May he seize what he has in lieu of what he is owed, take an oath affirming the debt, and keep it?

In both cases RHG permits the seizure (if accompanied by an oath), specifically basing his argument on Tosefta which teaches: "If one says: You have a maneh of mine, and the other replies: Indeed I do have a maneh worth of clothing or vessels of yours [which I'm withholding] on account of the maneh [you owe me], he is exempt" (T Šebuot 5, 5, according to RHG's reading. See TOSR iii, 178). The undisputed Tosefta, then, is RHG's source for allowing the creditor to take the matter of reimbursement into his own hands.

Elsewhere, it is a talmudic baraita which seems to serve as the basis of his decision, although he does not cite his source. Explaining how one can widen the circle of relatives who will share one's estate, RHG states: "The terms, 'he shall receive the bequest,' and 'he shall be heir' regarding one who is entitled to be his heir, are considered expressions of gifts" [and become the property of those designated] (DCA 290a, cited above 30). This is based on what is related in the Talmud: "In a baraita it was taught [the expression of] 'he shall receive the bequest' and 'he shall be heir' [are] also [legal] in [the case of] one who is entitled to be his heir" (BB 148b).

We have already stated our belief that RDG 241 which establishes RHG's and RSG's regard for principles of adjudication, talks of mishnah only because the question referred to mishnah, but that in reality "all that was applied to mishnah holds true equally for principles governing Gemara" (above p. 45). If we attempt to carry over to amoraic sources the principle just discussed, that laws transmitted in undisputed mishnayot, although neglected by the Gemara, serve as bases for legal action, we may anticipate something of this sort: Not only explicit amoraic decision but any undisputed legal statement of the Talmud or of a significant amora, should be considered authoritative and binding, and serve as a source for decisions. And in fact, such a principle is explicitly formulated by RHG (in a joint responsum with RSG): "Certainly in the whole Talmud . . . a statement explicitly uttered by an important man . . . cannot be shaken or appealed against" (MH 9, pp. 35-36).

Having thus established that this principle is a part of RHG's methodology, we can proceed to examine examples in which it is invoked. We begin with examples in which he cites or refers to the amoraic statements upon which his decision is based, so that it is clear from the responsum that, in accordance with his formulated principle, he is following an *amora's* statement.

A.   We have already seen (above p. 18) RHG's view (expressed in ŞZ 4, 3, 55) that in daily practice, gifts given with full intent are valid even though the donor does not use the "gift written in public" formula. One of his arguments is that "R. Seṣet stated: 'He shall take,' 'acquire,' 'occupy,' and 'own' [used by a dying man] are all legal expressions denoting gift" (BB 148b), and R. Seṣet mentions nothing about a public gift or the formula: Write the deed and sign it in some public place. Nonetheless, concludes RHG, R. Seṣet's formulae are no less acceptable than other formulae of gifts.

B.   X purchased gold from Y with the following stipulations: Delivery was to be in the month of Elul, and payment by the day before the Day of Atonement (i.e., the ninth day of Tiṣrei, the month after Elul). The price was set at twelve *zuz* a measure, with the additional stipulation that if the purchaser does not pay on time, he will then have to pay according to the actual market price at the time of the conclusion of the agreement which was thirteen and a half *zuz*. The gold was delivered as promised but X did not pay on time. Meanwhile the price of gold climbed, reaching fourteen and a half *zuz* by the end of Tiṣrei. When X finally sent Y *zuzim* from which to collect his due, Y took twelve and three quarters *zuz* per measure. X claimed that despite the agreement this was usury and forbidden (ŞZ 4, 2, 4).

RHG's responsum goes straight to the point, upholding X's claim: "This is our view, that this is outright usury as R. Nahman said: 'The general principle of usury is: All payment for waiting [for one's money[2]] is forbidden [BM 63b]. And since Y said, if you wish to withhold payment you will have to return gold pieces valued greater than the price agreed upon, that is payment for waiting, which is forbidden."

RHG, then, holds that any increment arising from an extension in time is usury and prohibited. He bases his decision on the above statement by R. Nahman. Interestingly, though he might have deduced the same conclusion from M BM 5, 2, he preferred using a decisive amoraic statement as his source.

C. In OG Ket. 203 (see above, pp. 35-36 and 39), RSG and RHG argue that if the witnesses were to testify that they had been told to write the qualifying notification (*modaà*) by the husband at the time he told them of the whole affair, then, even if they had not written it at the time, they may (and should) write it at a later date—even at the time of the court case. The source they cite as a basis for this argument is a statement by R. Nahman: "A *modaà* must be made in the presence of two persons, and they are at liberty to write it down only when being definitely[3] instructed to do so" (BB 40a).

D. RHG was asked about the propriety of entertainment at banquet halls by women with timbrels and choruses. He replied:

> If it is a company of men there is nothing so severe as this. Not only timbrels and choruses, but even entertainment by mouth is ugly and forbidden, because R. Joseph said, "When men sing and women join in it is licentiousness; when women sing and men join in, it is like fire in tow. For what practical purpose is this mentioned?—To abolish the latter before the former" [Sotah 48a]. So much more so in a banquet of men because it is an absolute prohibition. Whoever breaches this is placed under a ban (OG Gittin 18, p. 9 and OG Sotah 143).

RHG, then, cites R. Joseph's statement as his source for rather extreme punitive action.

E. In the case discussed in RDG 40 (see above, p. 33), the deceased's granddaughter— the daughter of his son from his first marriage—challenged the widow's right to maintenance from the property which had been destined for her father. RHG upheld the widow's right evoking the Talmudic narrative about Rabin: "As the sages said: 'For Rabin[4] had sent in his letter: If a man died and left a widow and a daughter, his widow is to receive her maintenance from his estate' [Ket. 49b]."

In the cases we have so far dealt with, RHG explicitly quotes the amoraic statement upon which he bases his decisions, demonstrating his use of the principle he laid down when still writing joint responsa with his father: statements of important men cannot be shaken or appealed against (above p. 50). We suggest that in the following responsa, too, amoraic statement serve as the basis of his decision, although he does not quote them, nor hardly refers to them. In each instance we will show which amoraic statement provided the basis for each ruling, and how.

A. According to Babylonian practice, after an animal is ritually slaughtered, its lung is inspected to verify that it did not have an infirmity which would render the animal *terefah* (see *OHM* 18). RHG rules: "If lobes of the lung do not adhere to each other [by fibrous tissue] [the animal is] kosher" (RDG 331, p. 159). This ruling is most certainly deduced from a statement of Rava: "If two lobes of the lungs adhere to each other [by fibrous tissue] no examination thereof can avail to render the animal permitted, but it is declared *terefah*" (Ḥullin 47a). Basing himself on Rava's statement, RHG arrives at his ruling by simple inference: If Rava states that it is the adherence of two adjacent lobes which renders the animal *terefah*, then certainly if they are non-adherent, the animal is kosher.

B. An assumption underlying the entire discussion in OG Ket. 203 (see above, p. 51), although not explicitly stated, is that a *modaà* affects bills of divorce as it does other contracts, agreements, and bills. The basis of this assumption is a statement of R. Šeṣet: "If one writes a protest [*modaà*] with regard to a document of divorce, then his protest is valid" (Àrakin 21b).

C. A claimant was told by the respondent, "I owe you nothing, but take an oath and collect your claim." The claimant declined, because he was pious and never took an oath —not an unusual practice. He asked, instead, that the court impose a ban on anyone evading paying him his due (RDG 333b). RHG was asked if the court should do so, if he might suggest a formula for the ban, and what constitutes taking an oath. In the course of his responsum RHG states: "We do not compel Simeon—the respondent—to answer 'amen' [after the recitation of the ban] because it is established that 'amen' is an oath."

Now in RHG's vocabulary, "it is established" almost always refers to some Talmudic source or law. In this responsum there is no intimation of how "it is established." The editor (RDG, n. 8) cites Šebuot 29b, no doubt referring to what "Samuel said: He who responds 'amen' after an oath—it is as if he uttered the oath with his own mouth, for it is written (Num. 5, 22), 'And the woman shall say Amen, Amen'."

Although Samuel's statement makes the same legal point as Hai's, the latter's formulation does not seem to be derived from the former. We suggest that his source is the statement of R. Jose b. R. Ḥanina (substantiated by the same Biblical verse), "Amen implies oath" (Šebuot 36a), a statement which differs from that of Rav Hai by only two

(Hebrew) letters (v. MPS, p. 38). In any case, we again find RHG relying on an amoraic statement as the source of his decision, without referring to it.

D. RHG closes OG Maschkin 79 (see above, p. 33) with the ruling that upon hearing of the death of one's mother or father he must rend his garments even if it is a distant tiding—as opposed to when hearing of the deaths of other relatives—even though the mourning obtains for only one day. The basis of this ruling seems to be a statement of R. Zeira: "In the case of father or mother one always rends one's garment" (MQ 20b).

All the above decisions comply with RHG's formulation of the principle of basing decisions on statements of specific "important" *amoraim*. We shall now see that in fact RHG went a step further and based decisions on statements of the *sugya*, the Talmud itself, a Talmudic editor or some anonymous voice from the Academy as well. This practice—basing decisions on statements found in the course of the Talmudic discussion— is known to have been used prior to the time of RHG and is encompassed in a sweeping principle found in *STA*, 42: "Every tradition ("ṣmáta") is law." We begin with responsa in which RHG specifically refers to amoraic statements (of no particular *amora*) as the source of his decisions.

A. RHG was asked about a court's suspicion that a seller and purchaser had used chicanery in order to circumvent abutter's rights (MH 16). He ruled that "if it has been definitely shown with clear proof that there has been trickery . . . the purchaser is removed from the property in favor of the abutter's rights. Proof of this is what we say: 'If one sold a *greiva* [a dry measure of land] in the middle of his estate, we see: if it is of the choicest or of the most inferior quality, the sale is valid; otherwise it is mere "evasion" ' [BM 108a]. Behold the matter is clear . . . that the sale is no sale." RHG, then, explicitly cites the statement of the *sugya* as his proof.

B. In a responsum chiefly exegetic in nature (RDG 333a, p. 160), RHG makes a number of digressions to rule on matters touched on by the Talmud in the discussions. He expresses the view that if one sells a field which is not his own, he must of course pay compensation, but is not obliged to provide the purchaser with the field even if it falls into his hands afterwards. His legal reasoning is that the purchaser never acquired rights to the field. He supplies proof for his view:

> Moreover, we [i.e., the Gemara] say regarding one who sold it [a field] when it was not his and subsequently purchased it from the

original owners: "It is obvious that if he [who stole a field and sold it]
subsequently sold it [to another person], bequeathed it to his heirs, or
gave it away as a present and then bought it [from the original owner,
we must assume that] he did [not][5] [in buying the field] intend to
secure it thereby for the [first] buyer. If it came to him as an
inheritance [we must assume this too, for an inheritance] comes of
itself [and he did not trouble himself to get it]" [BM 16a]. Behold he
is not obliged to produce it for the purchaser, because he never
intended to sell it.

Here too, RHG's "we say" is an overt reference to the statement of the Gemara which
provides the formulation for his view.

C. "We found in a responsum of our Rabbi Hai, o.b.m., that one recites the benediction
'who loosest them that are bound' when feeling around with his hands, and he wrote
there—and so wrote he in the Talmud—'When he opens his eyes, when he draws himself
up, when extending his side, when he dresses, etc.' But [adds the copyist] in all their
versions of the Talmud it was not found so [i.e., the benediction]" (Scribal addition to the
Oxford Ms. of SRA].[6] From the copyist's testimony it is obvious that RHG was citing his
version of the Talmudic pericope as the source for his ruling.

Having examined testimony from three responsa that RHG uses anonymous Talmudic
statements as sources for his decisions, we shall now present two others, where, in our
view, such statements serve as the basis of his decision even though he does not cite
them or even refer to them.

A. If, after slaughtering an animal, the routine check of the windpipe to see if it was
cut properly, shows "that the windpipe was pierced below the breast . . . it is considered
as if the lung was pierced. Just as, if the lung was pierced it is not valid, so if the
windpipe was pierced below the breast it is not valid, because it is like the lung itself"
(KGE 38). This ruling is based verbatim on a statement of the Talmud: "If the windpipe
was pierced below the breast it is considered as if the lungs were pierced" (Hullin 45a).

B. We have already explained in detail (above pp. 37-39) that RHG holds: Whoever
takes an oath should grasp a Torah scroll, and that this is based on a statement in the
Talmud: "The oath must be administered with a Torah scroll" (Sebuot 38b).

Having shown that RHG relies both on tanaic material and amoraic statements as
sources for his rulings, we now turn to combinations. When tanaic pericopae are
integrated, explained, or qualified by a significant *amora* or by a Talmudic discussion,

then these interpretations, explanations or qualifications are seen by RHG as authoritative. Hence, the tanaic pericopae together with the amoraic qualifications are binding. Here are some examples:

A. A congregational reader who had been suspected of improper conduct, but has since repented, may reassume his duties. However, he may still not conduct the services on a fast day, "because his youth was not unblemished, an evil reputation having gone forth in his youth" (OG Taanith 57-58, above p. 28). The reason, and consequently the ruling, is based on a tanaic source, a Talmudic *baraita*, and an amoraic explanation. The *baraita* says: "When they stand up to pray [on a fast day] . . . they place before the ark as reader only a man conversant with the prayers. R. Judah says . . . 'whose youth was unblemished.' Abaye said: This is one against whom no evil reputation had gone forth in his youth" (Taànit 16a-b). This combination can be traced precisely as the source of RHG's ruling.

B. Here now is a case of a mishnah with an amora's interpretation. We read in the Mishnah:

> As the testimony of two witnesses is void if one of them is found to be a kinsman or ineligible,[7] so the testimony of three is void if one of them is found to be a kinsman or ineligible . . . R. Jose said: This only applies in capital cases but in non-capital cases the evidence can be sustained by the remaining witnesses that are not ineligible. Rabbi says: It applies alike in non-capital and capital cases. When does it apply in capital cases? When they joined in warning the transgressor; but if they had not joined in the warning—what should two brothers do that saw one that committed murder? (M Makot 1, 8).

There is a Talmudic dispute as to the ruling: "It is stated: Rab Judah reported [his master] Samuel to have said that the *halakah* ["rule in practice"] was to follow the view of R. Jose while R. Nahman said that *halakah* ["rule in practice"] was to follow the view of Rabbi" (Makot 6a).

In a question to the geonic Academy, the questioners asked for a clear ruling in the dispute between Rabbi and R. Jose in light of the amoraic dispute about how to rule. If the law follows Rabbi, they added, is there any difference between oral testimony and witnesses signed in a legal document (RDG 236) i.e., if there are two consecutive signatures of valid witnesses, and, in addition, signatures of invalid witnesses and/or kinsmen, are we to invalidate the document? This problem often arose in the courts of the time (see below).

RSG and RHG responded to the request with a clear, detailed, and well documented response. They ruled that the law follows Rabbi and that, on principle, his stand holds true both for oral testimony and for witnesses signed on a document. Subsequently they cited in full Rava's interpretation of Rabbi. "Said Rava: We ask them whether they had come as mere onlookers, or to give evidence. If they say to give evidence, and one is found to be a near kinsmen, or a disqualified person, their entire testimony is void, but if they say they had come as mere onlookers, what could two brothers do that saw someone slaying a person? [i.e., the testimony is allowed to stand]" (Makot 6a).

Accepting Rava's interpretation of Rabbi as authoritative RSG and RHG understood him to mean that we are obliged to invalidate the whole group of witnesses only when we believe that the eligible witnesses intentionally joined the ineligible ones. Carrying Rava's interpretation one logical step further, they formulated the criterion of prearranged assembly ("noàdu"). This, then becomes their practical criterion—by taking Rabbi's view plus Rava's—in validating or invalidating groups of witnesses when one or more is ineligible or a kinsman. If we have reason to suppose prearranged assembly, then everything is void. If not, we can disregard the ineligible, and accept the testimony of the eligible. In writs or documents, if it is not established that all the witnesses converged, and we find two eligible witnesses signed consecutively, we may assume that they were the real witnesses, and the ineligible witnesses just added their signatures afterwards, thus not voiding the document.

This criterion, based on amoraic interpretation of a tanaic source is invoked not only in this responsum—where it was conceptualized and carefully worked out—but, once evolved, it served RHG as the guide in deciding other cases sent to him. In the following responsa, in all of which he again briefly discusses the *sugya*, he arrives at the same conclusions by using the same criterion.

1.   RDG 42—A *ketubah* was signed by three witnesses, only two of whom were known to the courts to be eligible witnesses.

2.   MH, p. 111—Four or five witnesses were signed on a legal document. The top two were ineligible or kinsmen.

3.   RLOW 3 (cited above pp. 37-38)—The *ketubah* of the widow who took the oath outside of court had been signed by three witnesses—two of whom were

kinsmen—placing its validity in question.

4-5.   RMBN BB 162b (cited in BY EH 120)—RMBN was familiar with two relevant responsa. In one RHG ruled that if the signatures of the ineligible witnesses come at the end, we assume that their signatures were appended. In the other he ruled that if the signatures were alternately of eligible and ineligible witnesses, we must assume prearranged assembly and invalidate the document.

In all these cases RHG applies his criterion, validating the testimony if there was reason to believe that the eligible witnesses did not prearrange to join the ineligible ones. RHG's principle of accepting tanaic pericopae together with their amoraic interpretations as authoritative units had far reaching results and eventually became the basis of some very important decisions of the Gaon.

We register this qualification to RHG's application of that principle: If a later *amora* did not draw upon the tradition of a predecessor when he might have, it is a sign that he did not deem that tradition authoritative. Once the tradition has been shunned, by an *amora*, its authority is shattered, and RHG did not rely on it as a source for his decisions. This approach manifests itself most clearly in this responsum which we find basic to understanding his legal methodology:

SZ 4, 5, 4. The questioners provide the background for their question by citing Mishnah: "If neither suitor was trustworthy the oath returns to its own place [to him against whom the claim is lodged (Danby ed.)]. So R. Jose. R. Meir says they share equally [half the claim only is paid (Danby ed.)]" (M Sebuot 7, 4). "It is established," add the questioners, "that our Masters of the Land of Israel and our Masters of Babylon disagree on how to interpret R. Meir, and the decision is to leave it to the discretion of the judges."

The questioners are referring to the Talmudic discussion revolving around the mishnaic phrase, "The oath returns to its own place." Here it is in full:

Whither does it return?—R. Ami said: Our Masters of Babylon said, the oath returns to Sinai [it cannot be applied]; our Masters of the Land of Israel said, The oath returns to him upon whom it devolves. R. Papa said: Our Masters of Babylon are Rab and Samuel . . . for we learnt: And so also orphans cannot exact payment except with an oath. And we discussed this: From whom? . . . But it means: and so also orphans from orphans cannot exact payment except with an

oath. And Rab and Samuel both said: They did not teach this, except
if the lender died during the lifetime of the borrower, but if the
borrower died during the lifetime of the lender, the lender was already
obliged to take an oath to the sons of the borrower; and a man cannot
bequeath an oath to his sons.

Our Masters of the land of Israel are R. Aba . . . (Ṣebuot 47a).

The decision to leave it to the discretion of the judges—mentioned by the
questioners—is thus:

(Ibid., 48b) R. Hama said: Now, since the law has not been stated
either in accordance with the view of Rab and Samuel or in
accordance with the view of R. Eleazer [who disputes Rab and Samuel
(ibid., 48a) and holds that the heirs swear the oath of heirs and receive
their due] if a judge decides as Rab and Samuel it is legal; if he
decides as R. Eleazar, it is also legal.

R. Papa said: This document of orphans [the borrower died during the
lifetime of the lender and then the lender died] . . . we do not exact
payment on it in case we agree with Rab and Samuel; and we do not
tear it up—for if a judge decides as R. Eleazer it is legal.

There was a judge who decided as R. Eleazer. There was a Rabbinic
scholar . . . he came before R. Hama who said to him: If a judge
decides as R. Eleazer it is legal.

With all this in mind, the questioners want RHG to rule on an issue which has led to
sharp disagreement among the local scholars. If a widow died without having taken an
oath, and her heirs claim her legacy from her husband's orphans, or if heirs of a creditor
claim a debt from the orphans, how should one rule?

RHG cites his version of another brief Talmudic discussion that the questioners did
not mention:

Rava said to R. Naḥman: "How did we learn in the Mishna" [was it R.
Jose or R. Meir who said that amount in dispute should be divided]?"
He said to him: "I do not know" . . . And R. Joseph b. Minyomi said
. . . that R. Nahman said, R. Jose says they divide. Some say in the
name of R. Joseph b. Minyomi that R. Naḥman decided a case
according to R. Jose who said they divide (ibid., 47a).

Now claims RHG, were this tradition to be relied upon, then the later amoraic
generations would have relied upon it. But behold, R. Hama is later and he decides to
leave matters to the discretion of the judges.

RHG's reasoning that the traditions regarding R. Joseph b. Minyomi were shunned, no doubt runs like this: Were either tradition regarded as reliable the issue would have been resolved in amoraic times. As RHG points out, had earlier *amoraim* accepted as verified, the reading of R. Jose in the Mishnah saying they divide, they would have ruled like him over R. Meir. So much more so had R. Nahman actually taken action and decided a case accordingly (see below, 64 ff.). Clearly, then, if later *amoraim* did not rule according to R. Jose they were purposely shunning R. Joseph b. Minyomi's tradition. Consequently, RHG too rules (in this responsum and elsewhere—RLOW 3, RDG 203 and MPS, pp. 79-80), that in the main we leave matters to the discretion of the judges. For if R. Hama and later *amoraim* did not draw upon R. Jose b. Minyomi's tradition to rule according to R. Jose, post-Talmudic generations too, should not accept the tradition as authoritative, and should not let it serve as the basis for their decisions.

Not all of RHG's predecessors were concerned with this reservation. RSdG was questioned about a similar case. A childless widow died. Her brothers and her husband's brothers contested the value of the *ketubah* and the property (OG Ket. 604). RSdG writes:

> We see: If the customary practice of the townsfolk is like R. Nahman, they [the husband's brothers] pay them [the widow's brothers] half their value. [As the basis of his ruling he cites the Mishnah (loc. cit.) and the tradition of R. Joseph b. Minyomi, then adds] And how do we know that we do not act according to R. Nahman except in places where they were accustomed to do so, because at the end of the discussion they said thus: "Rav Papa said: This note document of orphans, drawn up on other orphans [heirs], we do not tear it up [etc.] ... From this we learn that we do not divide the value between them except in places where they customarily did so" (ibid., pp. 247-48).

RSdG, then, did not reject the tradition of R. Joseph b. Minyomi outright, as RHG did. He did not claim, as did RHG, that if a later *amora* does not draw on a tradition of an earlier one, it is a sign that it is not authoritative, and should be rejected. RSdG rather saw both views as representing different traditions, both of which are legitimate and may be followed by those institutions or localities which have established a custom to follow one tradition or the other.

RSdG's approach, not to reject an amoraic statement even if later *amoraim* did not draw upon it, was the more classic geonic approach (see below). Among his Sura predecessors we find a responsum of Moses Gaon taking that approach. He, too, was questioned about a widow who died without taking an oath. In that case, the widow had willed gifts to her heirs from her *ketubah* or dowry (HGN 62). R. Moses discussed the relevant Talmudic material at length and commented regarding R. Joseph b. Minyomi's tradition about R. Nahman: "Whenever the judge does not feel comfortable about ruling neither according to R. Eleazer nor according to Rab and Samuel he may act like R. Nahman . . . behold R. Nahman already took into consideration both R. Eleazer and Rab and Samuel." He then viewed all the Talmudic traditions as possible alternatives for all judges. He did not believe as RHG, that it was enough that R. Hama and R. Papa ignored R. Joseph b. Minyomi's tradition, for contemporary judges to shun it as well. Nor did he agree with RSdG that the tradition be confined to just those localities which were accustomed to act accordingly.

In RHG's earlier years his opinion stood close to that of RSdG and R. Moshe Gaon, which seems to have been the traditional one in Pumbedita as well as in Sura. However, from the time he began composing responsa, his break with the traditional approach in this issue was total and he was relentless in invoking this qualification of "acceptance of later *amoraim*". One responsum in particular gives us further insight into his method of reasoning. In it he explains quite clearly why he maintained the stand he did.

Rabbi Zekharya Agamati *(Sefer Hanner*, p. 18) records statements of Rab and R. Yohanan. "Rab[8] said: One should never petition for his needs in Aramaic; and R. Yohanan said: When one petitions for his needs in Aramaic, the Ministering Angels do not heed him, for they do not understand Aramaic" (Shabat 12b). Regarding the authority of these statements, he quotes a responsum of RHG: "We have never heard of anyone paying attention to those statements of Rab and R. Yohanan. On the contrary, from a number of actions and statements found in the Gemara about Rabbis and angels that speak Aramaic, we learn that the sages disputed them, Rab and R. Yohanan, and rejected their statements as unintelligible. And just as the ancients did not heed them, so should we not pay any attention to them."

Again we find that RHG invoked the familiar principle: If statements of early *amoraim* (in this case Rab and R. Yohanan) were not drawn upon by later *amoraim*, who used Aramaic with the angels, then we, too, must not accept them as authoritative.

What RHG adds here suggests more clearly the reason for using this principle (or qualification of an earlier principle). By not drawing upon the earlier view, rather by ignoring it, the later *amoraim* are, in fact, disputing that view, albeit passively. Ignoring to RHG is tantamount to rejection. One cannot remain neutral. Since his principle regarding the acceptance of statements by important *amoraim,* and of the *sugya* as sources for decisions refers only to undisputed statements, it cannot apply when the tradition has been ignored (i.e., disputed or rejected). In these cases decisions must be reached through other principles of adjudication, particularly those governing disputes, and especially disputes between earlier and later *amoraim.*

Here is a case in which RHG does rule according to the pronouncement of an important *amora,* but only after taking pains to stress that the *amora* is not in dispute or conflict with a view of either a contemporary or a later *amora.* "R. Zeira said to his attendant: Put your mind to it and blow [the *shofar*] for me" (RH 28b). The Talmud deduces: "I gather from this that in his opinion the performer requires to put his mind to it [i.e., to perform consciously for the benefit of the listener]" (RH 29a). This pronouncement and deduction comes toward the end of a long discussion dealing with "intent" in which it would appear that both Rabah[9] and Rava hold that commandments do not require intent.

"Our Rabbai Hai ruled this [according to R. Zeira]. We must say that R. Zeira ... did not disagree with Rabah, but rather they both held that commandments do not require intent ... if so, the view or R. Zeira does not disagree with Raba and Rava and we act according to him" (OG RH 72). The justification for relying on R. Zeira is that he is not in conflict with *amoraim* who succeeded him. In other words, the principle of deciding according to an important *amora,* holds true only when his view is undisputed.

Both in the responsum just discussed, and in SZ 4, 5, 4 (the first responsum of this series) RHG considered conflicting views in the *sugya,* decided in the above case that there are none and therefore accepted R. Zeira, but decided in the latter case that there are, and therefore rejected R. Joseph b. Minyomi. The responsum from *Sefer Hanner* (discussed on p. 60) represents a departure and a development. RHG does not limit the field of his consideration only to the discussion in which the views appear, nor even to the "wider *sugya.*" Nowhere does RHG claim that there is any evidence in the *sugya* in Shabat that anyone takes exception to the view of Rab and R. Yohanan. On the contrary, he emphasizes "from a number of actions and statements found in the Gemara," i.e., that they lie elsewhere in the Talmud, outside of this particular discussion. This implies a "Beware!" sign for any codifier or judge wishing to invoke the principle of deciding according to an amoraic statement. He must first ascertain—and this requires extensive knowledge—that not only is the statement neither disputed or ignored in the *sugya* in which it appears, but that nowhere else in the Talmud is it rejected explicitly or implicitly,[10] by contradictory statements or actions, or by being shunned. This is what Hai means when he writes "from a number of actions and statements . . . *we learn.*" The scholar called upon for a decision must be able to draw conclusions from evidence strewn all through the Talmud, that the statement upon which he wishes to rely was indeed deemed authoritative by the Talmud itself and by all its contributors.

We can now go a step further. What we have been saying about individual amoraic statements holds true equally for complete *sugyot*. RHG believes that a law accepted throughout a *sugya* or resolved at its conclusion, should be accepted by post-Talmudic authorities as a basis for decisions, providing there is no other *sugya* to be found in the whole Talmud which is based on assumptions contradictory to that law or in which opposite conclusions are reached. RHG views the basing of a decision on the final opinion of a *sugya* as legitimate legal methodology and was wont to do so himself, but only when it is clear that there is no contradictory, refuting, or disputing *sugya* elsewhere. Because our sensitivity and erudition often falls short of that of the Gaon, we occasionally find ourselves wondering, when studying a responsum, why did RHG not draw his conclusion on the basis of this *sugya* or resolve the issue on the basis of that one. With closer scrutiny we often find the solution: a clear cut dispute with another *sugya*. Some cases are less obvious, and more careful sleuthing is required to discover which other *sugya* RHG may have felt opposes the given one, and obviates a decision according to it. Some decisions of RHG remain enigmatic because we are unable to uncover the *sugya* which may have led RHG to decide against the more obvious one.

Here is an example of *sugyot* clearly in conflict, taken from a responsum dealing specifically with that conflict: The displaced community of Fez asked RSG and RHG to decide between the contradictory conclusions of two Talmudic discussions (MH 9).[11] The conclusion of the discussion in BB 70a-b is: "If a man deposits an article with another and receives a written acknowledgement for it, and the other, subsequently asserts, 'I returned it to you' . . . we accept his word . . . on his taking an oath." On the other hand, in Sebuot 45b the Gemara claims that there is agreement that "He who deposits [an article] with his neighbour . . . by document, he must return it to him before witnesses," meaning that if he does not do so and claims "I returned it to you," he is not believed.

RSG and RHG entered into a detailed study of the discussion in Ṣebuot, which is the more complicated one, and claimed that it does not present clearly the stand of even one participating *amora*. But, they claimed, the discussion in BB is clear and open and they accepted its conclusion. In other words, they rejected the Ṣebuot *sugya* in favor of that of BB, and thereafter the whole Ṣebuot *sugya* no longer played a role in their rulings on the topic.[12] One should not rely on it because it is disputed elsewhere by another *sugya*—a *sugya* more acceptable to RSG and RHG.

In the above case the contradiction between the two *sugyot* was clear, and the geonim's rejection of one in favor of the other was explicit. Unfortunately it is not always so. Sensitivity to such contradictions might have saved a distinguished scholar, J. Shor, from unnecessary speculation. *Itim* (p. 44), quotes a passage from one of Hai's responsum in which the Gaon was asked how it was that the Israelites did not prepare *erubim* in pre-Salomonic times. RHG replied, "All those years that the Israelites were occupied with wars, enemies, and various troubles, they had not [opportunity to measure the distance] between cities . . . and to prepare *erubim* because they had to go out in camps and guard the border and there *erubim* are not practical, because they are exempt from preparing the *erubim* in military camps, as we learned in the mishnah, 'Four things have they permitted to men that are in a camp. They are exempt from . . . preparing *erub'* " (M Erubin 1, 10). The editor, Shor comments (n. 10) that from mention of cities it is obvious that RHG is referring to *erubei teḥumim*. In this Shor is undoubtedly correct. He then wonders: How can RHG say this, since the Talmudic discussion around the mishnah (Erubin 17b) notes that only *erubei ḥazeirot* were abrogated in camps, but not *erubei teḥumim*. Shor does not offer an acceptable solution to the problem he raised.

The real solution to Shor's query is that RHG most probably never accepted the *sugya's* distinction between the two types of *erubim*. Although nowhere in the discussion is there any hint of anyone having a reservation about that distinction, we still must ascertain whether it is universally accepted. The distinction between *erubei teḥumim* and *erubei ḥazeirot* is possible because in the *sugya* the prohibition of movement beyond the Sabbath boundary is said to be Mosaic (Biblical), while that of carrying between private domains is universally accepted as being Rabbinic. It is this distinction which is the basis of the assertion that only the principle of *èrubei ḥazeirot* was abrogated in the camp (since its prohibition is only Rabbinic). Now, there are other *sugyot* in the Talmud which take the view that the prohibition of movement beyond the Sabbath boundary is also Rabbinic. Most codifiers accept the latter view.[13] RHG, too, probably shared the majority view. If so, there is no difference between the two types of *èrubim*, and if one is abrogated in camp the other is too (Erubin 17b notwithstanding). Undoubtedly this is RHG's view as well. Although he cites the mishnah and bases his remarks on it, he rejects the Talmudic *sugya* revolving around it (that which caused Shor consternation) in favor of other, conflicting, *sugyot*, without specifically saying so.

Derivation from Actions

So far we have been dealing with statements and their authority, but "action speaks louder than words."[14] This holds true for RHG's principles of adjudication as well. The actions and deeds of a *tana* or *amora* which register a legal point are deemed by RHG even more authoritative than their statements, and become part of the legal material which serve him in adjudication. RHG draws this principle from the Talmudic formula: "An act [or practical decision] is weightier" (literally: "An act is a teacher"--Sabat 21a s.n.). We see how *amoraim* so esteemed actions when the Talmud suggests that R. Aba considered them a more significant source for decisions than even explicit rulings (BB 130b). RITBA comments on this suggestion: "And such is the manner of the Gaon to say that action is preferable."

RHG quotes the Talmudic "an act is weightier" formula verbatim on two occasions when ruling in favor of an act recorded in the Talmud:

A. RSG and RHG were asked to explain M Hullin 2, 2 and a number of passages in Hullin 30a-b, and to rule on their practical legal applications, since there was disagreement not only among *amoraim*, but among later codifiers as well (RDG 376). The mishnah reads: "[If] two people hold a knife and effect an act of slaughter [of a single beast], even one higher up and one lower down—their act of slaughter is valid." This mishnah is interpreted by some *amoraim* as referring to two people who slaughter with separate knives, one higher up and one lower down. Others interpret the mishnah as referring to two people holding one knife, one holds the knife at the upper end one at the lower, for

according to these latter *amoraim,* slaughter in two places simultaneously is invalid.

Other relevant pericopae are:

> Rab Judah said in the name of Rab: "If one cuts the throat in two or
> three places the slaughtering is valid. But when I reported the
> statement to Samuel he said to me, 'We must have a wide open cut and
> it is not so here,' Reiṣ Laqiṣ is also of the opinion that there must be a
> wide open cut." (The view of Samuel and Reiṣ Laqiṣ coincides with
> the latter interpretation of the mishnah, and that of Rav, with the
> former.)

> An ox was once slaughtered, its throat having been cut in several
> places and R. Isaac b. Samuel b. Martha came and obtained some
> choicest meat of this animal. Whereupon R. Zera said to him, "You
> have [by your actions] taught us, Master, that our mishnah deals with
> the case of two knives and two persons."

The *geonim* weighed the issues carefully to decide which principles of adjudication

could be applied. They eventually ruled in favor of Rab for three reasons, one of which

is: "The act of R. Isaac b. Samuel b. Martha, and it is established that an act is

weightier."

B. "Reuben donated stored barley to the poor before the Passover. The rains came and

leaked into the storehouse and into the barley. Circumstances prevented him from

selling it before the Passover" (OG Pessachim 14). Is it considered *hamez* which was in

his possession during the Passover and is now therefore prohibited? Must it be destroyed,

or may the barley be sold, and the money given to the poor?" RHG responds:

> The barley is to be inspected. If it was as *hamez* which was in his
> possession during Passover it is prohibited ... and what is the
> inspection of the barley? We see if they split because of the rains
> which fell upon them or not, as we say [Pesaḥim 40a] "Our Rabbis
> taught: One may not wash [moisten] before grinding the barley on
> Passover; and if one did wash [them] and they split they are
> forbidden; if they did not split they are permitted." And even though
> we observed in connection with that [ibid.]: "Mar Uqba said: It does
> not mean literally split but [if they reach] such [a condition] that if
> placed on the duct [spout] [15] they will split of themselves" then they
> are forbidden. Haven't we said [ibid.] "Samuel said: It means literally
> split." Samuel acted in the vicinity of Bar Ḥasuba [16] [on the view
> that] "split" is meant "literally." And it is established that an act is

weightier.

Having shown RHG's making explicit mention of the Talmudic term: "an act is weightier," let us turn to responsa where the term is not mentioned, but the principle is very much in force, since RHG explicitly refers to the action on which he bases his ruling.

A. To examine laws of mourning the Talmud relates a tale: "When Rab, R. Hiyya's brother's son—who was also R. Hiyya's sister's son—came up there [to Palestine], he [R. Hiyya] asked him [Rab] 'Is father alive?' He replied, [ask me whether] 'Mother is alive!' Again he asked, 'Is mother alive?' He replied, [ask me whether] 'Father is alive!' Thereupon he [R. Hiyya] said to his attendant, 'Take off my shoes and carry my things to the [public] baths.' (MQ 20a and Pes. 4a). The Gemara concludes that "From this we learn three lessons: We learn that a mourner is forbidden to don shoes; that a delayed report [of death, i.e., after thirty days] entails [formal mourning] but for one day; and that part of the day is [deemed] as an entire day['s mourning]."

Taking his lead from the Talmud that the action of R. Hiyya can serve as a basis for deducing three laws, RHG too deduces three laws from R. Hiyya's actions. One is identical to that of the Talmud, the other two are original: "Whoever received a delayed report of death after thirty days observes the formal mourning period for only one day, and is obliged to rend his garments in mourning over his father and mother . . . and need not sit in mourning position until comforters come to comfort him as we say, 'When Rab, R. Hiyya's brother's son' etc." (OG Maschkin, 79, cit. sup., pp. 33 and 53).

B. RHG was asked about the practice of sounding a long *shofar* blast after the New Year service (OG RH 82). He answered that neither he nor his forefathers practiced it as a custom ("*minhag*") in the technical-legal sense of the term. "However there are individuals who blow each according to his desire because (RH 30a), 'When R. Isaac b. Joseph came, did he not report that when the congregational reader had finished blowing in Yabneh, a man could not hear his own voice in his ears for the noise of the blowing of individuals.' We learn from this that the ancients were accustomed to individuals sounding the *shofar* after the service . . . blasting after the service is a meritorious deed . . . and it is a good thing to do." RHG, then, invokes the actions of the scholarly congregation of Yabneh to provide legal justification for what seems to have been fairly common practice, although in the *sugya* the action was related *en passant*, without normative intent.

C. Regarding the Biblical injunction, "No man shall take the nether or the upper millstone to pledge for he taketh life to pledge" (Deut. 24, 6), the Mishnah declares: "They spoke not only of the nether and the upper millstone, but of aught wherewith is prepared necessary food, as it is written, 'For the taketh life to pledge' " (BM 9, 13). RHG considers what constitutes vessels "wherewith is prepared necessary food": "Every vessel of handicraft which provides livelihood to the craftsman is called a vessel 'wherewith is prepared necessary food' . . ." This view is supported by the tale in BM 116a, "A certain man took a cobbler's knife in pledge. On his coming before Abaye, he ordered him: 'go and return it because it is a utensil used in the preparation of food' " (cited in DCA 158a). RHG could have supported his view by citing beraitot found in that very same sugya which state that if one takes in pledge a pair of barber's shears, he incurs a double penalty. Nevertheless, he chose to support his view with Abaye's action, undoubtedly because "an act is weightier."

D. SZ 4, 5, 4 (discussed in detail, sup. 57 f.). After ruling that the decision is left to the discretion of the judge, RHG informs the questioner, that for the most part his judicial decisions are according to Rav and Samuel. His concluding reason for acting thus is, "That case of a man who died and left a guarantor (borrower and lender both having died)." The reference is to Sebuot 48b where R. Papa and R. Huna the son of R. Joshua disagree as to whether to permit the heirs to take an oath in this case. RHG argues that in this actual case, "Both R. Papa and R. Huna b. Joshua followed the reasoning of Rav and Samuel (each interpreting differently)." The practical actions of amoraim become a consideration in RHG's deciding—qua judge—how to judge when the decision is left to his discretion.[17]

Having examined responsa in which RHG explicitly mentions the Talmudic principle, "an act is weightier," and then others in which, though he does not cite the principle by name, he does refer to the recorded actions which serve as the basis of his rulings, we require no further proof that this was one of his governing principles. We now therefore introduce yet other responsa, in which we believe that actions recorded in the Talmud served as the basis of his rulings, although RHG makes no specific reference to such action in the responsa.

A. RDG 323. A man died leaving sons and unmarried daughters. One daughter died within a year of the father. The sons then went about dividing the estate. They put aside the required sums for their sisters' marriage outfits (a tenth of the estate). The firstborn then demanded his rights to a double share of the remainder of the estate. His brothers granted his claim regarding most of the estate. However, they contended that there is no firstborn right to what would have been the marriage outfit (tenth of the estate) of the deceased sister. They argued that it was her due from the father, and upon her death it returned to the estate. Since it is well known and accepted that the firstborn right to a double share apply only to what is part of the estate at the time of the father's death, they continued, the firstborn brother in their case, had no special claim on her share. Not so claimed the firstborn. The sister had no due from the estate proper. What she did have was a claim on all the brothers, equal to that of a creditor. Since she could never materialize that claim, it remained part of the estate. Hence he was entitled to the firstborn's double share of that as well.

RHG replies: The law is just as the firstborn claimed, that the daughter did not inherit nor did she come into possession of anything that she might have left as legacy to her brothers. For it is established that a daughter, in her claim to her tenth, has the legal status of a creditor of the brothers, and it is incumbent upon the brothers to set her up properly when she is ready for marriage. But if she should die before then, she has nothing [to bequeath].

Let us now determine how RHG knows that *it is established* "that she is a creditor of the brothers." The Gemara (Ket. 69a) accepts the view that an orphaned daughter is indeed a creditor. The *sugya* then raises the question: Is she a creditor of the father or of the brothers? No clear answer is given. However, two incidents are recorded in which Rabina treated orphaned daughters as creditors of the brothers. No doubt, it was these recorded actions of Rabina which made it clear, in RHG's eyes, that "*it is established* that she is a creditor of the brothers."

B. RHG was asked, "May a Jew roast kosher meat in a gentile's oven used for roasting non-kosher meat?" (OG Pes. 208). He replies that when there is contact between the two kinds of meat the kosher meat becomes non-kosher. However, in cases where the kosher meat is on a spit, even if there is non-kosher meat in the oven simultaneously, the ruling would be dependent on the outcome of a Talmudic dispute between Rav and Levi: "Rab said fat meat of a [ritually] slaughtered [animal] which was roasted together with lean meat of *nebelah* [in the same oven on separate spits] is forbidden. But Levi maintained: Even lean meat of a [ritually] slaughtered [animal] which was roasted together with fat meat of *nebelah* is permitted. What is the reason? It is a mere smell and smell is nothing" (Pes. 76a-b). Rav Hai rules that the law follows Levi. Hence, if someone did already roast meat in such a fashion, it remains kosher, although one should take care not to do so to begin with.

Why does RHG rule in favor of Levi, who as the Gemara shows (ibid., b) was dependent on *tanaim*, which would normally be sufficient reason for the law not to follow him (v. inf., p. 81)? RHG's reasoning for favoring Levi seems to be thus: Regarding Rav's stand on this issue we know only his registered opinion. Levi, on the other hand, according to the Gemara (ibid.), "gave a practical decision in accordance with his view at the home of the Exilarch in the case of a goat and 'something else' (i.e., swine)." Since Levi actually took action, RHG no doubt invokes the principle of "an act is weightier" and rules in his favor.

The legal authority which RHG attaches to acts recorded in the Talmud, occasionally places him in an uneasy situation. If actions are authoritative, then they must certainly be compatible with the mainstream of accepted Talmudic legal tradition. How then is RHG to treat those actions recorded in the Talmud which seem to be contrary to the established law as he understood it (on the basis of one or more of the other principles of adjudication)? He has no option but to reinterpret those actions so as to harmonize them with what he deems to be the established Talmudic law, no matter how forced these interpretations might be. Here, then, are examples of such forced interpretations resulting from his adhering to the principle "an act is weightier."

A. An issue discussed widely in the responsa and legal works of the *geonim* is the propriety and permissibility of fasting on the Sabbath and Festivals.[18] In one responsum, RHG states his position that fasting on the Sabbath is prohibited, but on the Festivals it is permitted except for Pentecost (OG Jom-Tow 43). As his source, he cites Pesaḥim 68b.[19]

> All agree in respect to the Feast of Weeks [Pentecost] that we
> require [it to be] "for you" too . . . Rabbah said: All agree in respect
> to the Sabbath that we require [it to be] "for you" too . . . Rabbah
> said: All, agree that on Purim we require "for you" too. RHG
> continues, "and afterwards we say [ibid.], 'Mar son of Rabina would

fast the whole year except on the Feast of Weeks, Purim and the eve
of the Day of Atonement.' [He continues] Obviously then, on the days
of which was said 'for you too' he did not fast. And that is how Rabbis
came to say that on the Sabbath day he did not fast, because that is
what it says at the beginning of the discussion."

RHG was faced on the one hand with universal agreement, registered at the
beginning of the discussion against fasting on the Sabbath; agreement which ought to
make that stand authoritative. On the other hand, the same discussion concluded by
describing the actions of Mar, the son of Rabina, a description which apparently implies
fasting on the Sabbath, contrary to the law established by universal agreement. Since in
RHG's view, an action recorded in the Talmud is likewise authoritative, he had no choice
but to accept the interpretation of unnamed Rabbis that Mar, the son of Rabina, did not
in fact fast on the Sabbath. This interpretation is rather forced since the exceptions
were enumerated in the discussion (cited above) and Sabbath was not one of them. It was
RHG's high regard for the weight of an action which drove him to accept this forced
interpretation.

B.   In RDG 331 (cit. sup., p. 52) RHG discusses the *sugya* in Ḥullin 48a. He cites the
following traditions as authoritative (tendered with his interpretations).

1.   "R. Naḥman said: If the lung [which is being inspected after slaughter (v. loc.
     cit. sup.)] adheres to [literally: is close to] the chest wall, and there is an
     eruption of ulcers there is great fear with regard to it (i.e., whether it is kosher
     because there may be perforation)."

2.   In the same discussion, it is further stated: "R. Isaac b. Joseph was walking
     behind R. Jeremiah in the butcher's market. He noticed certain lungs with
     ulcers and he said: "I declare them permitted."[20]

Rav Hai, then, must extricate himself from an apparent contradiction between the
legal tradition he deems authoritative, and a similarly authoritative report of an *amora's*
action. He does so by interpreting R. Naḥman's tradition as dealing with ulcers on the
adhesion,[21] which raise doubt as to the animal's being kosher, while interpreting the
market tale as dealing with the ulcers in the lung proper,[22] which are permissible.
Again, his attaching great weight to Talmudic actions precludes his rejecting the legal
view found in the tale, and necessitates the somewhat forced harmonization.[23]

The "weightier acts" which serve RHG as sources for adjudication are usually those recorded in the Babylonian Talmud. However, this is not necessarily due to their carrying more weight than acts recorded elsewhere, but is most likely because BT is RHG's major source and chief frame of reference.[24] In fact, acts recorded in other Rabbinic works also serve Hai as sources for adjudication. They, too, are deemed authoritative.

This usage was already pointed out by medieval Rabbis in connection with RHG's ruling that when a fast day is due to begin at sundown, one who has concluded the repasts of the day, and has recited the grace after meals, may eat again before sundown, even though he originally had no intention of eating before the fast.[25] The source of the ruling is a tale in Lamentations Raba (3, 6) and cited in a question posed to R. Hai (OG Taanith 34):[26] R. Judah b. Beteira went to Nezivin on the eve of the Day of Atonement. He ate and ceased. The Exilarch came to invite him. R. Judah said to him, "I have already eaten and ceased." Eventually he yielded to the Exilarch's insistence and dined with him. The questioners asked how to reconcile this with the conclusion of the Talmudic *sugya* (Taänit 12a, Malter, p. 43 1.7 ff.), regarding fast days due to begin at daybreak, that once having said grace after the repast and before the advent of the fast, one may no longer taste food, even if there is still time left before daybreak.

RHG differentiates between those fast days beginning at daybreak and those beginning at sundown. The Talmud's prohibition applies only to the former. Indeed, it is precisely from the conduct of R. Judah b. Beteira that we derive the ruling that on fast days beginning at sundown, one may always eat again until sundown without hesitation. RHG repeats this ruling in another responsum (cited in Eṣkol 1, p. 126) but formulates the view without even mentioning the tale which served as its source (v. also BHM, Taänit 11 and sup., n. 25).

Having first seen that "acts are weightier" even than statements of significant *amoraim,* which in themselves are authoritative (see above p. 49) it is understood that RHG will rule according to a statement backed by an act. An example of this, one which leads him to an extreme and unpopular conclusion, is his ruling (cited RABIAH Ḥullin, p. 154 and The responsa of RDVZ, V. ii, 659): "Whoever does not give the priests' due[27] should be put under a ban like R. Ḥisda said [Ḥullin 132 b] 'A butcher[28] who does not give the priestly dues etc. [is to be put under the ban of the Lord God of Israel]'." Although the responsum is not cited in full, we do not doubt that RHG's view was strengthened by what follows in the *sugya:* "Rabbah son of R. Shila said, 'The butchers of Huzal have been under the ban of R. Hisda for the last twenty two years'." The action supporting that statement probably clinched the argument for RHG.

As we anticipated, then, RHG decides easily with a statement supported by an act. But how does he treat an act which qualifies a statement? From one ruling, which has already been discussed, it appears that RHG holds with the qualification.[29] We have noted (above p. 39) RHG's ruling that, if one claims: I repaid to you in the presence of X and Y, further evidence is required to prove the plea. This is ruling based on an actual court decision of R. Yizḥaq Nafḥa (recorded in BB 170a) who was basing on Rav's statement (ibid.): "Where one claims I repaid to you in the presence of X and Y, it is necessary that X and Y should come and give evidence." R. Yizḥaq is admittedly delivering judgment according to a qualification of Rav's original statement. Rav Hai ruled according to that qualification following R. Yizḥaq's action.

PRINCIPLES OF ADJUDICATION II

An Individual Opposed to More Than One

In the two preceding chapters we have seen how RHG uses Talmudic material as sources for his rulings on specific issues. The Talmudic material considered was either undisputed statements, explicit rulings, or acts interpreted as expressing established legal modes. We shall now turn to undecided Talmudic disputes, and show how RHG decides them, establishing those decisions as bases or proofs for his rulings to the questioners. His methodology is founded in principles of adjudication, as he writes in RDG 241 (cit. above, p. 45 f.), "We seize upon the principles ... and all the other principles which the Rabbis gathered," namely, all the intricate principles of adjudication. As we have already noted (ibid.), RHG, deals with tanaic material, because that is what the questioners asked about. It should, however, become clear in the successive pages, that RHG's approach is the same for undecided amoraic material and disputes. He readily invokes "all the principles" to decide matters whenever there is no explicit Talmudic decision.

Some of these principles referred to were established by Talmudic sages and can be found in the Talmud. Others were products of the geonic academies and formed part of the traditions transmitted to RHG by his geonic predecessors. In addition, although he doesn't indicate this in the responsum cited above, RHG added to these principles others which were his own innovation. He invoked them all to enable him to extract maximum utility from the Talmud as the main source of solutions to the problems posed to him. Even when the Talmudic discussions—though relevant to the issues facing RHG—did not offer a firm resolution per se, the principles enabled him to answer the inquiries with clear and precise rulings. Let us now discuss the principles one by one. We begin with one specifically mentioned by RHG in RDG 241 when attesting to his use of principles, one which the Talmud itself invokes both the tanaic and amoraic disputes:

"[Where] an individual is opposed to more than one, the law follows those more than one" (Berakot 9a s.n.).

This principle, accurately translated and formulated, applies even in cases of two against one, and is thus no different from another Talmudic principle: "The opinion of one cannot prevail over [the opinion] of two" (Ḥullin 36a, AZ 38b).[1] They are in fact alternate formulations of the same principle.[2]

RHG's responsum in OG Pessachim 40—in which he explicitly holds with two against one in accordance with this principle—casts light on his use of the principle in general and his understanding of its relationships to other Talmudic principles. The discussion centers around the Talmudic principle: "A casting vote of a third party is not decisive" (Pes. 21a s.n.). RHG claims that a casting vote of a third party is decisive when two are indispute and one decides in favour of one of the two. We then have two [one against one] and [the extra] one deciding, and the law follows those more than one."[3] RHG, then, refers to a case of two against one, and explicitly calls the principle he applies: "The law follows those more than one." His view that there is a decision in such circumstances in favor of the majority, seems to be based on yet another formulation of this theme by the Talmud (Sabat 39b): "Whenever you find two disputing and a third casting a deciding vote, the *halachah* is as the words of the deciding vote." When then—according to RHG in OG Pessachim 40—is a casting vote of a third party not decisive? "When the third party says partly what one says and partly what the other says, because that is really a third opinion."

To clinch our argument that RHG conceives of "two against one" as equalling "the law follows those more than one," we take note of RIF's formulation of AZ 38b:

> Salted fish and roasted eggs [prepared by a gentile] are permitted by Hezekiah and Bar Kappara, but prohibited by R. Johanan.[4] R. Hiyya Paruadàah visited the house of the Exilarch where he was asked, "How is it when an egg is roasted" [by a gentile]. He replied, "Hezekiah and Bar Kappara permit it but R. Johanan prohibits it, and the opinion of one cannot stand against that of two." Rabbi Zebid said to them, "pay no attention to him, because Abaye declared that the legal decision agrees with R. Johanan who prohibits." "And," continues RIF, "The Gaon [i.e., RHG (v. R. Yeruham I, 136a)] said: 'The law was decided according to R. Johanan only in the case of roasted eggs because Abaya's explicit ruling takes precedence [see above p. 46] but in the case of salted fish, the law follows Bar Kappara and Hezekiah [the two] who permitted, who are more than one against the one [R. Johanan]' " (RIF AZ 1246).

So, where there are two against one (and no explicit decision to the contrary), RHG invokes the principle: When an individual opposes those more than one, the law follows those more than one.

RHG refers to the ruling "two against one," in OG RH 72 (discussed above, p. 61). After having expressed his view that R. Zeira does not disagree with Rabyah and Rava he comments: "If you wish to claim that R. Zeira does disagree . . . then the law would not follow him, but would follow Raba and Rava—the *both* of them." His intent is clear. They are two and R. Zeira is one. Hence, we rule like the two. Unfortunately, RHG does not refer to the principle he invoked by its precise formulation, thus casting no further light on his equating the principle of "the law follows those more than one," with that of "one can not prevail over two."[5]

RHG's own testimony as to the employment of the principle, "The law follows the more than one"—cited above—and its appearance in the responsa examined, can leave little doubt as to its prominence in RHG's rulings. Following our usual outline, we shall now cite rulings for which we believe this principle served as a source even though it is not always explicitly mentioned in the responsa. We shall begin with cases in which it is clear at least that RHG is ruling in accordance with more than one sage. Afterwards we shall attempt to clarify rulings less obviously based on this principle.

A. RHG was asked if an inhabitant of an upper story which has a courtyard and w.c. may use the walls and apertures of the courtyard as the walls and apertures of his *Sukkah* by covering it with the required *sekak*. "And he answered: This is our view that the law follows the sages who taught that regarding the sides, two [walls] must be of the prescribed dimensions and the third [may be] even one handbreadth [in width]" (OG Sukkah 54, p. 27). Hence the *Sukkah* is valid (RHG favors setting it up in a way that the w.c. and cooking corner should not be seen from the *Sukkah*.) The sages RHG is referring to are those sages who are in dispute with R. Simeon. The Mishnah states that a *Sukkah* is not valid if it does not have three sides (M *Sukkah* 1, 1). Regarding this law the Gemara cites a *baraita*: "Our Rabbis taught, two [walls] must be of the prescribed dimensions, and the third [may be] even one handbreadth [in width]. R. Simeon says three [walls] must be of the prescribed dimensions and the fourth [may be] even one handbreadth" (BT Sukkah 6b, s.n.). No doubt, RHG rules like the sages, because they are more than one against R. Simeon's one. RHG repeats the view that "two must be of the prescribed dimension and the third even one handbreadth" in yet another responsum—OG Sukkah 53, p. 26.

B.   OG RH 11. RSG and RHG were asked for their commentary on RH 14a f. In the
course of the responsum they dealt with the dispute between Rabah and R. Humnuna.

> Rabah said: A citron tree which has blossomed in the sixth year and
> ripened in the seventh is not liable to tithes [i.e., in this it has the
> same law as fruit of the Sabbatical year] and not liable to clearance
> [in third and sixth years of the septemate, v. Deut. 26, 13, i.e., in this
> it has the law of fruit of regular (6) years]. Rabbi Hamnunah,
> however, said: A citron tree which has blossomed in the sixth year
> and ripened in the seventh is always reckoned as belonging to the
> sixth" (RH 15a).

> > (R. Hamnunah is consistent in that the blossoming is the
> > determining factor in establishing to which year the citron
> > belongs, and he applies to it all the regulations of that year).

Further on in the *sugya* we read:

> It has been stated, R. Johanan and Reṣ Laqiṣ both say that a citron
> tree which blossomed in the sixth year and ripened in the seventh is
> reckoned as belonging to the sixth year (RH 15b).

RSG and RHG rule in favor of R. Hamnuna over Rabah (OG RH, p. 25) because we find R.
Yoḥanan and Reṣ Laqiṣ are in agreement with him. In other words, if we take R.
Yoḥanan and Reṣ Laqiṣ together with R. Hamnuna, they are more than one against
Rabah's one, and the law follows them.

C.   The Rabbis of Kairouan asked RSG and RHG for a ruling in the case of a woman who
lost her *ketubah* document, and was then widowed or divorced. Is she still entitled only
to the statutory *ketubah*, to the additional jointure as well, or to neither. If she is
entitled to the addition, how does one determine what sum had been fixed in the
document (OG Ket. 161)?

RSG and RHG place the burden of proof upon the woman. In the cause of their
arguments they state: "We conclude that whenever we do not posit that [a woman who
has not claimed her *ketubah*] has remitted the statutory *ketubah*, we equally do not posit
that she has remitted the additional jointure." Nowhere in the entire relevant *sugya*
(Ket. 104a-b) do we find such a conclusion which makes non-remission of the addition a
function of non-remission of the statutory *ketubah*. The *sugya*, in the printed version,
deals only with the other side of the coin: Does the remission of the statutory *ketubah*
automatically carry with it remission of the addition?

The statement of RSG and RHG makes sense only if we assume that they had a reading (Ket. 104b) different from our printed version, a reading akin to that of RIF and the Munich Ms.:[6] "Bar Qapara said: [The non-remission of a woman who did not claim her ketubah] was taught only in respect of the maneh [100] and 200 [statutory ketubah of non-virgin and virgin respectively]. To any additional jointure, however, she is not entitled. R. Abahu in the name of R. Johanan, however, ruled, she is entitled to the additional jointure for R. Aibu has laid down in the name of R. Jannai: The additional provisions of a ketubah are subject to the same rules as the ketubah itself." The Gemara then relates a story, in which—according to RHG's interpretation (v. OG Ket., the commentaries 287)—Rav was asked about the issue and remained silent. So we remain with Bar Qapara's view that non-remission of statutory ketubah does not necessarily mean non-remission of the addition, in contrast to the view of R. Yoḥanan and R. Yannai who equate the addition to the statutory ketubah, i.e., non-remission of the latter assumes non-remission of the former. RSG and RHG ruled in favor of R. Yoḥanan and R. Yannai over Bar-Qapara (as did RIF) in keeping with the principle: "[Where] an individual is opposed to more than one, the law follows those more than one."

D.   In our detailed study of RDG 236 (above, p. 55 f.) we noted that RSG and RHG rule in favor of Rabbi against R. Jose. One of the reasons they give for this ruling is: Rabina places Rabbi in a line with the sages who say that "He that hath brought an evil name [must be judged] by three and twenty." Let us explain what they mean.

There is a dispute recorded in M San. 1, 1 regarding claims brought against one that hath brought an evil name (v. Deut. 22, 13 f.). R. Meir says that they are decided by three judges and the sages say by twenty three. The Gemara attempts to establish what is behind this dispute (San. 8a f.). Rabina claims that the point of contention between R. Meir and the sages is the same as that in which R. Jose and Rabbi differ (in the dispute discussed in RDG 236). Rabina equates the view of the sages to that of Rabbi, and the view of R. Meir to that of R. Jose (San. 9a). What RSG and RHG are then claiming is that since Rabbi is equivalent to those more than one, and R. Jose to the one, the law must follow Rabbi, because "the law follows those more than one."

E.   RHG was informed of a local custom of bringing spices to the synagogue on the Feast of the Law ("Simḥat Torah") and burning them (as incense) in the presence of the Torah scroll. The questioners wanted to know if this act of burning was permitted on the

Festival (OG Jom-Tow 62). Now M (Bezah 2, 7, Eduyot 3, 11) informs us that R. Gamaliel permits putting spices on the fire on a Festival day and the sages forbid it. RHG (OG loc. cit.) accepts the following amoraic interpretation of the dispute: "The dispute [between R. Gamaliel and the sages] is [only with respect] to smelling [spices] but when it is for perfuming [clothes] all [both R. Gemaliel and the sages] agree that it is forbidden (Bezah 22b)."

In relating to the custom in question RHG writes: "It is certainly perfuming and forbidden." Further on, he adds: "In this fashion it is certainly for smelling and forbidden." RHG then prohibits both burning for smelling and burning for perfuming with the same formula and certainty, even though one represents unanimous amoraic opinion and the other the view of the sages only, with R. Gamaliel deferring. We may deduce from this that in a case of one (R. Gamaliel, in our example) against those more than one (the sages in the example), RHG rules according to those more than one with the same firmness as if it were a unanimous Talmudic view.

F.   Rav maintains that the scroll of Esther, when read on Purim proper, may be read even in private (and the benedictions recited likewise). R. Asi disagrees and says it may only be read when ten[7] are present (Megillah 5a). In reply to a query, "whom does the law follow?", RHG states that the law as commonly practiced is like Rav, that the scroll of Esther is read even in private (OG Megillah 22-3). In support of his view (and the common practice), RHG cites another amoraic discussion: "R. Hiyya b. Abba said in the name of R. Johanan, if one reads the scroll of Esther in a volume containing the rest of Scriptures, he has not fulfilled his obligation. And they said this only regarding the public [when reading in the presence of a quorum]," inferring that an individual does fulfill his obligation.[8] "And we learn from this," continues RHG, "that it [the scroll of Esther] is read in private" (in R. Yohanan's view). Since R. Yohanan's view turns out to be the same as Rav's, we combine them. "And the law is like them" rules RHG. The reason, no doubt, because they are two to R. Asi's one.

G.   How should a judge rule when a monetary claim cannot really be decided? Symmachus says: "Money, the ownership of which cannot be decided has to be shared [by the parties] but the sages say: 'The onus probandi falls on the claimant' " (BQ 46a s.n.). In an anonymous mishnah (M BQ 5, 1) we find the view that it has to be shared. Samuel notes that this ruling in the anonymous mishnah is the view of Symmachus, but that here, too, the sages would say: "This is a fundamental principle in law that the *onus probandi* falls on the claimant," i.e., this mishnah is not an independent opinion concerned with Symmachus, but it is simply an illustration of Symmachus' opinion.

Normally, the law follows an anonymous mishnah. Despite this principle, RHG determines: "It is current law and a fundamental principle in law that the *onus probandi* falls on the claimant" (OG Ket. 161, cit. sup., p. 26). This determination gives us at once deep insight into RHG's methodology and reasoning, shows us how he analyzes Talmudic intent as to the principles of adjudication, and demonstrates how he resolves conflicts between them and qualifies them. It is not by chance that his ruling contained Samuel's *dictum verbatim*. By doing this he makes it clear that he is ruling the way he does, because Samuel pointed out that such was the view of the sages. In other words because it is the opinion of more than one against that of one. RHG reasons thus: If the Gemara or an *amora* specify that a view found in an anonymous mishnah represents the opinion of a single *tana*, their intent is that we (students, teachers, judges and codifiers) should treat it precisely as that: the view of one sage disputed by more than one. Consequently, invoking the principle "the law follows the more than one," one should rule against that view even though it appears in tanaic literature and tradition as an anonymous mishnah. The "more than one" principle predominates. So if the Talmud indicates that a particular view is of one sage only, we should reject that view in adjudication, when "more than one" hold differently.

That is why RHG consistently resolves the dispute between the sages (more than one) and Symmachus (one) in favor of the sages, as in the following examples.

A. The Gemara rules explicitly: "If one sold [a plot of land for the sole reason that he needed money for some specific purpose] but [on concluding the sale] he was no longer in need of money, the sale may be withdrawn" (Ket. 97a). R. Jacob b. R. Moses of Gabes asked RHG whether this applied to sale of moveable goods as well as immoveable ones. RHG replied: "Since the whole Talmudic discussion revolves around immoveable goods we must not ... carry it over to other types of goods without proof ... since the seller who desires return of the item is the claimant, the *onus probandi* falls on him ... and this is a fundamental principle in law" (OG Ket. 775).

B. OG Ket. 203 (discussed in detail above p. 35, et. seq.). "The husband is considered to have the status of her heir," claim RSG and RHG, "And now her [other prospective] heirs wish to come and claim that the matrimonial bond ceased to exist . . . and he did not

inherit [from] her at her death. Then the *onus probandi* falls upon them."

C. We mentioned (above p. 67) that in SZ 4, 5, 4 RHG informs us that despite his ruling

that the decision is left to the discretion of the judges, for the most part his judicial

decisions are according to Rav and Samuel. One of his reasons is, that were we to rule

according to R. Elazar, the claimant would be extracting money. RHG prefers to stay

clear of such a possibility since the *onus probandi* falls upon the claimant.

Interestingly above p. 41, we have found yet another case where there is an explicit

Talmudic ruling that the law is undecided and an individual has the right of discretion,

and where there, too, RHG opts in favor of complying with the view of those more than

one (against the one). The Mishnah teaches us: "The afternoon prayer [may be said]

until sunset. R. Judah says: Until midway through the afternoon. The evening prayer

has no set time" (M Ber. 4, 1). The corollary is that R. Judah permits the evening prayer

to be recited any time from midway through the afternoon, while the sages, who disagree

permit reciting it from sunset only. The Gemara concludes: "Seeing then that it has not

been stated definitely that the law follows neither the one nor the other, if one follows

the one he is right, and if one follows the other, he too is right" (Ber. 27a). So then,

according to Talmudic ruling, each individual may act as he chooses. RHG has occasion

to discuss this issue and writes:

> The law was not decided neither according to R. Judah nor according
> to the sages, as we say, "Seeing then that it has not been stated
> definitely that the law follows the one and not that the law follows
> the other,[9] if one follows the one he is right, and if one follows the
> other he is right," and this is the conclusion . . . since R. Huna and the
> other Rabbis did not pray the evening prayer till night time [ibid.] . . .
> it is best to do so, like the more than one (OG Ber. 173).

These cases in which the Talmud itself gives the individual (judge or layman)

discretion, and yet RHG opts in favor of those more than one, provide substantial

testimony to the significance that he attaches to the principle, "the law follows the more

than one."[10]

Rules Governing Tanaic-Amoraic Combinations

The principle of "the law follows the more than one" is valid not only for deciding a straightforward tanaic or amoraic dispute. When there is an amoraic dispute which is shown to coincide with a tanaic dispute ("*ketanai*"),[11] the tanaic dispute being of one against more than one, then we again invoke the principle of "the law follows the more than one," and rule in favor of the *tanaim* (together with the single *amora*) and reject the view of the *amora* who coincides with only a single *tana*. E.g., in OG RH 72 (discussed above, pp. 61 and 75) RHG, to bolster his contention that "if you wish to claim that R. Zeira does disagree . . . then the law would not follow him but would follow Rabah and Rava," advances the following argument: "His [R. Zeira's] tradition is the subject of a tanaic dispute ("*ketanai*") and he coincides with a single [*tana*], namely R. Jose, while the more than one disagree with him." He is saying: Even had R. Zeira's view differed, he would still rule with Rabah and Rava, since the *sugya* (RH 29a) shows that the dispute in which R. Zeira may be involved, coincides with a tanaic one, and—at best—R. Zeira coincides with a single *tana*, and we must therefore rule in favor of R. Zeira's adversaries who coincide with more than one *tana* (see below, p. 27).

This seems to be the principle behind yet another ruling of RSG and RHG, one which seems surprising at first glance. An ancient tradition regarding the search for ḥame*z* on Passover Eve states that two rows in the wine-vault are a place where ḥame*z* might have been brought, and needs searching. Each of the two old schools interpret the tradition differently. "The School of Shammai say: The two rows on the whole surface of the wine-vault. And the School of Hillel say: Only the two outermost rows that are uppermost" (M Pesahim 1, 1). The words of the School of Hillel, in turn, have also been given two varying Talmudic interpretations. "Rav said: [That means] the upper row and the one beneath it; while Samuel said: The upper row and the one on the inside of it." RSG and RHG ruled in favor of Samuel (Ms. Almanzi 1, 134) even though normally, in disputes between Rav and Samuel, the law follows Rav in non-monetary matters.

The reason for this exceptional ruling is, no doubt, to be found at the end of that Talmudic *sugya:* "R. Ḥiyya taught in accordance with Rav, while all [other] *tanaim* recited as Samuel" (Pes. 8b). Since the dispute between Rav and Samuel is also a tanaic dispute, RSG and RHG rule according to the *tanaim* who are more than one (and Samuel) against R. Ḥiyya, the lone *tana* (and his nephew, Rav).[12]

The cases just studied enable us to formulate another of RHG's principles of adjudication: When an amoraic dispute coincides with a tanaic dispute, we adjudicate by invoking principles governing tanaic disputes. The principle holds true only for coinciding disputes. RHG takes a different approach when *amoraim* do not offer independent views on a subject mentioned in a tanaic dispute, but they themselves consciously and explicitly wish to resolve a tanaic dispute and they disagree on how to rule. In these latter cases, RHG views the dispute as a straightforward amoraic dispute, and adjudicates according to his principles governing amoraic disputes (without considering the tanaic principles whatsoever). Here are some examples:

A.   RDG 236 (discussed above, pp. 55 and 77). The first reason for ruling in favor of R. Naḥman *(amora)* who ruled in favor of Rabbi *(tana)* is that "he is the conclusion of discussion and it is established that the law follows R. Naḥman in judicial and monetary matters whenever he spoke out." The prime reason, then, is a principle governing amoraic disputes.

B.   During the thirty-day mourning period the mourner may not wear new pressed clothes, according to Rabbi. According to fellow *tana*, R. Elazar b. R. Simeon only new white pressed clothes are forbidden (see MQ 23a). The Gemara relates that Abaye *(amora)* acted according to Rabbi and Rava *(amora)* according to R. Elazar b. R. Simeon (ibid.).   RHG claims: "The law undoubtedly follows Rava" (OG Maschkin 98). "Undoubtedly" RHG is alluding to the well known amoraic principle that in disputes between Rava and Abaye the law follows Rava (with certain exceptions). Although RHG's departure point was a tanaic dispute, since each *amora* consciously sided with one of the *tanaim*, RHG rules according to a principle governing amoraic disputes, and ignores the ones governing tanaic disputes (which would have "undoubtedly" led him to rule in favor of Rabbi).

C.   "If a man put to his own use what had been left in his keeping, the School of Shammai say: He is at a disadvantage whether its value rises or falls. And the School of Hillel say: [He must restore the deposit] at the same value, as when he put it to his own use. R. Aqiba says: As its value when claimed" (M BM 3, 12). RHG was asked directly: "That which we learned in the Mishnah: If a man put to his own use what had been left in his keeping; does the law follow the School of Shammai or the School of Hillel?" (SZ 4, 2, 31).   His response: "It is simple that although R. Judah said in Samuel's name: The *halakah* agrees with R. Aqiba [BM 43b], that is not the law. It is rather like Rava who said the *halakah* is as the School of Hillel [ibid.] because it is established that the law follows the latest." Since both *amoraim*, Samuel and Rava, consciously intended to decide a tanaic dispute, RHG treats it as amoraic dispute and invokes one of the classic principles for deciding amoraic disputes (and amoraic disputes only).

D. Raban Gamaliel, the patriarch and proponent of centralized authority and establishment rigidity in matters of law and prayer, declared the evening prayer to be obligatory. R. Joshua, a defender of individual freedom, often at odds with the patriarch, claimed it to be voluntary. The controversy eventually led to Raban Gamaliel's (temporary) expulsion from his post. Amoraic opinion differed as to whose view should prevail (see Ber. 27b). RSG and RHG were asked their opinion regarding the dispute and to explain why even those who favored R. Joshua recited the evening prayers nightly (OG Ber. 176).

Since their principles of adjudication governing both tanaic and amoraic disputes led them to the same conclusion in this case, RSG and RHG followed the same course as in RDG 236 (example "A" above) and invoked both types of principles. According to their reading and interpretation of the Talmudic text,[13] R. Judah transmitted in the name of Samuel that the law follows he who declared it obligatory while Rav said that the law follows he who declared it voluntary. Hence, treating it as an amoraic dispute they ruled according to Rav in non-monetary matters, and decided that the prayer is voluntary (like R. Joshua). They reached the same conclusion when invoking rules governing *tanaim*.

The previous discussion concerned decisions in amoraic disputes which were also tanaic disputes. We shall next investigate the weight RHG gives to an undisputed *amora*, who—as understood by RHG—did not consciously attempt to resolve a tanaic dispute, but did offer an opinion on a matter which happened to have been the subject of a tanaic dispute. Should we necessarily rule according to his stand, as if he had resolved the tanaic dispute? RHG's methodology provides an affirmative answer. He rules according to that *amora* even in cases where the principles of adjudication concerning tanaic disputes would have produced the opposite result. His stand is evident in OG RH 72 (discussed above, p. 61. See also above, p. 81). There, one of the possible interpretations he offers for understanding various Talmudic opinions in RH 28b is this: "Certainly if his [R. Zeira's] statement was only regarding blowing ... Then the *amora* tips the scales in favor of [the *tana*] R. Jose, because there is no *amora* disagreeing with him." RHG is claiming that, had the amoraic view been undisputed, it would have prevailed, even though it coincides with that of a *tana* R. Jose, whose view alone could never have prevailed since he was a single *tana* against the more than one.

Here is another example similarly structured. M Berakot (6, 1) teaches us: "What benediction do we say over fruit? Over the fruit of trees one says [Blessed art thou Lord our God King of the Universe] who createst the fruit of the tree ... over bread ... [Blessed ...] who bringest forth bread from the earth." These became the established formulae. In BT we read:

> If a man sees a loaf of bread and says, what a fine loaf this is! Blessed be the Omnipotent that has created it! He has performed his obligation. If he sees a fig and says, "What a fine fig this is!" Blessed be the Omnipotent that has created it! He has performed his obliga-tion. So R. Meir. R. Jose says: If one alters the formula laid down by the sages in benedictions, he has not performed his obligation. [The Gemara later relates this story:] Benjamin the shepherd made a sandwich and said, "Blessed be the Master of this bread," and Rav said, he has performed his obligation ... of the first benediction [of the Grace after food] (Ber. 40b).

Although the shepherd recited an original formula—not the standard one—Rav validated his benediction, taking a stand akin to that of R. Meir. "Regarding the dispute between R. Meir and R. Jose," we read in the Eşkol (1, 72 cited in part in OG Ber. the commentaries 176), "It would have occurred to us that the law follows R. Jose ... in all instances of disputes between R. Meir and R. Jose the law follows R. Jose.[14] However we saw that our Rabbi Hai of blessed memory wrote that the law follows not R. Jose but Rav who said 'He has performed his obligation of the first benediction,' like the act of Minyamin,[15] and we act according to Rav because we find no *amora* disputing him in this matter."

This ruling fits our formulation of the principle exactly. RHG rules in favor of an *amora* who he claims is undisputed (Rav), because that *amora*—while not consciously attempting to resolve a tanaic dispute—did venture an opinion on an issue (veering from the established benediction formula) which had been the subject of a tanaic dispute (R. Jose and R. Meir). RHG pays no heed to "tanaic" principles, which would have given the opposite result (in favor of R. Jose), but simply rules according to Rav, as if the latter had been resolving the tanaic dispute.

Having shown that RHG rules according to an undisputed *amora* even if the *amora* was not consciously resolving the tanaic dispute which pertained to that issue, we posit that the ruling we are about to examine is also based on that principle. According to tradition, drawn water is not fit for an immersion pool. Three logs of drawn water which fall into a pool containing less than the requisite volume of forty seah of fit water, make the water unfit.[16] Nevertheless, CP (16, 67a) testifies that RHG ruled that drawn water which has then been drawn entirely through a channel is ritually clean [fit for ritual purification]. The source of this ruling is R. Yohanan's statement precisely to that effect in Temurah 12b. In fact, RHG is repeating R. Yohanan's language verbatim. Although there exists a tanaic dispute pertaining to this issue,[17] RHG ignores the tanaic views and goes along with the undisputed *amora*, who was not consciously attempting to resolve that tanaic dispute.

A slight variation of this principle can help unravel the intent of a passage whose text and meaning were hitherto exceedingly difficult. According to OG Ket. 161 (discussed above, p. 76) RSG and RHG argue that one of the reasons a woman who lost her *ketubah* does not collect anything is, "perhaps payment has already, and we specifically learned in a baraita, 'If one finds a marriage contract in the street, if the husband admits [that he has not paid her the amount specified in the contract] it shall be returned to the wife' etc. (!) until the law follows R. Jose who apprehends that payment may have been made."[18]

In all likelihood the original responsum contained RSG and RHG's citation of the whole relevant *sugya*. Our text is the result of a copyist who abbreviated and replaced what he omitted by "etc, until". However, there is still one outstanding difficulty. Nowhere in the *sugya* do we find a ruling that the law follows R. Jose who apprehends that payment may have been made. No such statement exists in any known printed edition, ms. or medieval work (except for this responsum). It is difficult to imagine that RSG and RHG had such a unique reading. Hence, we must assume that the words "the law follows R. Jose" are RSG and RHG's own. Trying to reconstruct what happened, we imagine the following picture: A copyist was copying the responsum which quoted the relevant *sugya* in BM in its entirety. After citing the *sugya*, RSG and RHG ruled: The law follows R. Jose. The copyist decided that the *sugya* was well known and there was no need to copy it in its entirety. Hence he copied just the beginning added "etc." and thought he was copying the last few words of the *sugya* too. He failed to realize that the words: "The law follows R. "Jose" were not part of the *sugya* but instituted a decision of RSG and RHG. He thus mistakenly concluded the abbreviated *sugya* with those words, which in reality belong not to the *sugya*, but rather to the ensuing geonic decision.

This explains the text but not the ruling. It is quite understandable that RSG and RHG accept Rabina's interpretation, that R. Jose apprehends that payment may have been made (in the BM 7b *sugya*). What is difficult to comprehend is how they rule in favor of R. Jose in his dispute with the sages, who are, after all, more than one, to his one. Interestingly enough, RH—who relied extensively on geonic material (particularly that of RSG and RHG)[19]—also ruled in favor of R. Jose (OG BM RH commentary, p. 15, n. 3). Tracing RH's view in the question of "apprehending that payment may have been made," may shed some light on how RSG and RHG approach the issue.

This question of whether we apprehend that payment may have been made, arises on two further occasions in the first chapter of BM. In the Talmudic *sugya* BM 13b-14a, both Samuel and R. Eleazar wish to explain tanaic views with the notion that "we are not afraid that the debt has already been paid" while R. Yohanan holds, "we do apprehend that the debt has already been paid." The stand of Samuel and R. Elazar is refuted by the amoraic *sugya*, and is rejected. The views of Samuel and R. Yohanan surface again in another *sugya* (BM 16b). In this instance RH explicitly rules that the law does not follow Samuel because he was refuted and it is established that we apprehend that payment has been made (OG loc. cit., 28). This explains why RH, in the same vein, ruled in favor of R. Jose, who likewise held that we apprehend that payment has been made.

It seems quite likely that similar reasoning lies behind the decision of RSG and RHG in favor of R. Jose. They were faced with a tanaic dispute which was also the subject of amoraic contention, thought—to be sure—the *amoraim* were not consciously trying to resolve the tanaic dispute. Normally in such cases we would expect (RSG and) RHG to invoke a principle governing the tanaic dispute (see above, p. 82). However, since Samuel (and R. Elazar) was refuted and rejected, for all intents and purposes the *geonim* found themselves not with a true amoraic dispute (in need of resolution), but rather with the view of one lone *amora* which remained firm—that of R. Yohanan (after the rejection of the others by the Gemara). Hence, they treated R. Yohanan as a lone *amora* who sounded an opinion on a matter which had been the subject of a tanaic dispute without consciously desiring to resolve that dispute. True to their principle, they ruled according to the view of that *amora*, which happened to coincide with the view of R. Jose, although purely on the basis of the tanaic dispute the decision would have gone the other way. Since the *sugya* (BM 7b) which RSG and RHG found pertinent to the discussion of the problem, raised in the responsum presently under scrutiny (OG Ket. 161), did not contain the amoraic material relevant to their ruling, they were perfectly satisfied simply to lay down the ruling: The law follows R. Jose who apprehends that payment may have been made.

OG Megila 36 (discussed above, p. 18) also involves an *amora* whose views coincides with one party to a tanaic dispute. RHG was asked if the law follows Samuel who claimed that [the scroll] "of Esther does not make the hands unclean" (Meg. 7a—and is thus not considered among the Holy Scriptures). He answered, "The law does not follow Samuel who is placed with one individual. The law rather follows the anonymous mishnah." RHG is referring to the amoraic *sugya* (loc. cit.). R. Joshua is recorded as not considering the scroll of Esther as part of Holy Scripture as opposed to other tanaic sources which do. Among the latter, in RHG's opinion, is an anonymous "mishnah." Although the Gemara states that "Samuel concurred with R. Joshua" RHG rules, not like the *amora* who is in agreement with a *tana*, but like the anonymous "mishnah" which is considered authoritative.

The obvious question we must ask ourselves now is: Why did RHG have recourse to principles governing tanaic sources at all? Since there is no registered amoraic opinion disagreeing with Samuel, if our formulation of the principle is correct, shouldn't RHG have treated this case as one of an undisputed *amora* entertaining a view in a matter which had also been the subject of tanaic controversy? According to the way we have understood his principles, he should then have ruled according to Samuel without considering "tanaic principles" at all.

The solution to the dilemma lies in the words "*who is placed* with one individual". RHG emphasized that Samuel was placed by the Gemara in a line with R. Joshua. In all the previous cases we had examined, where RHG ruled according to the lone *amora*, it was the Gaon who perceived that the *amora's* view coincided with a tanaic view. Here, however, it was the Gemara itself which explicitly determined that we identify the amoraic view (Samuel) with a particular known tanaic opinion (R. Joshua). It is as if the Gemara was teaching us—so RHG's reasoning seems to run—that we should not treat this amoraic view as a lone, independent amoraic opinion. Treat it instead—the Gemara tells us—as auxilliary to the tanaic view. If, because of principles governing tanaic disputes, we should reject that tanaic view—and such indeed is the case here since R. Joshua's is a minority opinion—then it is the Gemara's intention that the amoraic view, too, should fall by the wayside.

An *Amora* who contradicts a *Tana*

We continue our discussion of principles covering *tana-amora* combinations with one of the most basic of all such principles: An *amora* may say (or do) nothing contradictory to a *tana* unless there is also a *tana* who agrees with him. This principle is fundamental to much of amoraic discussion and is well documented in all works on Talmudic methodology.[20] Throughout the Talmud the standard method of discrediting amoraic opinion is by showing that it is contradicted by a "mishnah" or a "baraita." It is universally acknowledged that one may not accept the view of an *amora* who disagrees with a *tana* without having another on his side. Hence, we need not go to great lengths to prove that RHG, too, adopts this principle. We shall merely draw attention to a responsum in which he demonstrates his usual extreme caution in ascertaining that the *amora* toward whose view he leans, does not indeed violate this principle.

The responsum we refer to is OG RH 11 (discussed above, p. 76). RSG and RHG cite a number of tanaic sources quoted in the course of the *sugya*, none of which are in agreement with R. Hamnuna. Therefore, when they finally introduce their ruling in favor of R. Hamnuna (OG RH, p. 25), they preface it with a justification of their ruling in face of this tanaic contradiction:

> Although among these *tanaim* there is none who is in complete agreement with R. Hamnuna who said, "We always reckon according to the blossoming of the fruit", however regarding the Sabbatical year (year of release) itself the first (anonymous) *tana* does reckon according to the blossoming of the fruit, [and] there are other *tanaim* who hold that regarding tithes[21] we reckon according to the blossoming of the fruit, as we learned in a *baraita* [RH 15b] . . .so that R. Hamnuna stands in accord with the former (the first *tana*), regarding the Sabbatical year [of release] and with the latter [*tana* of the *baraita*] regarding tithes.

So RSG and RHG take great pains to come up with a combination that will show tanaic agreement with R. Hamnuna. Only then do they declare: "and the law follows R. Hamnuna." Had they not demonstrated tanaic agreement with R. Hamnuna, they could never have ruled according to him. Had there been only tanaic disagreement, they could have found no justification for a ruling in his favor. The law can never follow an *amora* who disagrees with a *tana,* unless he has tanaic support.

Tanaic Support for an *Amora*

The other side of the coin in this: If we can point to undisputed tanaic support for an *amora* involved in an amoraic dispute, that *amora* predominates. The support may stem from a mishnah or even from a *baraita*—so long as the *baraita* is reliable. A reliable *baraita* is one whose legal traditions are authoritative. And what is an authoritative *baraita* according to RHG? One cited in an amoraic discussion by an *amora* or by the Gemara, for purposes of support, refutation or arriving at decisions (see in further detail, below, p. 97). Amoraic opinion supported by such tanaic material will be sustained even where the principles governing amoraic disputes would have gone against that amoraic view. RHG formulates this principle in RDG 79 (p. 48), "It is established that if there is tanaic support for an *amora,* the law follows him even though the principles of adjudication[22] [for amoraic disputes] would not have decreed in his favor."[23]

RHG makes explicit use of this principle on deciding a number of disputes involving Rav.

A.   In RDG 376 (discussed above, p. 64), one of the arguments RSG and RHG set forth for deciding in favor of Rav is that "Our Mishnah is . . . in agreement with what Rav said" (RDG 376, p. 193).

B.   Rav is again the beneficiary of this principle in OG Meg. 22. R. Hai was asked if the law followed Rav who said, "On the actual day of Purim the scroll of Esther can be read even by an individual" (Meg. 5a as opposed to R. Asi who requires ten). RHG replied, "This is our view, that the law follows Rav . . . for behold our Mishnah supports him."

C.   RDG 327. RHG rules that if an intended purchaser tells his fellow to pay the purchase price of an article, for him, to that article's prior rightful owner, the intended purchaser may no longer change his mind, "Because a *baraita* was brought in support of Rav who said, 'If man says to another take to so-and-so the *maneh* which I owe him . . .

he is not at liberty to retract the commission' " [Gittin 14a]. Samuel disagrees with Rav
and holds that "he is at liberty to retract the commission" (ibid.). Now, although the law
would normally follow Samuel in monetary matters, RHG, in this case, ruled in favor of
Rav, purely because of the tanaic support (the *baraita*) which the Gemara (loc. cit.)
brought down in his favor.

Here are other instances where RHG veers from the principles normally governing
disputes between Rav and Samuel probably because of the tanaic support which he found
in the Talmud for the one or the other:

A.   OG Sanhedrin 623 (cit. above 38). In answer to "A"'s monetary claim, "B" stated: I
owe only one *prutah*, if you so wish, take an oath and collect the *prutah*. "A" countered:
You take an oath that you owe me no more than a prutah and be absolved. RSG and RHG
were asked to prescribe the proper court procedure for this case. They ruled that "B"
must take an oath. To bolster their claim they drew upon the case of "that claimant who
claimed two silver coins and a *prutah* and the respondent admitted a *prutah*, whereby he
[the respondent] is liable to an oath, like Rav, since the law follows him [Rav]."

RSG and RHG are referring to the discussion in Sebuot 39b: "Rav said: The denial [in
regard to] the claim must be [at least] two silver [coins—*maàhs*]; and Samuel said: The
claim itself must be [at least] two silver [coins—*maàhs*]; even if he denied only a *prutah*
or admitted only a *prutah*, he is liable". Since they ruled in favor of Rav, RSG and RHG
needed to ascertain that—in our case—Rav's minimum requirement was met, before
determining whether the respondent could or could not legally evade taking an oath.[24]
Since this minimum was clearly met in our case, they proceeded to rule that it was, in
fact, incumbent upon "B" to take the oath.

RSG and RHG's acceptance of Rav's view as the basis for determining the
incumbency of the oath is somewhat surprising at first glance. Since the issue is judicial
procedure and monetary claim, we would anticipate that Samuel's guidelines supercede.
No doubt, here too, their decision was based on the tanaic agreement with Rav cited in
the *sugya:* "Rava said our Mishnah is evidence in support of Rav ... R. Hiyya taught in
support of Rav" (Sebuot 39b-40a).

B.   A query of RHG from Tlemcen posed the following questions: One of the pillars of
the community died leaving two sons. The elder had been managing the household and
engaging in commerce with the father's money, and had been a part of the household.

The younger had gone abroad to engage in commerce, at which time the elder had given him money which the latter had in hand, for purposes of commerce. Upon the younger's return, the elder claimed that the money he had given had been his own—a gift he had received from his grandfather. The younger argued: It had been understood, and was obvious, that the money received was our father's, who had been a man of great wealth (RDG, p. 347).

RHG rules that since the elder brother had been managing the household, then he must furnish proof that he had independent means, from which he had given money to his younger brother (RDG 37).

This stipulation too is subject to a dispute between Rav and Samuel:

> It has been stated: [If a number of brothers live together and] one of them has the management of the house, and if there are deeds and bonds current in his name and he asserts: They are mine, and I obtained them from the legacy of my maternal grandfather; Rav says that the *onus probandi* lies upon him and Samuel says that the *onus probandi* lies upon the brothers (BB 52a).

So once again RHG ruled according to Rav where we might have expected him to favor Samuel. Here too, the reason seems to be tanaic support—R. Naḥman having furnished a *baraita* which agrees with Rav in every detail (ibid., b).[25]

C. Here is a case in which Samuel's opinion gains from this principle. RHG was asked if it is permissible to wash one's body in the Sabbath or a Festival with hot water prepared on the Sabbath (or Festival) eve. He replied:

> Regarding hot water heated on the Sabbath eve, it has been made plain to us that it is forbidden to wash one's whole body in it [on the morrow] (cited, Eṣkol 1, p. 7).

Where and by whom has it "been made plain to us?" We would think by the Gemara in BT, where "It was stated: If hot water is heated on the eve of the Sabbath—Rav said: On the morrow one may wash his whole body in it, limb by limb; while Samuel ruled: They [the sages] permitted one to wash his face, hands and feet only" (Sabbath 40a). However, since this is not a monetary issue, but one of prohibition, we might have thought that the law should follow Rav. Why then did RHG feel that the law is plainly like Samuel? Once again, the opinion was almost certainly prompted by what is found further on in the *sugya* (cited above): "It [a *baraita*] was taught in accordance with

Samuel: If hot water is heated on the eve of the Sabbath, on the morrow [the Sabbath day] one may wash his face, hands, and feet therein, but not his whole body limb by limb". Plainly then, RHG rules according to the *amora* with tanaic support (even though another principle of adjudication would have given different results).

D.   According to the laws of usury, "No bargain may be made over produce before its market-price is known" (M BM 5, 7). A borrower of produce must have the prospect of repaying it at current cost, though it may not, at the moment, be available to him. It follows, that if one already possesses same, he may borrow even before the market-price is known. Such a borrower "may say, 'Lend it to me until my son comes' or 'until I find the key' " (ibid., 9). Of the cases permitted even before the market price is known, "R. Huna said: If he possesses a *se'ah* he may borrow a *se'ah*; two *se'ahs*, he may borrow two *se'ahs*. R. Isaac said: Even if he has only a *se'ah* he may borrow many *kors* against it" (BM 75a).

At the close of SZ 4, 2, 4 (discussed above, p. 50) RHG adds the following ruling: "And the law follows R. Isaac who said, 'Even if he has one[26] *se'ah* he may borrow many *kors* against it'." The reason for RHG's favoring R. Isaac is undoubtedly that "R. Hiyya taught the following, which is in support of R. Isaac. '[One may not borrow wine or oil ... because] he has not a drop of wine or oil.' Surely then, if he has, he may borrow a large quantity against it" (BM 75a), i.e., tanaic support for R. Isaac.

E.   We have already had occasion to discuss in detail RHG's view that a document signed by both eligible and ineligible witnesses (or kinsmen) may be validated if there is no reason to suppose prearranged assembly (above, p. 55 f.). In the responsa cited in the discussion he validates documents in which the blank space of two lines between the text of a deed and the signature of the witnesses is filled with signatures of kinsmen. This ruling represents the view of Hezekiah who held "[If] it [the blank space ...] was filled with [the signatures of] relatives [the deed] is valid" (BB 162b s.n.). RHG, no doubt, validates that particular type of document because the Gemara states (ibid.) that a baraita cited in the *sugya* "affords support to [the view of] Hezekiah."

Amoraic Questions and Answers According to the View of a *Tana* or Earlier *Amora*

If *amoraim*[27] posed questions and gave answers according to the view of a *tana* (or earlier *amora*), the law then follows the *tana* (or earlier *amora*), even where other principles of adjudication would call for a contrary decision. A classic example of RHG's implementation of this principle is in deciding the dispute in M Ket. 6, 1 (see *TEQUFAT*, p. 235, par. 37). The Mishnah relates that

> [if] a married [woman] ... [receives compensation for] indignity and blemish, it falls to her. R. Judah b. Bathyra says: If it was done to a hidden part [in her body] two-thirds [of the compensation] fall to her and one-third to him; if in a manifest part two-thirds fall to him and one-third to her.

> Raba son of R. Hanan demurred: Now then, if a man insulted his fellow's mare would he also have to pay him [compensation for the] indignity? [This is refuted:] But is a horse then susceptible to insult? [The questions persist:] This, however [is the objection] If a man spat on his fellow's garment would he also have to pay him [compensation for this] indignity ... [if it] is really so ... only [where it touched] the body ... [The defense:] [An insult] to his garment involves no indignity to him [but an insult to] his wife involves an indignity to him.... If a man insulted a poor man ... where all the members of the family are involved in the indignity, must he also pay ... to all the members of the family? He [R. Aṣi] replied ... one's wife is like one's own body (BT Ket. 66a).

All these questions and answers are comprehensible only in the perspective of R. Judah b. Bathyra's view that a husband receives part of his wife's compensation. It is quite understandable that someone confront this view with the legitimate question: Since when does one receive compensation for an indignity committed against someone (or something) outside his own person? However, this whole discussion makes no sense whatsoever according to the first *tana* who holds that the woman alone receives all her compensation.

> Because the Gemara asks these questions in perspective of R. Judah b. Bathyra's view Rav Hai o.b.m. wrote, "This is what they came up with in the Academy. Even though normally when an individual is opposed to more than one, the law follows those more than one [see above, p. 73], in this case the law follows R. Judah b. Bathyra. Since our Rabbis [i.e., *amoraim*—see n. 27] posed questions and answered them according to the view of R. Judah b. Bathyra, we may deduce from this that the law follows him" (OG Ket. 495).[28]

RHG explicitly invokes this principle in resolving another dispute found on the very same folio of BT (Ket. 66a). R. Yoḥanan explained that there is a dispute between R.

Àqiba and the "first *tana*" as to who is entitled to the surplus of a woman's work, above
the amount required for her maintenance, obtained through undue exertion, "The first
tana being of the opinion that this belongs to her husband while R. Aqiba maintains that
it belongs to herself."

Here is the way the *sugya* closes:

> R. Papa raised the question: What is the law where she performed for
> him two [kinds of work] simultaneously? Rabina raised the question:
> What is the ruling where she did three or four [kinds of work]
> simultaneously? These must remain undecided.

In reflecting on the dispute, RHG could not but recall the Talmudic principle, "The
law is always in agreement with R. Àqiba when he differs from a colleague of his"
(Erubin 46b, s.n.). Nevertheless, we read in RASBA's novellae to Ketubot (p. 202, cited
OG Ket. 497),

> Rav Hai Gaon o.b.m. ruled in favor of the first *tana* and said that the
> questions of R. Papa and Rabina appertain only to the Rabbis [i.e., the
> first *tana*] and they were asking thus: Perhaps the Rabbis [i.e., the
> first *tana*] have been saying that the surplus obtained through undue
> expectation [belongs] to her husband only because, at any rate, it
> entails only one labor, and the husband is entitled to whatever his wife
> produced in one act of labor. However the Rabbis never decreed that
> he receive the produce of two simultaneous labors, because it is
> unusual to produce so much at once. Then came Rabina and said:
> Even if you wish to claim that two simultaneous labors are common,
> and their produce reverts to the husband, what about three or four
> simultaneous labors, which is really not common.

Since, according to Rav Hai's interpretation of the amoraic questions, they were
asked only according to the view of the first *tana*, the law follows him.[29]

RSG and RHG apply this principle even where there is amoraic agreement with one
of the tanaic disputants, i.e., even if there is explicit agreement between an *amora* and
one of the *tanaim*, but the Gemara—or some *amora(im)*—poses questions and gives
answers according to another (disputing) *tana*, then the law follows the latter. They do
so explicitly in a responsum dealing with Israel's script. Now, "R. Jose said . . . writing
[script] was changed through him [Ezra] . . . Rabbi said, the Torah was originally given
to Israel in this [Ashshurith] writing. When they sinned, it was changed into Roàz.
[Samaritan script]. But when they repented the [Assyrian characters] were re-

introduced ... R. Simeon b. Eleazar said ... on the authority of R. Eleazar of Modin this writing was never changed at all." (Sanhedrin 21b-22a). An amoraic tradition transmitted by R. Ḥisda in the name of Mar Ùqba[30] reads: "Originally the Torah was given to Israel in Hebrew characters and in the sacred language; later, in the times of Ezra, it was given in Ashshurith script and Aramaic language" (ibid.). This, of course, is in agreement with R. Jose. The *sugya* closes by questioning how R. Simeon b. Eleazar would interpret the verse, "But they could not read the writing" (Daniel 5, 8). Interpretations are offered in turn, by Rav, Samuel, R. Yoḥanan, and R. Aṣi.

RSG and RHG reject the view of Mar Ùqba, claiming: "The law does not follow Mar Ùqba because it [his view] has been established as being subject to a tanaic dispute [*ketanai'*]" (OG Sanhedrin 338-39. Such a view is not held in high esteem—particularly here where it agrees with only one *tana*). RSG and RHG favor the view of R. Eleazar of Modin, one of their arguments on his behalf being: "Rabbis posed questions and answered them according to him, . . ." and each of the *amoraim* offered his interpretation of R. Eleazar of Modin (OG, loc. cit.) They refer of course to the close of the *sugya,* which we cited above.

Exclusive Amoraic Interpretation of a *Tana*

The last comment of RSG we cited, suggests the next of the cognate principles in this section. If *amoraim* interpret or explain the view of one disputing *tana* exclusively (i.e., excluding commenting on other disputants), then the law follows that *tana.* The underlying reason for this principle—and the other related ones in this section—is probably that if the Gemara records interpretation and explanation of the view of a particular *tana,* it seems to be ample indication that the message is: treat that view as authoritative and binding. We are meant to rule according to it regardless of other principles of adjudication. This message is tantamount to an explicit amoraic decision, hence overriding any of the other principles (see above, p. 46).

This appears to be intimated by RHG when discussing a tanaic dispute regarding defects in animals which render them *terefah* and forbidden food. "If the innermost stomach is pierced or if the greater part of its outer coating is torn. R. Judah says: A handbreadth in large cattle, or the greater part in small cattle" (M Hullin 3, 1). The view of R. Judah is discussed and interpreted by the Gemara.

> R. Benjamin b. Japhet reported in the name of R. Eleazar, "large"
> does not mean a large animal, nor "small" a small one, but the
> meaning is: If it was torn to the extent of a handbreadth but this was
> not the greater portion [of the rumen, it is *terefah*] and this is what
> the mishnah teaches us by stating "A handbreadth in large cattle," and
> if the greater portion was torn but it was not the extent of a
> handbreadth [it is *terefah*] and this is what the mishnah teaches us by
> stating "the greater part in small cattle" (Ḥullin 50b).

After explaining what is meant by the different "stomachs," RHG remarks,
"Regarding the law since we [the Gemara] forego discussing the reason of the first *tana*,
but do explain the reason of R. Judah, we deduce from this that the law follows him."
(KGE 36). RHG is referring to R. Benjamin's report (cited above). He intimates that
although we would normally decide in favor of the first *tana*, whose remarks comprise an
anonymous mishnah, since amoraic tradition interprets only the view of R. Judah, the law
follows him.

We now posit that, although not cited explicitly, this principle lies behind the rulings
of RHG listed below.

A. A husband may take forth his wife against her will "from a bad dwelling to a good
one, but not from a good dwelling to a bad one. Rabban Simeon b. Gamaliel says: Nor
even from a bad dwelling to a good one, since a good one puts her to the proof" (M Ket.
13, 10). The Gemara doesn't take up the view of the first *tana* but does elaborate on the
statement of Rabban Simeon b. Gamaliel: "What [is meant by] 'puts her to the proof'?
In agreement [with a saying] of Samuel. For Samuel said: A change of diet is the
beginning of bowel trouble" (Ket. 110b).

It seems quite certain that it is because of this amoraic passage that we find: "Rav
Hai ruled that the law follows Rabban Simeon b. Gamaliel" (OG Ket. 837). Again, he opts
for the view explained by the Gemara over the anonymous mishnah (i.e., first *tana*),
despite the common principle.[31]

B. In OG Taanith 57-8 (cited above, pp. 28 and 55), RHG permits a reader who was
suspected of intimacy with a married woman, but has since repented and reformed, to
continue to lead the prayers. However, he adds this stipulation: "But on a fast day we do
not place such a person before the ark [as reader] because his youth was not unblemished
and an evil reputation had gone forth in his youth." This stipulation is based on the

personal opinion of R. Judah in a *baraita* as interpreted by an *amora*.

> Our Rabbis have taught: When they stand up to pray [on a fast day]
> although there may be present an elder and a scholar, they place
> before the ark [as reader] only a man conversant with prayers. R.
> Judah says an old man whose youth was unblemished. [The Gemara
> asks:] What is meant by "an old man whose youth was unblemished?"
> Abaye said: This is one against whom no evil reputation had gone
> forth in his youth (Taànit 16a).

Since R. Judah's personal opinion was interpreted by an *amora*, R. Hai ruled accordingly.

An Amoraic Question Posed from a *Baraita*

To continue with RHG's principles pertaining to tanaic-amoraic combinations, we
turn now to amoraic use of tanaic pericopae. Not only does amoraic interpretation of a
particular *tana* lead RHG to decide in favor of that *tana*, varying usage of tanaic
pericopae by *amoraim* also leads RHG to view those pericopae as law. The first of this
group of principles that we formulate to suit RHG's implementation of the principle is
this: If the Gemara (or an *amora*) posed a question from a *baraita*, it is a clear sign that
the *baraita* is law, and we must rule in accordance with it.[32] Here are some examples:

A. RHG states that when the courts administer an oath they say to the one taking the
oath: Know that we do not adjure you according to your own mind, but according to our
mind, and the mind of *Beth Din* (RLOW 3 cited above, pp. 37 and 56, and mentioned
briefly in MH 3, p. 18). This is based verbatim on a *baraita*, from which the Gemara
poses a question (Nedarim 25a s.n.).

B. In this example RHG bases his ruling on the first part of a *baraita* from which the
Gemara posed a question, even though it is rather clear from the continuation of the
sugya that part of the *baraita*, at least, is not in line with the accepted *halakah*. After
having introduced a tradition in the name of R. Yoḥanan, the Gemara reports:

> An objection was raised [from a *baraita*]: He who makes a *lulab* for
> his own use shall recite the benediction "Blessed. . . ." When he takes
> it to fulfill therewith his obligation, he shall say, "Blessed [art thou]
> . . . who has sanctified us . . . and commanded us concerning the
> taking of the *lulab*;" and even though he has recited the benediction on
> the first day, he must again recite it on all seven days. He who makes
> a *sukkah* . . . when he enters the *sukkah* to take up his abode therein
> he shall say . . . "who has sanctified us by thy commandments and

commanded us to dwell in the *sukkah*," and once he has recited the
benediction on the first day, he has no need to repeat it [on subsequent
days] (Sukah 46a).

It is clear from the ensuing discussion that the accepted *halakah*, and common

practice, is to recite the benediction upon entering the *sukkah* throughout the seven days

contrary to the view of the *baraita*. So the end of the *baraita* is naturally not accepted.

But what about its beginning? Should it be discarded with its end, or should we relate to

what is written there as authoritative law? RHG's answer comes through loud and clear

in this responsum:

> The Master Rav Hai Gaon was asked: If one takes the *lulab* in order to
> carry it to or from the synagogue, is he meant to recite the benedic-
> tion "concerning the taking of the *lulab*," or should he turn it over [in
> such a manner that he is clearly not fulfilling the commandment].
> Furthermore, if he recited the benediction at the time of taking [it to
> fulfill his obligation] is he—or is he not—required to repeat it during
> the *Hallel*?[33] Likewise is a congregational reader who has already
> recited the benediction meant to repeat it. . . .
>
> He answered: If one takes the *lulab* in order to carry it . . . is only out
> of love of the commandment and there is no need to be a stickler.
> This is the crux of the matter: When he takes it to fulfill therewith
> his obligation he shall recite the benediction. And it is our view that
> there is no need to recite the benediction over the *lulab* . . . more than
> once a day (Eṣkol 2, 103).

Clearly, then, RHG bases his rulings regarding the benediction on the *lulab*, on the

first part of the *baraita*. "When he takes it to fulfill therewith his obligation he shall say,

'Blessed' etc." i.e., the benediction is recited only when it is taken to fulfill therewith

this obligation, which is once a day. We note that although the latter part of the *baraita*

was virtually dismissed by the Gemara, RHG, nevertheless, bases his general ruling on

(the first part of) that *baraita*. We learn from this that he feels strongly about the

principle: if the Gemara poses a question from a *baraita*, that *baraita* must be

considered binding and authoritative. If certain sections of the *baraita* were dismissed by

the Gemara, then those sections—and those sections only—may be disregarded. All other

sections must be deemed authoritative and binding; otherwise, the Gemara would not

have used that *baraita* for posing the question.

Amoraic Use of a *Baraita* to Resolve a Question or Doubt

The next in this series of principles, on which RHG bases his rulings on amoraic use of tanaic pericopae, we formulate thus: If the Gemara uses a *baraita* to resolve a question or doubt, then we rule according to that *baraita*.   RHG probably reasoned that any amoraic attempt to resolve an issue from a source which is not authoritative, would no doubt have encountered amoraic opposition.   Hence, a *baraita* used for resolution—and not evoking reaction—must be authoritative.   We formulate this principle on the bases of the following examples:

A.   RDG 39 (cited above, p. 36).   A man died leaving a widow and son.   The widow—who had a large *ketubah*—sold immovable goods from the estate, ostensibly to provide her with money for maintenance.   The son later claimed that she had enough money and did not really have to sell just for her maintenance.   He requested invalidation of the widow's sale.   Neither side can furnish decisive proof to substantiate their claims.   The question posed to the gaon is: Who is to be believed?   In his responsum RHG cites a *sugya*.

> R. Yohanan asked: If the heirs say: We paid [the widow's mainten-
> ance].   And she says: I have not received [it] . . . is the estate [of the
> deceased man] in the presumptive possession of the heirs, and
> consequently it is the widow who must produce the proof, or is the
> estate rather in the presumptive possession of the widow, and the
> proof must be produced by the heirs.   [The principle as to who must
> produce proof would be the same in our case].   Come and hear what
> Levi taught: [The Gemara wishes to resolve the question from a
> *baraita* dealing with a dispute on the maintenance of] a widow, the
> heir, must produce the proof so long as she is unmarried, but if she
> was married the proof must be produced by her.   R. Simi b. Asi said:
> . . .   This is subject to a tanaic dispute ["*ketanai*"] . . .   [The *sugya*
> concludes that R. Simi has no proof for his contention] (Ket. 96 a-b).

RHG writes that since none of the other tanaic pericopae introduced in the course of the *sugya* furnish a clear resolution to the original question—being given to various interpretations—and since there is no conclusive evidence that Levi's *baraita* is subject to tanaic dispute the conclusion must be, "that which Levi taught was not rejected, so we learn from it that the estate is in the presumptive possession of the widow and proof must be produced by the heirs that [in the case of the question in RDG 39] her sale is not valid.   Barring such proof her sale is presumed valid."

We see then, that a *baraita* used to resolve a question in the course of a *sugya* (although challenged), is binding, so long as it has not been conclusively rejected by the Gemara *(sugya)*.

B.   Among the instructions RHG gives for writing legal documents is "Elaborate, so that the final line and a half should be free from anything new" (MH, p. 111). The reason is that what is written in the final line and a half is not taken into consideration. It was in the Gemara itself that

> The question was raised: What about a line and a half? [Don't we rule that we do not take what is written there into consideration, and subsequently, if the signatures of the witnesses were removed a line and a half from the text, the deed is nevertheless valid since even if unauthorized matter would be forged and added it would not be taken into account] ... What about an answer to the question? Come and hear what has been taught [in a *baraita*. If] the [signatures of the] witnesses were removed two lines from the text [the deed] is invalid; [if] less than this it is valid [because we anyhow do not take into account new material written in the final line and a fraction] (BB 162b).

It is on account of this *baraita*—used by the Gemara to resolve the question—that RHG instructs not to include new material in the final line and a half, since it will not be taken into account.

C.   We conclude this series of examples with a *baraita* through which the Gemara wishes to choose between two conflicting traditions. The Gemara attempts to pose a question from the *baraita* in one tradition. When answered, it then suggests that it might serve as corroboration for the other tradition. This, too, is thwarted, and the Gemara reaches no conclusion.   Nevertheless, its mere use of the *baraita* is sufficient for RHG to draw conclusions from it for the questions he was dealing with, as he himself explained.

Conflicting traditions are reported in the name of Samuel as to whether, in the Passover Eve *Seder*, after having eaten the mazah, one may partake of fruits, nuts, sweets, etc. (Pesaḥim 119b-120a, as understood by RHG in RGA pp. 44-45, cit. sup., p. 27). The *sugya* introduces this *baraita* to support the negative stand, and when answered, repeats it to attack the positive stand—again unsuccessfully. The *baraita* reads: [As for] sponge cakes, honey cakes, and rich mazah—a man may fill his stomach with them, providing that he eats as much as an olive of unleavened bread at the end.

RHG (loc. cit.) was asked for his view on the matter of one who had only one measure of properly processed mazah on Passover Eve. Should he eat it at the beginning of the meal or at its end? (The questioners reported that HP and HG had disputed the issue). RHG cites the aforementioned *sugya* and declares: "We deduce from it [the discussion] that according to both the first version and the latter version [of the Samuel tradition] one is obliged to end his meal with a measure of mazah but is not obliged to begin his meal with a measure of mazah." RHG's view is, of course, based on the closing statement of the *baraita:* "providing that he eats as much as an olive of unleavened bread *at the end.*" RHG thus bases his view on the *baraita,* even though the *baraita* did not prove conclusive in determining what the *sugya* wished to determine.

This sharpens our understanding of RHG's reasoning. The authority of the *baraita* in RHG's eyes stems from the Gemara having esteemed it enough to have posed questions from it, resolved doubts with it, brought proofs from it, etc. Its ultimate influence on the outcome of the *sugya* is of no consequence. It is the fact that the Gemara uses it which shows that the *baraita* is an authoritative one, and its word, law.

A *Baraita* Appearing as an Integral Part of the *Sugya*

Based on our appraisal of RHG's understanding of the use of non-mishnaic tanaic pericopae by *amoraim,* we can formulate another principle. It would seem to be RHG's view that, in the course of a *sugya*—as an inherent part of its give and take (questions and answers, proofs and solutions)—the Gemara makes use of only such *beraitot* which contain what the Gemara thought to be the accepted and authoritative *halakah.* Hence, in RHG's eyes, such *beraitot* are ipso-facto binding upon us as well. This is not to say that we do not find *beraitot* whose laws are not accepted ones strewn throughout the Babylonian Talmud. Indeed we do. However, we do not find such *beraitot*—RHG thinks— as an integral part of the *sugya* construction, unless, somewhere along the way, it has clearly been noted that part or all of the legal assumptions of that *baraita* are either rejected, or, at least, subject to dispute. Such a signal is necessary for an exception to the rule. The rule is: A *baraita* which appears as an integral part of the *sugya* represents the accepted *halakah.*

The following two decisions of RHG at first glance, seem to run contrary to the principle as we have formulated it. Closer scrutiny, however, reveals how consistent RHG's decisions are with our formulation of the principles.

A. The mishnah relates a dispute regarding a merchant's rights when defrauded

> Just as the private person has the right to retreat because of *onaah*
> [defrauding by overreaching], so has the merchant the right. R. Judah
> says: The merchant has not the right. (M BM 4, 4).

> [The Gemara wonders:] Because he is a merchant he has no claims
> for *ónaáh* [according to R. Judah]?! [Two explanations are offered:]
> Said R. Naḥman in Rav's name: This was taught of a *safsar*
> [speculator or merchant middleman] ... R. Aṣi said: What is meant
> by "There is no *ónaáh* for a merchant?" He is not subject to the laws
> of *ónaáh*, i.e., he can withdraw even for less than the [normal
> recoverable standard of] *ónadh.* [The ensuing discussion ends by
> furnishing proof to R. Naḥman from a *baraita*]. It has been taught in
> accordance with R. Naḥman: R. Judah said: There is no *ónadh* for a
> merchant, because he is an expert (BM 51a).

If we have correctly formulated the principles which guide RHG, we might—at first
glance—anticipate that he holds the following:

1) The *halakah* follows R. Judah, because the law follows a *tana* according to
whom *amoraim* posed questions and answers.

2) The view of R. Naḥman should be accepted, because he has tanaic support.

3) The law contained in the concluding *baraita* should be the accepted one, since
the Gemara brings support only from such authoritative *beraitot*.

In fact, we read thus in RHG's abridged responsum:

> And regarding R. Judah who said the merchant has not the right to
> retreat because of *ónadh* the Rabbis have said that R. Judah's view is
> to be rejected, because even if "it has been taught in accordance with
> R. Nahman who said in Rav's name,"[34] This is how it has been
> taught: "R. Judah says" (SZ 4, 6, 26).

Careful scrutiny of the *sugya* discloses how RHG exercised disciplined reasoning and
textual sensitivity to reach his conclusions which were totally consistent with the
principles as we formulated them. R. Naḥman is indeed supported by a *baraita*.
Consistent with our principles, we therefore accept his view. But what is his view that
the *baraita* comes to uphold? He claims that R. Judah is talking about a merchant who is
a *safsar*. Very well, we accept that R. Judah is talking about a *safsar*. Now to the
baraita. It was utilized by the *sugya* as proof. According to our principles this means
that the *baraita* is authoritative and must be accepted. Again all is well. We accept

what it tells us, namely that R. Judah holds that a merchant has not the right of retreat, and that his reason is: "because he is an expert."

So we have accepted the *baraita* and R. Naḥman—who are in virtual agreement—as authoritative, and we conclude that theirs is the correct interpretation of R. Judah. They never claimed anything more. RHG, too, certainly goes along with this. In fact, this is precisely what he means when he writes, "even if 'it has been taught in accordance with R. Naḥman'." There is no denying that such a teaching binds us in accepting both the *baraita* and R. Naḥman as authoritative. However, continues R. Hai, "This is how it has been taught, 'R. Judah says'." R. Hai is telling us that both R. Naḥman and the *baraita* are only interpreting R. Judah. Their interpretation we certainly accept as authoritative.

However, the correct interpretation of R. Judah is not the crucial question. The crucial legal question is once we have arrived at the proper interpretation of R. Judah, do we establish the law according to him? In a "first glance" we tend to answer affirmatively since the *sugya* includes an explanation of R. Judah's opinion. Why then does RHG identify with the opposing view? The answer lies in the last discussion of the previous mishnah. In the course of the *sugya* a question is posed from the view of the first *tana* in our mishnah: "But did we not learn, 'Just as the private person has the right to retreat, because of *onaah*, so has the merchant the right' " (BM loc. cit.). So, there was a conflict between the two principles from the same group. *Amoraim* discussed the view of R. Judah on the one hand, and on the other hand, the *sugya* posed a question from the view of the first *tana*. RHG resolved the standoff by resorting to principles governing straight tanaic disputes and decided in favor of the first *tana*.

B.   Here now is a case which not only deepens our understanding of this set of principles but also has wider implications in respect to one of the most basic principles of adjudication in Talmudic literature, that governing disputes between the Houses of Hillel and Shamai.

> If a woman awaiting levirate marriage inherited property, the School of Shammai and the School of Hillel agree that she may sell it or give it away and the act will be valid. If she died, what should be done with her *ketubah* and property that comes in and goes out with her? The School of Shammai say: The heirs of her husband share with the heirs of her father. And the School of Hillel say . . . the *ketubah* falls

to the husband's heirs and the property that comes in and goes out with her falls to her father's heirs (M Yeb. 4, 3).

[The Gemara asks] Wherein does the first clause in which there is no dispute between them differ from the final clause in which they do dispute? (Yeb. 38a).

In answer to that question, the Gemara introduces a long *sugya*, containing various opinions, all explaining the view of the House of Shamai.

Were RHG to invoke the principle: "If *amoraim* interpret or explain the view of one disputing *tana*, the law follows that *tana*" (above, p. 95), he would have ruled according to the House of Shamai. In fact, however, he writes,

> In all events these replies and presumptions are all according to the School of Shammai, "Wherein does the first clause in which there is no dispute between them differ from the final clause in which they do dispute," but according to the School of Hillel the ketubah is considered to be in the presumptive possession of the husband's heirs no matter where it is, and the property that comes in and goes out with her are considered to be in the presumptive possession of her father's heirs. And thus do we act, and so are we accustomed, and barring this we know nothing (RDG 80, p. 50).

So, RHG decidedly and emphatically rules in favor of the School of Hillel. It is left for us to explain why he does so despite his noting that the whole *sugya* revolves around the School of Shamai. Why does he abandon the aforementioned principle and rule in favor of the School of Hillel?

This question can be answered in two ways, each way representing a different approach to understanding this group of principles. The first approach differentiates between the *sugya* at hand and those others in which RHG applies the principles. All the latter *sugyot* flowed in regular *sugya* fashion. Only careful analysis of the *sugya's* give and take leads us to realize that it makes sense only according to one of the tanaic opinions. It is as if the Gemara assumed that there is only one tanaic view which really needs to be considered, thereby posting a clear sign that it is that tanaic view which represents the accepted law, and all subsequent students of the Oral Law are to follow this lead.

Our *sugya*, on the other hand, does not consist of a discussion which just happens to make sense only according to one view. From the onset it is clear that the sole purpose of the whole *sugya* is to explain the theory of the School of Shamai, and to determine what prompted them to dispute the latter part of the mishnah. The *sugya* consciously concerns itself with only one of the views, but, simultaneously, it is cognizant of the fact that there is another—that of the School of Hillel. The *amoraim* deal with the view of Shamai not because it is the accepted one, but because it is the problematic one, while that of the School of Hillel is clear and requires no elucidation. It is precisely because of the difficulty in the view of the School of Shamai that the *sugya* deals solely with that view and not because the Gemara believes it to be the authoritative view. Now, although normally we claim that if *amoraim* trouble themselves to explain a particular tanaic view, they must have felt it to be law (see above, p. 95), in this case the reasoning has already been accurately analyzed by one of the great medieval Talmudic commentators: "Although the law does not follow the School of Shamai, their opinion is worthy of arousing interest and discussion" (RITBA to the *sugya*, s.v. Gemara).

The second approach treats this *sugya* no differently from any other. With no other principles to refer to, we would have favored the School of Shamai since the Gemara discusses their view. However, when a dispute between the schools of Hillel and Shamai is at hand, one of the oldest Talmudic principles of adjudication comes into play, and takes precedence over all other principles. That principle is: The view of the School of Shamai is regarded as having no authority [literally: is not a mishnah] when it conflicts with [literally: in the place of] that of the School of Hillel. The only exceptions are those cases specifically noted as such by the Gemara.

The leading proponent of this approach in all disputes between the schools of Hillel and Shamai was Sa'adya Gaon. His position is most clearly stated in a response to a question dealing with a case very similar to one discussed in a mishnah.

> A question [came] before our Master Sa'adya, the Head of the Academy: A house fell down on a man and his wife, and they died. It is not known who predeceased whom, and after their deaths the heirs came quarreling with one another. The husband's heirs say: The wife died first and her inheritance already fell to the husband in his lifetime. The wife's heirs say: The husband died first, and the property of the woman had already become her own [with no attachment] during her lifetime. Moreover, we demand her *ketubah*.
>
> [RSdG's response:] It is our view that the claims of these heirs of the husband and heirs of the wife were the subject of a dispute between

the Schools of Shammai and Hillel [i.e., in a similar case] . . . as our
Rabbis have learned: "If the house fell down on a man and his wife the
husband's heirs may say, the wife died first and the husband died
afterward, and the wife's heirs may say, the husband died first and the
wife died afterward. The School of Shammai say: Let the claimants
share. The School of Hillel say: Possessions [are to remain with those
who are] in presumptive possession" [M BB 9, 9] . . . Even though we
say later on [continues RSdG:] "R. Simeon b. Laqish in the name of
Bar Qapara said [the estate in dispute] is to be divided" [BB 158b],
this is not the law, because this statement is like the School of
Shammai, and it is established that the view of the School of Shammai
is regarded as having no authority when it conflicts with that of the
School of Hillel, except for those ten cases, some of which are
specified in the mishnah and others in the Talmud, and our case is not
among them (RDG 558).

RSdG then, holds that we always rule in favor of the School of Hillel over the School of
Shamai, regardless of other principles of adjudication which might apply. The absolutely
only exceptions are those cases specifically and explicitly specified by the Talmud.

An earlier Gaon of Sura, Natronai, had already taken a similar stand. He had
pondered over the same *sugya* in Yeb. (cited above, p. 104) which RHG had recourse to in
RDG 80 (ibid.) and he considered a question which ultimately occupied RHG as well:
What should practical judicial procedure be in cases similar to that discussed in the
sugya? His conclusion was: To rule in accordance with the School of Hillel, "That all
property which had clear origins should be left in the possession of their presumptive
possessors, the *ketubah* falling to the husband's heirs, and the property that came in and
goes out with her falling to her father's heirs." His reasoning was: "The law follows the
School of Hillel, first and foremost because the view of the School of Shammai is
regarded as having no authority when it conflicts with that of the School of Hillel" (OG
Yeb. 158). R. Natronai never even considered the amoraic discussion, demonstrating that
it bears no significance when the School of Shamai-School of Hillel principle can be
invoked. When a clearcut and practical ruling is called for, this ancient principle of
adjudication holds sway over all others, and swings the ruling in favor of the School of
Hillel.[35]

All-Amoraic Combinations

We have so far considered principles establishing the authority of tanaic pericopae or opinions which have been the source of amoraic discussion, usage, or reliance. For the most part, the principles we have formulated in these pages are true not only of tanaic pericopae or opinion but hold for early amoraic pericopae or opinion as well.

Amoraic Questions and Answers According to the View of Earlier *Amoraim*; Interpretation of Earlier *Amoraim*; Questions Posed or Resolved from Amoraic Statements

Here, for example, is a ruling by RHG which demonstrates that if amoraic (or Talmudic) give and take revolves around the opinion of one particular earlier *amora*, then the law follows that *amora*, and if the Gemara uses an amoraic opinion to resolve a question, then the law follows that amoraic opinion. At the center of RHG's ruling is the view of Rav that:

> If "A" sold something to "B" when it was not his and then went and purchased it from the original owner [C] . . . He [Rav] said . . . [we posit that] the first [A] sold the second [B—in advance] every right that he [A] might subsequently acquire [the purchase from (coming to legalize the sale to B)]. For what reason? [Asks the Gemara] Mar Zutra said: [Because] he wished that he [B] should not call him a robber. R. Aṣi said: [Because] he [A] wished to indicate his honesty. Further on, the question is raised, whether Rav's statement holds equally in a case where the original owner—[C] gave it [the robbed object] away as a present to him [A]. R. Aba and Rabina differ (BM 15b-16a).

Elsewhere (ibid., 72b) the Gemara uses the views of Mar Zutra and R. Aṣi to put down a question.

RIF testifies that although

> In MQM [Ch. 29] he [RHG] said that the law does not follow Rav's view . . . he [RHG] changed his mind in a responsum and said that the law does follow Rav in this matter, because since we see that Mar Zutra and R. Asi and Rav Aba and Rabina—who are last—give and take according to Rav, we learn that the law follows Rav. Moreover, we learn in the chapter [beginning] "What is usury" [BM Ch. 5] . . . and we answer, "How now? There, whether on the view that he [the vender] is anxious not to be called a robber, or on the view that he is desirous of retaining his [the purchaser's] trust. . . ." Behold the law

follows Rav, for were it not law, they [the Gemara] would not have
used it for giving an answer (OG BM 75).

In this ruling, then, RHG clearly treats amoraic usage and discussion of earlier amoraic
opinion, precisely as he treats usage and discussion of tanaic opinion.   In another
responsum too (RDG 333a and OG BM 76, cited above, p. 53), RHG again works on the
premise that the law follows Rav in this case.

Here is another example involving a ruling in favor of Rav. In a responsum dealing
with the laws of *terefah* we find the following: "Rav said: If a rib was dislocated
together with the vertebra in which it is fixed, or if a rib was dislocated from one side
and from the other side and the vertebra remains—in the sequence of the vertebrae—[the
animal] is *terefah* and such is the law" (KGE 36). Muller has already pointed out in his
footnotes to the responsum:

1)   That this is not a verbatim citation of Rav's statement as cited in the Talmud (Hullin
52a), but is rather a reformulation of Rav's statement based on the amoraic discussion
and interpretation of that statement (ibid.), and 2) That many codifiers did not rule
according to Rav.   Now, as to RHG, there can be little doubt that it was precisely
because there was amoraic discussion and interpretation of Rav's statement that led
RHG to decide that "such is the law." That is in effect why he formulated the law—and
the statement—according to the amoraic discussion.[36]

We see, therefore, that the principle that the law follows *tanaim* whose view has
been discussed by the Talmud, or according to whom *amoraim* give and take, is true of
earlier *amoraim* as well.[37] The same is undoubtedly true of the other related principles
dealing with amoraic-Talmudic use of tanaic material; e.g., the *sugya's* use of earlier
amoraic opinion for questioning or answering is a sign that the law follows that *amora*—
just as it is true of tanaic material. In fact, we shall now disclose that RHG's explicit
formulation of one such principle is in connection with amoraic material.

According to the tradition of the Oral Law one may not carry an article four cubits
in public ground on the Sabbath (see Shabbat 96b). According to Rabbinic tradition the
acts of "work" prohibited on the Sabbath are derived from—and consequently must be
similar to—the work that was required and performed in connection with the building of a
Tabernacle in the wilderness (v. e.g., ibid., 49b and introduction to Soncino edition).
Now, "R. Samuel b. Judah said in R. Abba's name in R. Huna's name in the name of Rav:

If one carries [an article] four cubits in covered public ground he is not liable because it is not like the banners of the wilderness" [which were carried in non-covered ground in the Israelite encampment] (ibid., 98a). RSG and RHG cite this tradition in a responsum[38] and add the following comment: "And this tradition is law for behold we learn from it in the chapter 'goings-out on the Sabbath' [Sabbath Ch. 1] and we provide an answer in order to maintain it" (OG Shabbath 282, p. 92).

The reference is to Shabbat 5a where the *sugya* poses a difficulty based on this tradition, and then offers an answer, keeping the tradition intact. From this RHG concludes that this tradition is law. His reasoning runs thus: If an amoraic pericope is the source of a *sugya's* question (and is not rejected), or, if a *sugya* takes the trouble to argue difficulties raised about that pericope, it is a sure sign that the pericope in question should be viewed as authoritative law. Formulating this as a more general principle: If in the course of a *sugya* a question is asked—based on amoraic opinion—and then resolved, RHG views it as a sign that the Gemara accepted that opinion, and he will invariably rule in accordance with it (qualifying it only by any qualification the Gemara might have added while resolving the question).

RHG expresses this with youthful exuberance and hyperbole in an early work. Talmudic tradition attributes to R. Nahman the introduction of the consuetudinary (court imposed) Rabbinic oath of inducement into the judicial procedure (Sebuot 40b). There are however, conflicting traditions (ibid.) as to the case in which he instituted the oath. One tradition claims that R. Nahman was commenting on M Seb. 6, 1: "[If the claimant said,] 'Thou hast a maneh [100 dinars] of mine, [and, the other said] 'I have nought of thine,' he is exempt." And "said R. Nahman: But they impose upon him the consuetudinary oath," i.e., according to this tradition the oath is imposed in all cases of denied claims. According to the other tradition R. Nahman was commenting on M Seb. 6, 2: "[If the claimant said] 'Thou hast a maneh of mine' [and the other said] 'Yea,' and on the morrow the first one said to him, 'give it to me' [and the other said] 'I have given it to thee already,' he is exempt." Only then did R. Nahman add: "But they impose upon him the consuetudinary oath," i.e., only when there is money "at stake," where money has already been admitted, or where there is agreement—at least—that some sort of a transaction has taken place.

RHG in a monograph, upholds the first tradition, bringing proof from the following

Talmudic passage:

> There was a shepherd to whom people entrusted cattle every day in
> the presence of witnesses.   One day they entrusted without
> witnesses.   Subsequently he completely denied [receipt of the
> cattle]. But witnesses came and testified that he had eaten two of
> the cattle ... [Asks the Gemara:] Should we not impose an oath
> [upon the shepherd] because of the view of R. Naḥman as we have
> learned, "Thou hast a maneh of mine ... I have naught of thine ..."
> but R. Naḥman said: "They impose upon him...." (BM 5a).

The Gemara answers that R. Naḥman's ruling is not applicable in this case. It never
challenges the validity of the ruling. On the surface, the tradition the Gemara cited is
the first tradition in the transmission of R. Naḥman. Hence this is a classic case wherein
the Gemara poses a question based on amoraic tradition, and then takes great care to
answer the question, while maintaining the integrity of the tradition. Hence, RHG, in
keeping with his principle as we formulated it, rules according to the first tradition of R.
Naḥman while formulating the principle. So he comes out in favor of the first tradition,
and adds:

> And so much more so since in the Gemara [on the mishnah] of "Two
> laid hold of a cloak" [BM 1, 1] in the [discussion of] "There was a
> shepherd to whom people entrusted [etc.]" we find the words of R.
> Naḥman cited according to the first way [tradition] ... and they ask
> and answer ... now were it necessary for there to have been a
> transaction between them [the claimants] in order [for an oath] to be
> incumbent [i.e., the second tradition in R. Naḥman] they [the
> Gemara] should have brought it up in their answer. And it is well
> known that they pose questions and answers only regarding what is
> correct[39] (MPS, p. 37). . . .

> This discussion [BM 5a cit. sup.] favors whomever establishes the
> consuetudinary oath without a previous transaction or agreed money
> at stake, establishing it on the first part of the mishnah, "Thou hast a
> *maneh* of mine ... I have nought of thine, he is exempt," and R.
> Naḥman said: "But they impose...." This is a great proof in that
> they [ibid.] agreed and posed questions and answers according to this
> [tradition] as we have already prefaced [in the passage cited directly
> above] (MPS, p. 61).[40]

Amoraic Statements Used by the *Sugya* for Posing Questions, Qualified or Limited by the *Sugya's* Answer

Here now is an example of amoraic statement used in a *sugya* for posing a question. The question is answered, but the answer in effect, qualifies and limits the statement. True to the principle we have formulated, RHG rules according to the amoraic statement with its qualification.

In a number of places we have cited and discussed at length RSG and RHG's responsum in OG Ket. 203 (e.g., above pp. 51, 79, et. seq.) in which the crucial issue is the declaration of a witness that the bill of divorce upon which he was signed, was not really meant to be valid. A relevant Talmudic discussion is found in BB 48b. The Gemara asks:

> Seeing that R. Naḥman has said: If the witnesses [to a deed] say . . . we wrote only [under reservation of] a modaà [ascertaining before signing that the principal was acting under duress and intended the deed to be void] their word is not accepted. [And answers:] This is the case where they make a verbal statement to this effect . . . but if they write a deed [a written *modaà*] then one deed [the *modaà*] can invalidate another.

If our formulation of RHG's principle is accurate, then we would expect him—based on this Talmudic discussion—to disqualify an oral *modaà* but to accept and validate a written *modaà* or one intended to be in writing.

Indeed, toward the end of their intricate responsum (OG Ket. 203, cit. sup., p. 75) RSG and RHG rule that since the directive of the husband was given in a manner intending to have the witnesses commit it to writing, the witness should yet now do so, making it a written *modaà* and only thus the witness' claim: "I wrote the divorce under the reservation of a *modaà*" should be accepted, the divorce ruled void, and the woman granted return of the property. This is a fine example of using the principle to help resolve what we have seen to be an intricate legal question.

An Amoraic Statement Used by the Gemara to Resolve a Difficulty

A final principle of adjudication which we include in this group is: If the Gemara uses an amoraic statement to resolve a difficulty in the course of a *sugya*, the law follows that statement. The assumption behind the principle is that the Gemara would not use non-authoritative material for legal resolutions. Here are examples of RHG's use of this principle:

A. While discussing restrictions meant to make it difficult to forge documents, the Gemara asks: "Is [there no] apprehension that he might erase the [original] 'firm and established' [formula][41] and add whatever he wished, and then write 'firm and established'?" The Gemara answers: "Surely R. Yoḥanan said: A suspended [word that has been] confirmed is admissible; an erasure [however] is inadmissible although it had been confirmed." Consistent with the principle, RHG views R. Yoḥanan's statement as authoritative (since it was used by the *sugya* to resolve a difficulty). Hence, when drawing up instructions regarding additions and corrections in drawing up documents, RHG writes: "If something occurs in the middle of the document which must be suspended, we change the document, or we . . . repeat at the end that this line has such and such suspended" (MH, p. 111 top).

This first example was one of an amoraic statement (which had originally been uttered by R. Yoḥanan in a particular context) which was known to later *amoraim* (those who were discussing the view of R. Huna in BB 160b) who chose to refer to it in order to resolve a difficulty which had arisen in the course of their discussion (ibid.).[42] RHG reasons: If they esteemed the statement enough to resolve their difficulty with it, obviously they deemed it authoritative. Therefore, we do, too. A more complex case would be that of an amoraic statement first made in the course of a particular discussion with the express purpose of resolving a difficulty which arose in the course of that same discussion. Would RHG view that statement as just a stop-gap measure, not bearing authority, or would such a case still fit the principle? His reasoning in the latter instance is: If the statement went undisputed among the participants in the discussion, and if it is satisfactory enough to them and to the *sugya* for resolving their difficulty, that in itself makes it authoritative. The next example shows that these cases, too, can be adjudicated by the same principle.

B.   R. Jose ruled, if the first day of the Festival [of Tabernacles] fell on the Sabbath, and a man forgot and carried out his *lulab* into a public domain [such carrying being forbidden on the Sabbath] he is not culpable, since he brought it out with permission [i.e., being influenced by the performance of a religious act] (M Sukkah 3, 14).

       Abaye stated [qualified R. Jose's ruling]: They taught [that he is not culpable] only when he had not yet fulfilled his obligation [of taking the *lulab*] but if he had already fulfilled his obligation [prior to carrying it out] he is guilty of a transgression. [Abaye's colleagues raised a difficulty:]   But has he not fulfilled his obligation the moment he lifted it up? [to carry it out—so how could he ever be "not culpable?"   To resolve this difficulty] Abaye answered: Where he held it upside down [when lifting it—implying that in such a manner one does not fulfill the obligation of *lulab*].   Rava replied, You may even say that he did not hold it upside down, but here we are dealing with a case where he carried it out in a vessel (Sukkah 41b-42a).

Now, Abaye's statement was obviously intended for the express purpose of resolving the difficulty raised by his colleagues regarding his qualification of R. Jose's rule and in the framework of the discussion cited. The statement has wide legal significance since it implies that one fulfills the obligation of taking the *lulab* only if it is held right side up. Should we discount the implications since Abaye made it only to defend his qualification, or, since it is undisputed in the discussion—Rava offered an alternative suggestion, but did not reject Abaye's—should the statement and its implications, be deemed authoritative?   RHG follows the latter course and rules that whoever holds the *lulab* upside down at the time he takes it, is not to recite the benediction because in that manner he is not fulfilling his obligation (Eṣkol 2, p. 103, cited above, p. 98, cf. OG Sukkah 117-130).

Earlier Amoraic Material Commented Upon, or Used, by Individual *Amoraim*

So far, in this latest group of principles the term "amoraic" use or "amoraic" discussion, has been employed to the *sugya* or the whole body of participants in the discussion. Here now is a case where RHG accepts the authority of an amoraic opinion, seemingly because it was later used by a particular *amora* (rather than the *sugya* as a whole). In ṢZ 4, 2, 4 (discussed above, p. 50) RHG argues that the agreement is not binding because it is usury. He adds: "Even were it not usury it is an *àsmaḵta*[43] and it is established: 'No "if" is binding'."   The truth is that this view is not so "established" in the Talmud (and there is certainly no other source for it). It appears verbatim in only one Talmudic discussion and even there it is not clear that it is indeed the authoritative view. Here is the discussion: "R. Papa thought to argue, where do we rule that an *àsmaḵta*[43] is not binding, only in respect of land . . . but as for wine . . . it is just the same as money. But R. Huna, the son of R. Joshua said to R. Papa: Thus is it stated in

Rav's[44] name: No 'if' is binding" (BM 66b).

RHG had already incorporated this short amoraic discussion into his codification of the laws of purchase and sale (MQM, Ch. 17), where he explains why he feels that this *sugya*-qua *sugya* should be given preference over other *sugyot* (which clearly hold that *ásmaḳta* is binding). What he does not explain is why it is so clear to him that this discussion "establishes" that an *ásmaḳta* is not binding. Such a formulation by RHG usually means that he is hinting at some principle of adjudication. This one might be phrased so: If a tradition (or statement) of an *amora* is cited by another *amora* to set some matter straight, it is a sign that the tradition is authoritative.

An *Amora's* Qualification of an Amoraic Statement

Continuing with principles concerning reactions of particular *amoraim* to earlier amoraic statements, we now set forth a number of rulings which RHG based on one *amora's* qualifying the statement (or opinion or tradition) of another (or of one which arose anonymously in the discussion). The number of available examples justify our determining that in these cases, RHG was invoking one of his principles of adjudication, one which we would formulate thus: If an *amora* qualifies another amoraic statement (or opinion or tradition) the law follows the statement (or opinion or tradition) with the qualification.

A. MH 16 (cit. above, p. 53). RHG brings proof for his decision that if it is clear to the judges that there was a purposeful evasion of the laws of preemption, they may cancel the evasion (and the deal) and invoke preemption. He accomplishes this by first explicitly citing the Gemara: "A gift is not subject to the law of preemption. Said Ameimar: But if he [the donor] promised [wrote][45] security of tenure [in case it is seized for the donor's debt another will be supplied] it is subject to the law of preemption" (BM 108b). RHG then continues: "Now you know that we evict the purchaser from a gift containing security of tenure and give it over the abutter." Obviously, he is telling us that he was ruling according to the Gemara's statement with the *amora's* (Ameimar's) qualification.

B.   In his [Rav's] name has the following dictum been reported, viz., if,
          after slaughtering [the windpipe] was found to be torn loose, the
          animal is permitted for it is impossible to have cut through an organ

that had been torn loose. R. Yohanan, however, said, he should bring and compare it.[46] R. Nahman said, the rule holds good only if the slaughterer did not grasp the organs [when slaughtering], but if he did grasp the organs [the slaughtering is invalid for] then it is possible to cut through the organ that had been torn loose (Hullin 54a).

The traditional commentaries are divided over the explanation of this pericope. Some view it as a three-way dispute. Others see R. Nahman as qualifying the two previous statements. Others yet believe that R. Nahman is qualifying only Rav's statement.[47] This amoraic discussion is treated in a "responsum" which is actually a series of rulings regarding laws of *terefah* attributed to RHG. He cites the statement of Rav then skips that of R. Yohanan, quoting R. Nahman instead, as if it were a direct continuation. He then adds: "And this is the law" (KGE 36). An analysis of the reasoning behind this clever construction gives us this picture: He holds that there is a dispute between Rav and R. Yohanan, with R. Nahman qualifying the statement of Rav. Hence, although the law normally follows R. Yohanan in disputes with Rav, in this case the law follows the *amora* whose statement is qualified by another—together with the qualification, i.e., Rav and R. Nahman. Therefore, in order to lay down the law—in adhering to the principle—he need do nothing more than to note those two statements (Rav and R. Nahman), which is just what he did.

C. "R. Nahman said, if [after the slaughtering of an animal it was discovered that] the lung was pierced, but the perforation was covered up by the [chest] wall it is permitted. Rabina added, provided it had grown into the flesh" (Hullin 48a). Now Rabina is commenting directly on R. Nahman's statement, and calling for greater stringency. RHG—as we might have anticipated—does indeed accept the view of R. Nahman with Rabina's qualification (RDG 331, p. 159), again in compliance with the principle.[48]

The Gemara's Qualifications of an Amoraic Statement

To complete the cycle and to close our discussion of this group of principles here now is a case of the statement of a particular *amora*, qualified not by a fellow individual *amora* but by the amoraic discussion (*sugya*). Here too, RHG accepts the statement together with its qualification as authoritative. In RDG 323 (cited above, p. 67) RHG contends that an orphaned daughter's right to one-tenth of the estate (marriage outfit allowance) should not be viewed as passing into her possession automatically. As proof, he points to the case in which—so he claims—she loses this right in her lifetime, namely when after having attained adolescence and having married she is not maintained by the estate (her brothers) and did not lodge a protest (a claim). To substantiate his contention he cites part of the Talmudic discussion found in Ket. 68b. However, that portion of the discussion reaches a firm conclusion only regarding her not having lodged a protest. How, then, does he construct the total picture? No doubt, from the continuation of that Talmudic discussion, in which the following tradition is transmitted in the name of Rava: "If she attained her adolescence she need not lodge a protest [claim]. If she married she need not lodge a protest. But if she attained her adolescence and was also married it is necessary for her to lodge a protest." To avoid a contradiction with a different statement of Rava, the *sugya* qualifies the aforementioned tradition: "One is a case where she is maintained by them, the other where she is not maintained by them." RHG therefore concludes from this discussion that the tradition amended by the qualification, is authoritative. His conclusion is: If she is neither maintained, nor did she lodge a protest, then—and only then—does she lose her rights to the marriage outfit allowance.

EPILOGUE

This study was designed to provide a glimpse at the functioning of the Babylonian *geonim*. We focused on Rav Hai, the last of the major *geonim*, whom the *rishonim* considered the greatest of them all. (Hence the pinnacle and finest example of geonic accomplishment). We studied his performance and practice when responding to questions on matters of Jewish law, custom and thought, and affairs both public and private. These responses of Hai comprise a major portion of what is generally considered to be the *geonim's* major contribution to Jewish literature and tradition, geonic responsa. We observed that the Babylonian Talmud was the Gaon's major source, inspiration, and guide. From this observation we gained insight into the process that determined the Babylonian Talmud's central position in traditional Judaism. We were spectators to the earliest development of what is now the standard, time-honored procedure for the traditional Jew to seek guidance: questions posed to the legal expert and religious authority. The wide range of topics covered in the queries impressed upon us the breadth of the Gaon's expertise and authority, and the many facets of life in which he served as shepherd and arbiter to his flock. The names of the communities from which the questions were sent, map out the extent of the Gaon's influence. The later Rabbinic literature which furnished us with many of the responsa, provided as well a glance at medieval Rabbinic legal codes and Talmudic commentaries, and gave us some idea as to the extensive use of geonic material by the later Rabbis. The accompanying comments often reminded us of the esteem in which the *geonim* were held by ensuing generations.

Much of this was "by-the-way." The express purpose of this study was to clarify RHG's methodology: The principles by which he arrived at his decisions. The first and major group of these were principles of adjudication, his guides in reaching conclusions based on the texts which we have seen to be his primary sources, i.e., *sugyot* of the Babylonian Talmud. The limitations necessarily imposed by the size of the present work, enabled us to deal only with the "basic" principles. We showed—through examples from his responsa—how Rav Hai invoked these principles. Hopefully, future volumes will provide opportunity to deal similarly with more principles, as well as with the methodology Rav Hai applied when Talmudic sources were insufficient for arriving at solutions to the problems the questioners posed.

T.G.

APPENDIX

Identification and Attribution of Responsa

In our Introduction we explained why we specifically chose responsa as the best subject for an analysis of RHG's methodology (or the methodology of any responder). True to our purpose we have done our utmost to construct our study of Hai's methodology from his responsa, using his other works only as examples or supplementary proofs. These other works—which do not form the main basis for our study—include his legal monographs, commentries to Tractates or chapters of the Talmud, epistles and poems (even when written at the request of a petitioner or questioner). Citations and fragments of undeterminable origin were not assumed to have derived from a responsum, unless their form and subject matter precluded their stemming from one of the above. If, despite our precautions, some extra-responsa material does somehow appear, it does not really alter our conclusions. After all, these other works, too, are representative of R. Hai's methodology.

We determined RHG's authorship of responsa (or fragments) in the following ways:

a. If a *rishon*—particularly one from a region with historical ties to the Babylonian academies—attributed a responsa to RHG or cited a section of one in RHG's name. We never questioned such an attribution unless we had compelling cause for doing so.

b. If an authentic heading was found on an individual responsum or in a group of responsa within a collection.[1]

c.- d. If the responsa is part of a pamphlet (of responsa) *("darj"; "quntres")*, or group, emanating from RHG (see below).

e. When certain *rishonim* cite a passage in the name of The Gaon or Gaon, we can know that RHG is meant (see below).

f. When we found sundry proofs for individual cases (see below).

The first two methods of attribution are self-evident, and can be employed or checked upon by anyone glancing at the printed text. We will therefore devote this appendix to pamphlets, groups, citations from *rishonim* and sundry responsa whose attribution to RHG is not immediately apparent.

Responsa attributed to RSG and RHG are included in this study. It was RHG who actually authored those "joint" responsa.[2]

Pamphlets

In terms of methodology of identification the most interesting, if not the most numerous, are those responsa which can be shown to have belonged to the same original group (scroll or pamphlet, *"darj"* or *"quntres"*) emanating from RHG, or RHG in collaboration with RSG. In the Introduction (p. 3) we described how the questions and responses were collected and dispatched in groups—thus forming a pamphlet. Later collections put together responsa from various pamphlets, hence creating collections from different authors. All collections of geonic responsa published before the Genizah are either such collections, or simply collections from the writings of *rishonim*. Some pamphlets have remained "pure"—without the infusion of responsa from other pamphlets. (They are not necessarily complete, i.e., some responsa from the original pamphlet may now be missing). Original pamphlets can be identified and reconstructed through lists (see Groner, ALEI SEFER 2, p. 5 f.). These lists were compiled while the original pamphlet was still intact (often at the request of a scholar wishing to know what was "available" but unable to afford copying all the responsa).

We have shown elsewhere (ibid., p. 7 f.) that the following pamphlets are authored by RHG (or RHG and RSG). All the responsa they contain should, then, be attributed to RHG.

1.   RDG 16-36 + RIF BM 527 + Marmorstein, pp. 53-55 (=GEONICA, pp. 208-09, RGA 82-3).

2.   RDG 59-67 + GRA 105-07+ SINAI 75, p. 19 + GEONICA 284-85 + GNK 1, pp. 1-4 + GNK 5, p. 33 f. + SZ 4, 2, 31 and 4, 6, 29.

3.   RDG 230-264 + RIF Sebuot 1158 + DCA 128a + SZ 3, 2, 15.

4.   RDG 315-28 + GRA 101-04 + DCA 304b + The fragment of a list published in GEONICA, p. 56 (and see OG Jom-Tow, p. 39, n. 6-7).

5.   The responsa represented by the fragment of a list published in "Marmorstein", pp. 45-47 (GNS 427-31), + GNS, pp. 49-68 + OG Jom-Tow 5 + Abramson, *INYANOT*, pp. 205-07.

To these we can add the following:

6.   RDG 37-43

RDG 37-38 appear together in HSG V. 2, p. 31 f. and in RLOW 133-36.[3] Here, the original heading is intact.[4] RHG is named as respondent and Tlemcen as the place from where the questions were sent (as in RDG). RDG 43 is attributed to RHG in DCA 171a and is found in an Aramaic version in ITTUR V. 1, 23a, where it is likewise attributed to RHG. Scholars have designated this and other responsa from the group as stemming from the pamphlet sent to Tlemcen, thereby postulating the unity of the group and its inclusion in the pamphlet.[5]

7.   RGA, pp. 60-62; 102-03 + SINAI JUBILEE VOLUME, pp. 412-17 + GRA, pp. 117-18, no. 19 + MORIAH 7a (5737), p. 3 + DRG 79 (b) + RDG, 434-35; 439.

This pamphlet was discussed in detail by Prof. Abramson.[6] The heading precedes RDG 434 and informs us that the pamphlet was sent by RSG and RHG to Judah b. Joseph *"Rosh Kalla."* Our formulation (in the heading) of what constituted the original pamphlet is based on the conclusions of Abramson (ibid.) which, in turn, are based on a list found in an Adler Ms. and on a fragment found in Cambridge.

8.   The responsa forming the pamphlet from which a fragment of a list was published in GEONICA, p. 60.

This fragment is part of a typical list, listing all the responsa found in a specific pamphlet (see p. 119). Unfortunately, the heading which would normally identify the questions and responder is missing.[7]   Only nos. 7-15 have been preserved in this fragment.   No. 9-11 of the list have been preserved in consecutive order in a Ms. published by Assaf in RGA, pp. 104-05, 144-46.[8] RDG 181 and 182 (!) were also copied from this group, being 9 and 13 in the list.

Although the heading is missing, we can nevertheless determine that RHG was the responder. There is testimony of the Eshkol attributing no. 10 in the list to RHG (see RGA, p. 103). Moreover, in nos. 13 and 14 the responder is asked about what he wrote in the Treatise on Oaths which he had compiled. The reference is to RHG's Treatise on Oaths (the complete responsa are found in RDG 182 and SZ 4, 5, 6). Since, as we have explained, all the responsa in a pamphlet came from the same gaon, we conclude that RHG was the author of all the responsa in the pamphlet.

9.   RDG 345-350.

This group bears the heading: "Questions asked by R. Jacob b. R. Nissim of the city of Kairouan". RDG 350 is followed by the date: "Shevat (1) 302 (Ptolemic-991). This group is certainly not a complete pamphlet. In the original pamphlet between what are now RDG 346 and 347 there was another responsum. B. M. Lewin published the three responsa, in proper order, copied from a different Ms. in GNK 2, pp. 18-19. This "middle" responsum was published again, copied from yet another Ms. in GRA (p. 127) where it bears this heading: "A responsum of R. Şerira Gaon and his son R. Hai, the head of the Court, of blessed memory, who responded to R. Jacob b. Nissim of Kairouan in the year 302". This "middle" responsum is, then, undoubtedly part of the original pamphlet, as are those two which flank it.[9] Since, in addition to this, RDG 345 carries the heading and RDG 350 the closing date, we may safely conclude that the whole group in RDG is indeed part of the original pamphlet (as did Prof. Abramson in his introduction to RNG, p. 18).

10. RDG 68-81.

"It is clear that the whole pamphlet is from R. Hai's" responsa to R. Joseph (S. Abramson, BEMERKAZIM, p. 46 and reiterated, p. 44; see his detailed discussion, pp. 46-55).

11. The responsa referred to in the list published in *MISIFRUT HAGEONIM*, pp. 225-27 which is the equivalent of the list published as "The Fourth Pamphlet," in "Marmorstein", p. 39 f. (and GNK 2, pp. 43-44 and GNS, pp. 425-27).

This is a list of the responsa in an original pamphlet. The responsa published in RDG 282-309 were all part of the original pamphlet from which this list was made. They are referred to by the following numbers in the list: 1, 4, 13, 16, 17, 21, 22, 24, 27, 28, 30, 33, 40, 41-43, 57, 60-69.[10] According to the heading at the beginning of the list in *MISIFRUT*, the pamphlet was sent "to Abu Jacob of Andalusia, and are responsa of our Master Şerira and his son the head of the Court, of blessed memory" (RHG).

12. The responsa referred to in the list published by Prof. Abramson in *INYANOT*, pp. 211-15 (Wolfson Jubilee Volume [Hebrew], pp. 18-21). This, too, is a list of the responsa in an original pamphlet (the listmaker's ninth). According to its superscription it was sent by "Şerira Gaon and Hai the head of the Court, of blessed memory." (See Abramson's Introduction and Notes for a full discussion of the list).

13. The responsa referred to in the list published in GEONICA V. 2, pp. 57-58.

This is a list of the responsa in the listmaker's fourth pamphlet. According to its superscription the questions are "from R. Meshulam b. Master R. Kalonymos from the city of Luca to R. Şerira Gaon and Hai the head of the Court." The known responsa among those which formed the original pamphlet were edited by B. M. Lewin in "RAV

ṢERIRA, MITQUFAT HAGEONIM", p. 32 f.

14. The responsa referred to in the list published in GEONICA V. 2, p. 69.

The original pamphlet from which this list was made (the listmaker's ninth) contained "questions from R. Judah b. R. Joseph to R. Hai Gaon of blessed memory."[11] All the questions in the list are in Arabic. The first responsum noted in the list is that which is also noted in RDG 207. It is rather certain that RDG 208—which is also in Arabic and contains a salutory ending—was the final responsum in the original pamphlet. Unfortunately, the list in GEONICA extends only until no. 10.

15. The responsa referred to in the list published in GEONICA V. 2, p. 71.

The original pamphlet from which this list was made (the listmaker's twelfth), was comprised of "questions which reached Rav Hai from Basrah." They all deal with (sundry) matters from the tractate BT BB. The pamphlet has been discussed in the introduction to GKT, p. 25. RDG 221-22 were part of this original pamphlet.

16. The responsa referred to in the list published in GEONICA V. 2, p. 67.

The original pamphlet from which this list was made was comprised of "Questions of R. Jacob b. Nissim to Rabbi Ṣerira Gaon and Hai the head of the Court, of blessed memory." It was discussed by Prof. Abramson in the introduction to RNG, p. 18 and n. 16.

17. The responsa referred to in the list published in *"MISIFRUT HAGEONIM"*, p. 227.

The original pamphlet from which this list was made (the listmaker's third), was sent to Egypt, to R. Elḥanan b. R. Shemaryah, by RSG and RHG, and was discussed by Prof. Abramson, in *Bemerkazim*, pp. 119-21

18. The responsa referred to in the list published in *"MISIFRUT HAGEONIM"*, p. 229.

The original pamphlet from which this list was made (the listmaker's second) contained responsa of R. Hai to R. Joseph, all of which were in Arabic. We might add the following beyond what Assaf noted in his notes: Responsum number seven in the list refers to the responsum printed in OG Shabbath 12. Assaf missed it because he did not fill in the lacuna accurately. His reconstructed opening read, "One who is [obligated (*"lzm"*)] to fast on Sunday." He should have rather filled in [wishes], using *"ram,"* or perhaps *"rad,"* or *"rgb."* That opening of the question would then have read: "One who wishes to fast on Sunday," just like in OG loc. cit. Assaf was further misled because the translation in OG differs slightly from the translation he employed.

Question no. 15 in the list concerns the passage in Ḥullin 64b regarding abortive eggs. It most probably refers to the responsum found in Samuel b. Jama's LAWS OF SLAUGHTER (HS) 38b (and in an abridged Aramaic form in KGE 59).

19. GEONICA V. 2, pp. 230-31.

Prof. Abramson concluded that this is a fragment of a pamphlet containing responsa of RHG (BEMERKAZIM, pp. 49-52; 55). The citation from RHG quoted by ITTUR published in OG Gittin 383 [cf. 384] is probably taken from responsum four of this fragment.

20. RDG 329-335 + GRA, pp. 98-101.

These were part of a pamphlet, sent to the honorable Rabbi Alfasl b. Berachya of Kairouan in the year 1333 (Ptolemic-1022), which contained 24 responsa. The pamphlet was scrutinized in detail by Prof. Abramson (INYANOT, p. 119 f.). RDG 333a may be the uncopied responsum mentioned in STMQ BB 136 b.

21. RDG 351-369 (?)

The subscription reads: "Questions of the people of Qabes before our master R. Serira and Hai, his son, the head of the Court." As to the details about these responsa, see Prof. Abramson, BEMERKAZIM, p. 101, who treats this group as a pamphlet. However, we have some reservations as to whether this group actually represents the whole and original pamphlet, since RDG 357-58 seem to appear on a list from a different pamphlet (MISIFRUT, pp. 225-27. Above p. 121, no. 11). See, also, the remarks of J. N. Epstein, DEVIR 2, p. 323.

22. ALEI SEFER 8, pp. 9-19.

Groups

We have said (above p. 119) that the pre-Genizah collections of geonic responsa are not made up of original pamphlets, but are groups drawn from various pamphlets. Much of the material went through many hands and many stages before reaching their present state. Some of the usual criteria of those who arranged the groups in the various stages, were: common topic, gleaned from a common source (e.g., a work of one *"Rishon"*), or common author. In the latter case the name of the author was sometimes appended to the group. Wherever such an attribution seemed authoritatively applicable to the whole group,[12] we treated the group as we treated an individual responsum from the collection when it carried a heading (see above, p. 118). But, unfortunately, groups do not always carry a heading or superscription, and are not always readily identifiable.

In his introduction to RNG, Prof. Abramson identifies three groups of responsa—not readily identifiable as groups—and also as attributable to RHG.

a.   RDG 223-226.

b.   RDG 227-229.

> On page 29 f. of RNG he identifies both groups as groups of responsa sent to Kairouan by RHG. The first group contains responsa sent to R. Nissim b. Jacob and the second to the head of the community in Kairouan, R. Abraham b. R. Nathan.

c.   ṢẒ 4, 5, 4-8.

> On page 31 f. of RNG he establishes that this group should be attributed to RHG.

Citations of RHG by Rishonim Using the Term "Gaon" in "Hai Gaon"

It has long been held by scholars of Rabbinic literature that certain early and important Rabbis of the North African and Spanish schools were referring to RHG when they wrote just plain "Gaon." Our view, that this was done by RḤ, RIF, and RMBN,[13] is reflected in this work.

1. *RIF*

David Conforte points out[14] that when RIF mentions "the Gaon" or "so wrote the Gaon" he is referring to RHG. He brings an example from HGHM Berakot 5, 6, "The RIF explained in a similar fashion in the name of the Gaon, who is," adds HGHM, "Rav Hai." What RIF attributes to a gaon (Ber. 177) is indeed attributed by many medieval authors to RHG (see OG Ber. The commentaries, 225, 227-8, and sources cited in Lewin's notes).

Malachi b. Jacob Hacohen expands upon this view in the fourteenth paragraph of the section of *Jad Malachi* entitled "Principles of the RIF." Bamberger calls this "The *Jad Malachi*" view, and in a note in *PEQUDAT HALEVI* to Taanit (p. 8) adds a clear and noteworthy example of this: RAH (ibid.) refers to a statement as "coming from what was sent by Rav Hai," while RIF attributed it to "just plain gaon" (OG Taanith 37). This view is also elaborated upon by R. Abraham Aligry in *LEV SAMEAḤ*,[15] and by ḤIDA in *SZEM HAGDOLIM.*[16]

With the advent of modern, "critical," scholarship, B. M. Lewin establishes the principle anew: "Just plain 'gaon' in Alfasi [RIF] is in fact Rav Hai Gaon" (GNK 2, p. 30). J. N. Epstein, bringing Lewin's remarks in his review of GNK *(Devir* 2, p. 330) registers his agreement through silence.

Indeed, in numerous instances where RIF refers to "just plain gaon," it can easily be shown that he means RHG. Here are just a few of many examples:

a. BB 787: "and so we saw that the [or "a"] Gaon [wrote]." RIF is citing MQM Ch. 35 (discussed at length by many medieval authors).

b. Makot 1062: "and we saw that the [or "a"] Gaon [wrote]." RIF quotes from RLOW 3, which is a responsum of RHG.[17]

c. Sanhedrin 1000. The Gaon—RHG—is named by BHM in his comments.

See also the following examples where the collated material in OG demonstrates that "Gaon" in RIF is RHG (references are to OG): Berakoth 144 and note 9; ibid., commentaries 135 and p. 47, n. 1; ibid., 227 and n. 16; Gittin 15 (taken from 18); Nedarim 85 and n. 6; Sotah 112 and n. 5; Taanith 37 and n. 7.

2. RḤ

Twentieth century scholarship has identified just plain "gaon" in the works of RḤ with RHG. Lewin first spelled it out: "Rav Hai Gaon ... he is the just plain 'gaon' in RḤ."[18] Prof. Abramson reiterated it more recently: "a segment of the responsum was quoted in RḤ BM 50b, in the name of 'Gaon' and he ['Gaon'] is Rav Hai" *(BEMERKAZIM,* p. 54). And again, in dealing with a passage from OZ: "from the commentary of RḤ, the Gaon wrote, i.e., Rav Hai Gaon" (LEṢONENU 36, p. 145).

Numerous other mentions of "just plain gaon" by RḤ clearly refer to RHG.[19] Here are just a few outstanding examples:

a. OZ AZ 142: "In the commentary of RḤ, of blessed and righteous memory, he wrote, 'we saw Gaon of blessed and righteous memory who said ... that it is permissible to rent to a non-Jew....'" The reference is to RHG, cited by name in OZ Shabbat Eve: 2[4].

b. RḤ BM 48a: "This is the explanation of the Gaon of blessed memory." The explanation is drawn from RHG's MQM Ch. 41.

c. RḤ cited in DCA 28a: "Our Rabbi the Gaon in his Treatise on Oaths." The reference is to RHG's MPS.

In the case of RḤ, too, the structure of OG enables us at a glance to identify references to "Gaon" as RHG. See, for example: OG Taanith 112 (a reformulation of 111); ibid., 68 and n. 2; OG Yoma 29; OG Sukkah, The commentaries 233; OG Taanith 37 and n. 7 (The passage is from "The Gaonic Novellae to Taanith," and it forms—together with the text printed in section 36—a continuation of the long responsa printed in section 34).[20]

3. RMBN

RMBN himself informs us who is meant by "Gaon": "Our Rabbi, the Gaon who is Our Rabbi Hai of blessed memory was accustomed to say . . ." (OG BQ 320). On a number of occasions, he cites "The Gaon" in his Treatise on Purchases. RMBN's Novellae to Gittin 52 (s.v. amen), BB 93b (s.v. ha ditnan) and OG Nedarim 121. The references are all to RHG in MQM.

Prof. S. Abramson[21] has assembled those citations from RMBN which combine the appellation "The Gaon" with that of "The Father of Israel," all of which refer to RHG while not mentioning him by name.

Here are more examples in which "Gaon" in RMBN can be shown to be identical with RHG.

1.   From RMBN's Novellae:

   a.   BM 112a "In a responsum of our Rabbi, the Gaon." The responsum was authored by RHG (v. OG Gittin 46).

   b.   BB 5a (s.v. Hazoreà), "The Gaon of blessed memory in a responsum." The same responsum is attributed to RHG by DCA (171a).

2.   From "MILHAMOT"

   a.   BM Ch. 4 (p. 26a). In the course of discussing what was said by the gaon, RMBN mentions "Gaon"—"The Gaon" a few times. The statement (and hence "The Gaon") under discussion is specifically attributed to RHG—on the spot—by RIF and BHM.

   b.   Qiddusin Ch. 2 (p. 42), "Our Rabbi, Gaon" is RHG, cited by BHM on the spot.

See also OG Berakoth, the commentaries 167 and p. 54, n. 7; OG Sanhedrin 463 and n. 3; and TARBIZ 19, p. 195.

Needless to say that when RMBN mentions RHG by name at the onset of a discussion, further on in the same discussion he commonly refers to him just by the appellation "Gaon." E.g. OG Ket. 207. "And this explanation is that of RHG ... This is the text of the Gaon's words." RMBN San. 26, 3: "In the responsa of our Rabbi Hai Gaon of blessed memory ... some support to what the Gaon said." RMBN BB 63 (s.v. *Omer*): "I saw that our Rabbi Hai Gaon of blessed memory ... the words of The Gaon of blessed memory;" *MILḤAMOTH* BM Ch. 1(7a), "Our Rabbi Hai wrote ... The words of The Gaon."

All that we have said until now regarding "Gaon" in RMBN holds true only for his novellae and *MILḤAMOT*. In his monographs the appellation just plain "Gaon" is not reserved for Rav Hai alone, e.g., *Torat Haádam* 28d: (Immediately following a citation from RHG), "[a citation from] Gaon. Regarding eulogy,—the commonly ... "; ibid., 50b: "So said Gaon, our custom is to remove ourselves from the cemetery. ..." Both quotations are from a responsum of R. Natronai, ṢS V. 2, p. 44.

The appellation "Geonim" (plural) in RMBN refers occasionally to RHG or to RHG and RSG, e.g., OG Shabbath 282, p. 191 and n. 3, 388 and n. 5, the commentaries 90 and 48; OG Pessachim 25 and n. 12; (cf. OG Shabbath, commentaries 93 n. 5). However, "Geonim" is not always confined to these two and may even represent an opposing viewpoint, v. e.g., RMBN Qid. 65a, "The Geonim agreed. ..." This refers to a view not shared by RSG and RHG (OG Qid. 357).

We were in a quandry how to treat the appellation just plain "Gaon" appearing in *The Geonic Novellae* to Taănit. In the sections of these novellae published in OG Taanith, just plain "Gaon" is mentioned thirty-three (33) times in twenty-two (22) different entries (OG Taanith 5, 7, 8, 9, 11, 12, 19, 26, 29, 34-37, 43, 61, 62, 68-71, 73, 95, 112, 127, 152). In eight cases (4 separate entries) the reference is to RHG.

1.   OG 29 - Identified by a superscription in the parallel.

2-3.   OG 34-37 and OG 68 - Portions quoted by medieval authors in the name of RHG.

4.   OG 112 - is a paraphrase of OG Taanith 111, where RHG is explicitly mentioned as the responder.

In addition, we know that "Gaon" in OG 95 refers to RSG and RHG since a shortened version of the responsum appears as part of a pamphlet sent by them, in RDG 249 (v. above 119). OG 69 (attributed to "Gaon") was authored by RSG and/or RHG as is attested by the list published by Prof. S. Abramson in THE WOLFSON JUBILEE VOLUME (Hebrew section), p. 20, number 23 (and note 12).

Except for these identifications of "Gaon" with RHG (and/or RSG), we were unable to make any other positive identifications of any of the other mentions of "Gaon" in these novellae. Furthermore, we were unable to distinguish any geonic material in these novellae originating from any gaon other than RHG (and/or RSG), whether attributed to (a) "Gaon" or not. There have indeed been scholars who have assumed that just plain "Gaon" in these novellae should be identified as RHG, e.g., S. Assaf—discussing the Ms. of these novellae—writes "just plain Gaon is Rav Hai" (GRA, p. 126). B. M. Lewin (n. 10 to OG Taanith 26, cit. sup.) comments, "This 'Gaon' is Rav Hai."

With all due respect to these scholars, and despite the evidence submitted above, we do not feel that there is sufficient proof to allow an unquestionable identification of RHG with every mention of "Gaon" in these novellae. Although every identifiable "Gaon" seems to be RHG, let us not forget that absolutely no Gaon is cited by name, that the percentage of successful identifications is relatively small, and that the identification of sources is extremely difficult. Hence, although we believe that it is very likely that "Gaon" in these novellae does refer to RHG, in this study where we wish to construct RHG's methodology based on responsa *undoubtedly* authored by him (or jointly with RSG), we did not include in our corpus of responsa citations from "Gaon" in these novellae, except where the identification of RHG is positive (as above).

We had similar hesitations regarding mention of just plain "Gaon" in RSHBA (particularly in his novellae to BT). Although on many occasions the reference is indeed to RHG (following one of his mentors, RMBN, see above p. 126), on others it is not so. Hence regarding RSHBA we did not posit that every mention of "Gaon" necessarily refers to RHG.

Sundry proofs of attribution

A. RDG 376 – This responsum is the source of citations in a number of works[22] to the effect that R. Serira (!) holds that, "If one slaughters (i.e., cuts the throat of an animal) in two or three places the slaughtering is valid," and other particulars related to that ruling. At first glance, then, we might conclude that R. Serira is the sole author of this responsum. However, RABIAH writes, "that slaughtering cut [slanting] like [the cut of] a writing reed or [sawtoothed] like [the teeth of] a comb, is valid, and I found that so ruled our Rabbi Hai and his father R. Ṣerira Gaon" (RABIAH, 1086, Ḥullin, p. 37, *Introduction to RABIAH*, p. 225). Now (contrary to what Aptowitzer wrote in the introduction, ibid.), both these rulings are found in our responsum, and it is precisely our responsum which is the source of RABIAH's statement. "A comb" (masreq) is discussed on p. 192, except that it is written *masruq* ("MSRUQ") instead of the usual masreq *("msrq")*. The responsum states: "A slaughtering cut like a comb is not [considered] a wide open cut . . . and is valid." Thus for "comb"; now about a "writing reed." On page 193, line 8, we read: ". . . establishes [BT Ḥullin 30a–b] that [the Tanaic text refers to a case] of a slaughtering cut like a [line 9] comb, where he began below, slanted, and ended above." The problem with this passage is that "like a comb" ("KMSRQ") makes no sense and is obviously a copyist's error. The first word on line 9 should read *"kqulmus"* ("like a writing reed"). The proof of this is rather simple:

    a.   This "slanting" is *not* the way the responsum (above) explains "like a comb." On the other hand, this *is* the accepted explanation for "like a writing reed."[23]

    b.   There is no known reading in the Talmudic text that has the *sugya* establish a reference to "a slaughtering cut like a comb." On the contrary, there is unanimity in the reading (BT loc. cit.) "of a slaughtering cut like a writing reed."

So we conclude that both of RABIAH's rulings stem from our responsum, which, according to his testimony, is a joint responsum of RSG and RHG.

May we offer quaint support for the case of joint authorship? All the medieval authors of the RABN school, beginning with RABN himself,[24] know a contradictory tradition regarding this ruling of RSG and RHG, namely, that "if one slaughters in two or three places . . . the slaughtering is invalid." We find it very difficult to accept the authenticity of this tradition, because of two reservations:

    a.   It stands opposed to the tradition of a number of different—and usually reliable—authors (cited note 22).

    b.   This tradition is not Pumbedethean, but is a Suraean tradition, as stated in HGB (p. 518), "They sent a responsum from the Academy of Sura . . . and we act like Samuel" (who ruled: "invalid" as opposed to Rav, BT loc. cit.). Indeed, we find a chain of *geonim* of Sura holding this view: R. Sar Shalom (TMI loc. cit.); R.

Amram (Commentary to RIF Ḥullin, loc. cit.; *HAMAKRIA* 4); R. Samuel b. Ḥofni (RABN loc. cit.).

We must conclude therefore, that confusion reigned in the sphere of RABN. They confused the view expounded by the questioners in RDG 376 with that of the responders.[25]

What we gain from the confusion is, at least, the knowledge of testimony as to a tradition that there was a joint responsum of RSG and RHG on this issue. It is now obvious that the reference is to our responsum, RDG 376, and it is established that RHG participated in its composition.   Hence, we can safely view its methodology as representative of RHG's methodology for our purposes.[26]

B.   RDG 210 (OG Ketubot 161, pp. 51-52)—Again it is RABIAH (957, Introduction, p. 229) who furnishes proof that RHG had at least some part in composing this responsum. He writes, "The Rabbis of the Academy sent this responsum of R. Zemaḥ to R. Hai Gaon of blessed memory, and he disputed it, and said that whenever we do not have the *ketubah* before us, we apprehend that payment may have been made."   Clearly the citation is from the responsum under discussion (OG Ketubot, p. 52, lines 2-3) in which the questioners indeed confronted RHG with the responsum of R. Zemaḥ (ibid., p. 51, lines 3-4). It is almost equally certain that the questioners to R. J. Migash also had this responsum (ibid., p. 52, line 3) in mind, when they wrote, "We saw in a responsum of our Rabbi Hai Gaon of blessed memory ... she collects the *ketubah* ... when the debtor admits" (ibid., 805 and n. 2).

I wish to go a step further and claim that this very same responsum is the one referred to by the ITTUR (V. 1, p. 41a), "So we saw by our earlier Rabbis, our Rabbi Serira and our Rabbi Hai, in responsa." This statement introduces what follows in the ITTUR: "A woman who lost her *ketubah* and was widowed or divorced not only does she surely receive the 200 zuz coming to her, since we say that she collects, but she even collects the addition to her *ketubah*, and what do we do [to assess the addition] we take out two or three *ketubot* of her relatives and we collect for her according to the lowest of them, requiring her also to swear under oath." Although this seems to contradict the ruling of RSG and RHG in the responsum under discussion, in fact it does not really reflect a conflicting tradition.   What happened here is similar to what we just saw regarding RDG 376 (above p. 129).   ITTUR confused the issue by quoting only the question, which really represents the view of R. Ẓemaḥ.[27]

C.   RDG 55 - Attributed to "Rav Hai in a responsum" in Tur HOSM 171 (25, 139a).

D.   RDG 202-03 - The parallel in SẒ (4, 4, 53, OG Ketubot 766) carries the subscription, "our Rabbi Hai Gaon."

E.   RDG 206 - Attributed to "our Rabbi Hai" in RSHBA responsa, V. 7, 455.

F.   RDG 387 - Identified by S. Abramson (SINAI 75, p. 10) as part of a pamphlet sent by RSG and RHG to Kairouan in the year 992.

G.   DRG 87 (OG Pesachim 360) and RGA, pp. 44-45.   The conclusion of the many scholars who have discussed this anonymous responsum is that RHG was its author. See, e.g., S. Assaf, RGA, p. 38 and KRS 29, p. 64; A. Epstein, *MIQADMONIOT HAYEHUDIM*, p. 379-80; B. M. Lewin, OG loc. cit. n. 5; S. Rapoport, Introduction to DRG, p. 12; S. Sassoon, Introduction to *HALACHOT PESUQOT*, p. 24, n. 57.

H.   SẒ 4, 2, 4 - The superscription in Ms. Halberstam identifies RHG as the author. Noted by Hildesheimer, "Komposition", p. 88.

I.   SẒ, 4, 6, 26 - As above. Ibid., p. 90 and previously by J. Müller, *Einleitung*, p. 243, n. 3.

J.   RLOW 3 - The end of the responsum is quoted verbatim by RḤ (Sheb. 48b) introduced by "our Rabbi Hai Gaon wrote."

K.   RLOW 133-36 - RDG 38 see above, p. 119, section 6

L.   ST 65 (OG RH 82) - A portion of the responsum is quoted by SS (part I, p. 42) and by other medieval authors (v. *IYEY HAYAM* to ST 65) in the name of RHG.

M.   MH 16 - Segments of the responsa are quoted in the name of RHG in DCA 149a.

N.   TMI 180 (OG Megillah 23) - Is a different version of the responsum in OG Megillah 22, which is superscribed "R. Hai Gaon."

NOTES

Chapter 1

[1]Perhaps originally pronounced "Haya" or "Hayey." The name means life, like the names "Hiyya" or "Hayim." See S. Morag, TARBIZ 31, pp. 188-90.

[2]RHG died in Nissan (Passover) 1038 according to SEFER HA QABBALAH, p. 43 and an addition to IGRSG. See T and S, p. 109, n. 2. SEFER HA QABBALAH also states that he lived 99 years. This is corroborated by Samuel Ha Nagid's elegy (Harkavy, STUDIEN U. MITTEILUNGEN 1, p. 45 f.) which says that he was about 100 years old at his death.

[3]E.g., Hai b. Nahson b. Zadoq and Hilai b. Natronai in Sura; Nehemiah b. Cohen Zedeq in Pumbedita. The father-son gaonates were not necessarily consecutive.

[4]See J. Mann, HEBREW UNION COLLEGE JUBILEE VOLUME, Cincinnati 1925, p. 258, and INYANOT, p. 107, n. 20.

[5]See e.g., BEMERKAZIM 75, n.7; J.N. Epstein REJ 64, pp. 210-12; SAADYANA, p. 118; TEQUFAT, p. 198 and n. 2; T and S 87, and the following note.

[6]For the pertinent dates see IGRSG, pp. 2 and 121; SEFER HA QABBALAH, pp. 43-44 and the editors' comments, pp. 201-02, 204; BEMERKAZIM, p. 88, n. 25; T and S, p. 84, n. 65 and p. 109, n. 2.

[7]See the Epistle of R. Samuel b. Hofni, T and S, p. 158, and the Introduction, p. 148.

[8]The abode of the Academies since the end of the ninth century, see SS 1, p. 64; J. Mann, RESPONSA, pp. [17-18], [50]; BEMERKAZIM, p. 15.

[9]See e.g., S. Abramson, RNG, the introduction section [A]; Mann, RESPONSA, p. [3] f.; HILKHOT HANNAGID, Introduction, pp. 58-59 and n. 48.

[10]See, e.g., Mann, RESPONSA [7] f; Hahiluqim, Introduction, p. 12 and n. 69; T and S, pp. 118, 199; BEMERKAZIM Chapters 9-10.

[11]See, e.g., Mann: THE JEWS V. 1, pp. 40, 67, 107, 115, 119 and passim; Responsa, p. [24]; T and S, pp. 91-92 and the material cited there.

[12]See TEQUFAT, pp. 43, 56, 198; Mann, RESPONSA, [54]; HALACHOTH KEZUBOTH, p. 5, n. 42; and the previous note.

[13]Saadya Gaon was the first Rabbinic author to compose legal monographs. Since there is no such Rabbinic tradition, it seems safe to assume that RSdG borrowed the idea from the world of Islamic law (RSdG was intimately familiar with all phases of Islamic culture). Indeed, the monographs (as well as most of his other works) were composed in Arabic (the Judeo-Arabic dialect: Arabic written in Hebrew characters). RSdG was also the first Rabbinic author to write a proper introduction to his works. This too, seems to have been influenced by Islamic works.

[14]On the monographs, see S. Assaf, Hazofeh 7, pp. 277-87, and S. Abramson, J. N. Epstein Jubilee Volume (TARBIZ 20), p. 296 f.

[15]See TEQUFAT, p. 202, paragraph 7, and the Responsa of R. Abraham, "The Son of Maimonides," p. 169.

[16]See TEQUFAT, p. 201, paragraph 5.

[17]Ibid., p. 202, paragraph 12, and S. Assaf in the PROCEEDINGS OF THE FIRST CONFERENCE OF JEWISH STUDIES, Jerusalem, 5712, p. 391.

[18]See TEQUFAT, p. 202, paragraph 10.

[19]See T and S, pp. 573-74; *BEMERKAZIM*, p. 82.

[20]See, most recently, E. Hurvitz in HADAROM 46 and 49.

[21]See Poznanski, JQR NS 3, p. 411; *TEQUFAT*, p. 141, S. D. Goitein, KRS 31, pp. 68-70.

[22]v. *TEQUFAT*, p. 141.

[23]v. J. N. Epstein, REJ 64, p. 210 f.; TARBIZ 5, 45-49; Mann, T and S 68; S. Abramson, SINAI 12, p. 58.

[24]v. *TEQUFAT* 142, paragraph 7; *BEMERKAZIM*, p. 121 bottom.

[25]See, Müller, Einleitung, p. 202 and n. 9.

[26]See RUNDREISE DES *R. PETACHYAH*, edited Grünhut, p. 41, n. 71.

Chapter 2

[1]This is reminiscent of *'ijma al-úma* in Islam.

[2]Affirming the absolute authority of the community's traditional practice, indirectly enhançes the gaon's status as traditional head of that community. However, RHG's record of intellectual honesty added to the firmly entrenched position of leadership he attained before he succeeded to the gaonate, remove any suspicion that his approach in this matter might derive from any personal interest.

[3]Literally: "Transcribed." The author was translating (consciously or not) from the Arabic *NQL* which can mean both "transcribe" or "transmit," and used the Hebrew $^c TQ$—which means only "transcribe," where *MSR* ("transmit") was called for. The phenomenon commonly occurs where Jews spoke Arabic.

[4]I.e., during the recitation of the *ÀMIDAH* of the Additional New Year's service (*Musaf*).

[5]See p. 50.

[6]See Meg. 7a and J. Neusner, A HISTORY OF THE MISHNAIC LAWS OF PURITY, xix, 140 f.

[7]RHG's text of this passage in the Talmud obviously differed from ours—in that it mentioned a fifth cup. See OG PES 351 f. and M. Kasher, *HAGADAH SHELEMAH*, p. 94 and n. 36.

[8]"[Even if] he did not write [in] her [marriage contract]: 'Male offspring that you will have from me, they shall inherit the money of your dowry, in addition to their portion which is with their brothers' [i.e., if you predecease me and I inherit you, upon my death your sons shall inherit your dowry] he is bound [by it] because it is a court stipulation" (M Ket. 4, 10).

Chapter 3

[1]The "we" in the phrase "*we* conclude" ("ásiqinan") used by RSG and RHG in this responsum referring to the Talmudic discussion, as well as in similar phrases used in countless other responsa, e.g., "*we* ask," "*we* answer," designates, of course, not themselves but the *amoraim* who participated in the *sugya*. From this, too, we see how they viewed themselves as an extension of the *amoraim* and totally identify with the Talmudic discussion. There are cases of *geonim* interpolating their own questions and comments into the Talmudic discussion, using these very same terms with which they

refer to the Talmud, or the Talmud's own terms. Again, it is because they see their own academies and amoraic ones as a continuum. This style left its mark to some degree on later Rabbinic style.

[2]This is the correct reading. See VL Pes., pp. 357-358 and n. 10.

[3]See Deut. 21, 17 and SUA HOM 277.

[4]We hope to investigate RHG's method of drawing parallels and analogies in a further study.

[5]RHG's reliance on practice and custom will be the subject of a future study.

[6]Their custom differed from our common custom of each individual reciting nine benedictions in the silent prayer (see glossary).

[7]See below, p. 23 "The law follows the majority," and Erubin 46b, "The halakah is always in agreement with R. Akiba when he differs from a colleague of his," implying: "but not when he differs from several colleagues."

[8]For a discussion of conflict between principles of decision-making and explicit rulings, see p. 45.

[9]RSG and RHG were not certain that this was indeed the case, and go on to discuss other possibilities as well. That is why they deal with many aspects of the divorce's validity. See e.g., pp. 39 f., 57 f., and 79 f.

[10]Codifiers and commentators argued if—accepting R. Eleazar's view—they should actually invalidate a divorce which was proper in every respect just because it was not delivered in the presence of two valid witnesses. RSG and RHG seem to follow traditional geonic opinion in ruling that it is indeed void (see OG Gittin 466-467).

[11]RHG's readings predominate in geonic and Spanish sources. See VL BB, p. 450 letters l-m and p. 452 letter d and BBA, pp. 198-199 variants to lines 388 and 428.

[12]Our reading is: "Seeing then that it has not been stated definitely that the law follows neither the one nor the other," which seems to be RHG's reading in his commentary published in OG Ber., the commentaries, p. 3 f. See also SHEELTOT iii 171, variant to line 30 from the Merzbach Ms. and see p. 80.

Chapter 4

[1]According to a principle of adjudication: The law follows an anonymous mishnah.

[2]"For one's money," literally "is to me," in Aramaic "Liy," which is RHG's reading, and the correct one. See VL BM, p. 181, n. 7. The printed editions have ley—"to him."

[3]Wezarik, literally "and he must." This is RHG's reading as is borne out by his quote of the passage in MQM (Ch. 31, 66a). Our traditional reading is weayno zarik—"without being," literally "and he does not have to." Cf. VL BB, p. 144 note sin.

[4]"Rabun"—in this text—is a unique reading, instead of the usual "Rabin." Both refer to one and the same person. See TTV i, 89, b, "R. Abin—Rabin—R. Bun" and EJ iii, 971.

[5]"Not" (lav) was omitted in our responsum, no doubt through a copyist's (or printer's) omission. Without it the Talmudic passage would prove precisely the opposite of what RHG holds. The word is found in all known editions, mss., and citations of the Talmud. Furthermore, RHG himself cites this passage elsewhere (MQM Ch. 29, 62 b), and there, naturally, the word appears. Other variants in this text are inconsequential, since RHG is paraphrasing and not necessarily quoting the Talmudic passage.

[6]Bodleian 4° 28, Neubauer 1095, copied with sundry errors by Azulai, Frumkin, Marx

(= OG Ber. 361), Hedegard, and Goldschmidt. The copyist found that RHG ruled to recite the benediction "who loosest etc." as part of the morning benedictions—and also included it in his Talmudic text—as opposed to *SRA* and many versions of the Talmudic text which omit it (see VL Ber., p. 346 n. ^{c}*ayīn*). RHG's reading in the brief Talmudic passage is different from ours and seems to bear some similarity to that of RSdG who writes: "When he extends his hands he should recite the benediction, 'who loosest them that are bound' " (*SRSG*, p. 88). There are other minor variants in RHG's text as compared to our readings (see VL loc. cit., n. *nun*).

From this responsum it is clear that RHG recites the benedictions at the time of the action, unlike the custom—which eventually prevailed—to recite all the morning benedictions in order, at home or in the synagogue. This refutes what was reported by the questioners to R. Abraham b. Maimonides, that RHG ruled to recite the benedictions in the synagogue.   R. Abraham correctly responded that one does not learn from "reports" (Responsa of R. Abraham 83, pp. 120-122. See the editor's note, p. 120 n. 3).

[7]Two is the minimum number of witnesses normally required for valid testimony in Jewish law (see EJ xvi 585). For disqualification of kinsmen and other ineligibilities see M San. 3, 3-4; SUA HOM, 33-37; EJ loc. cit.

[8]The printed editions read "R. Judah." "R. Judah in the name of Rav" is a common variant. See VL Sabath, p. 10, n. 8, and OG Shabbath 16, p. 4. RHG attributes the statement to Rav, but his reading may have been "R. Judah in the name of Rav said."

[9]"Rabah" appears to be the reading of Hai—and other medievalists—in RH 28 a, and, "Rava" in 28 b, as opposed to the printed editions and mss. which read "Rava" in both cases. Cf. VL RH, p. 73, n. B.

[10]An example of explicit rejection is when an amoraic view is accountable to only one tanaic opinion (see p. 81).

[11]Re. the community see EJ vi 1256. The community's involvement in Talmudic learning despite its deportation is noteworthy. See also RLOW 133 n. a. The question was raised because the traditional approach viewed the whole Babylonian Talmud as one unit, thereby making contradictions problematic.

[12]For other approaches solving conflicts between sugyot see the remarks of RSG and RHG at the close of the responsum and the editor's notes, p. 34, n. 6.

[13]See e.g., OG Erubin 24, and the *sugyot* and codifiers noted in the editor's references.

[14]The talmudic equivalent of the maxim was coined by Shammai: "Say little and do much" (Abot 1, 15).

[15]Bib. In the printed editions: "wine cask." See OG n. 6 and VL Psachim, p. 112, n. *mem*.

[16]Similarly in the Munich MS of BT and elsewhere. The printed editions read: "The house of Bar Haska." See VL loc. cit., n. *nun* and OG n. 7.

[17]In his earlier years when he decided according to the view of R. Jose, one of the determining factors was, "The conclusion, R. Joseph b. Minyomi said that R. Naḥman decided a case thus according to R. Jose who said they divide." R. Nahman's action was crucial to RHG's decision.

[18]See, e.g., OG Jom-Tow 39-49 and the editor's references.

[19]We cite the *sugya* according to the readings in RHG's responsum, which vary only slightly and insignificantly (for our immediate purpose) from those in our printed editions.

[20]We have quoted RHG's version of the report (akin to that of HG 128, 3, HGB, p.

528). It varies significantly from our printed version in that it specifically mentions lungs, and that they are clearly declared permitted. We assume that he cited original readings and not paraphrases nor readings checkered with interpretations (v. inf. and n. 22).

[21]*Semukah* ("close"), in this context, according to transmitted authoritative interpretation, implies adhesion. Hence the ulcers discussed are that type of adhesion (cf. VL Chulin, p. 53a, n. 5).

[22]More feasible according to his reading—which actually mentions lungs—than according to ours (v. n. 20).

[23]RHG commonly harmonizes inconsistent pericopae, an approach which exerted great influence on his interpretations, as we hope to show in an independent study.

[24]v. Ch. 1. Present work. RHG's sources are the topic of an anticipated work.

[25]v. OG Taanith, p. 18, n. 2.

[26]We quote from the version of the questioners which varies from our printed editions as noted by Lewin (ibid., n. 1).

[27]The shoulder, the cheeks, and the maw of slaughtered animals. v. Deut. 18, 3; M Hullin 10, 1.

[28]RHG's reading is unique. The printed editions read: "Priests," meaning priests who are butchers. See also VL Chulin 182 b, letter *tet.* RHG's reading leads him to a stringent view not universally accepted. Cf. RABIAH and RDBZ, loc. cit.

[29]Just like—in RHG's view—if an amoraic statement is qualified by another, the qualification is accepted.

Chapter 5

[1]See also Nedarim 57b and Bekorot 42b.

[2]On the other hand, the principle: "The law is like an anonymous mishnah" is an independent principle. In fact, the Tosaphists (Yeb. 10b, s.v. *ho'il*) claim that "an individual and more than one" is a weaker principle than "an anonymous mishnah," because the view of the individual can sometimes be accepted, if his argument is more convincing. cf. *MQM* Ch. 13 (33b), "the law follows the first *tana* because where an individual is opposed to more than one, the law follows those more than one."

[3]See ET 9, p. 346.

[4]He equates them with food cooked by a gentile, which is prohibited, v. SUA YOD 113.

[5]Interestingly, we do not find RHG carrying these principles a step further and invoking "majority rule." The *geonim* and early *rishonim* are not normally prone to head-counting in order to decide the *halakah*, neither of Talmudic sages nor of the *geonim* and Rabbinic predecessors. This method of deciding the *halakah* became common only later, although it has Biblical antecedents regarding court decisions, and is just a stone's throw from the "more than one" principle. The only place RHG even alludes to considering it is in RDG 376 (discussed, p. 64). Before offering their reasoned decision in favor of Rav, RSG and RHG comment that were we to take a head-count, we should find that there are no more *amoraim* leaning toward Samuel than towards Rav. The impression gained is that had the head-count been in Samuel's favor they would have either ruled in his favor or would have taken much greater pains to justify their ruling in favor of Rav.

[6]In the Munich Ms. there is an obvious lacuna in the statement of Bar Qapara, which must be completed as in the RIF.

[7]The usual quorom for public prayer.

[8]This seems to be RHG's reading in the talmudic text, similar to that of RIF. Cf. Price, Megillah, p. 30 and VL Megillah, p. 106, n. *samek*.

[9]See Ch. 2, n. 12.

[10]There are, nonetheless—even in RHG's view—limitations to the predominance and even use of this principle. See our discussions regarding an *amora* who decides a tanaic dispute (p. 82) and the standing of an *amora* when there is a coinciding tanaic view (p. 89).

[11]See p. 83.

[12]RH specifically cites, "all [other] *tanaim* recited as Samuel" as the reason for his exceptional ruling like Samuel in this case (OG Pes. 2). It is common knowledge that RH made extensive use of the responsa, commentaries, miscellaneous writings and traditions of RSG and RHG (see the citations p. 125). The additional explanation offered by Meiri (OG loc. cit.) is not accurate, as can easily be discerned from the course of our discussion. Nor is this a case of an explicit Talmudic ruling. Although our texts conclude: "And the law is as Samuel," R. Isaiah Berlin has already pointed out in a gloss printed on the page in all common editions, that none of the early codifiers or commentators had such a reading. This is easily verified by the fact that such a large number of them actually ruled in favor of Rav. The phrase is also missing in mss. (See VL Pessachim, p. 22, n. 5).

RHG's ruling is cited by a number of later Rabbis (see OG loc. cit.). However, RH's interpretation of the dispute which Lewin printed in brackets parallel to these citations —because he assumed it to be based on the interpretation of RSG and RHG—is in fact, in this instance, different from that of RSG and RHG.

[13]For their variant reading see the marginal note in the standard editions of the Gemara, and the sources cited by Lewin in note 7.

[14]The Eskol himself, then, would have used tanaic principles (even) in this case.

[15]A common variant reading of the shepherd's name in medieval works and in mss. See VL Brachoth, p. 218, note "zadiq."

[16]See J. Neusner, A HISTORY OF MISHNAIC LAW OF PURITIES, V. 13, p. 2.

[17]Temurah 12a-b. See Neusner op. cit., p. 106, and V. 14, p. 33 and *passim*.

[18]So in our text of the responsum, translated literally without any additions or abbreviations (except for the translator's brackets in the Talmudic text BM 7b).

[19]See p. 125.

[20]See, for example, the formulation of HALIKOT OLAM, Gate 2, Chapter 2: The *amora* has no power to dispute the *tana* under any circumstances whatsoever.

[21]What was gathered in one year may not be given as tithe for the produce of another year.

[22]In the original, "*sugya bealma*." The translation of this term in accordance with RHG's understanding and use of the term was the subject of careful analysis in our unpublished (Hebrew) Dissertation, RAV HAI GAON HIS HALACHIC METHODOLOGY (Jerusalem, Hebrew University, 1974).

[23]See TEQUFAT, p. 234, par. 35-36. It follows that any undisputed *baraita* explicitly designated in the Gemara as supportive of our *amora* assures that the law follows that *amora*. It stems from RDG 79 that all this holds even if the tanaic source is introduced by the disputant himself. As to whether tanaic support of one disputant constitutes total

refutation of his adversary, see *HALIKOT OLAM* (and the appended *KLALEI HATALMUD* of R. Joseph Qaro) Gate 2, Chapter 2.

[24]This point seems to have been lost on the editor or copyist of SZ, who incorporated this responsum into his collection (4, 5, 3) so he skipped the whole passage.

[25]It is, however, just possible that RHG favors Rav in this case, because his view is discussed in the course of the *sugya* (see p. 107).

[26]"One" (!). See VL BM, p. 209, n. 5-7 for variants in the whole passage.

[27]*Amoraim* are often referred to as "Our Rabbis" by RHG.

[28]This view was acknowledged by later codifiers. See also Rashi BQ 49a s.v. "*samin.*"

[29]Ironically RH (cited by RASBA in his opening remarks, OG Ket. part 3, 95-6) invokes the same principle for resolving the dispute. However, since he interprets the questions as having been asked in the context of R. Aqiba's view, he rules in favor of R. Aqiba.

[30]This is the reading of the questioners, the responders, medieval commentators and mss. The standard editions read: Mar Zutra or as some say, Mar Uqba said. See, also, VL Synhedrin, p. 52, n. *lamed*.

[31]According to RABAD we could list another example when RHG ignores an anonymous mishnah in favor of a *tana* whose view is explained by the Gemara. The mishnah, discussing an oath extracted from a woman regarding her husband's property or estate, opens with an anonymous mishnah and closes with the view of R. Simeon (M Ket. 9, 4-8). RIF cites "the Rabbis" who ruled in favor of R. Simeon (RIF Ket. 344, 46a). RABAD (to RIF) identifies those "Rabbis" as *geonim*. RMBN names R. Hai as leader of those "Rabbis" based on his views in MPS, p. 26, Gate 5 (RMBN, *SEFER HAZEKUT* to RIF, loc. cit.). In fact, R. Hai continued to hold that view in his responsa (OG Ket. 666, pp. 282 and 766, p. 337, where twice the reading is "R. Simeon b. Gamaliel [!]" like in the Cambridge Ms. of M). RABAD claims that the "Rabbis" (i.e., RHG) rule in favor of R. Simeon because the give and take of an amoraic *sugya* (Ket. 88a-b) explains his view. Therefore the Rabbis prefer his view over the anonymous mishnah principle favored by RIF.
However, RMBN (loc. cit.) has already noted that the initiators of the ruling in favor of R. Simeon were the HP-HG school (OG Ket. 653). Neither in their statements nor in those of RHG is there anything to confirm RABAD's interpretation. On the contrary, there are hints at other principles of adjudication. RMBN's explanation that RHG opted for R. Simeon because he was the compromiser is contradicted by RHG's view that the law does not follow such a type of compromise (OG Pes. 40).

[32]Although RHG did add his own nuances, others, before him, had already derived such a principle. See *TEQUFAT*, p. 234, par. 35, and above, p. 48.

[33]When the *lulab* is shaken. See M Sukkah 3, 9.

[34]"Who said in Rav's name" seems to be his reading in the text—agreeing with Ms. Hamburg—unlike the printed editions. See VL BM, p. 143, note *taf*.

[35]RHG's formulation—cited in our text—seems to point in the same direction, though we cannot be certain. We cannot test RHG's view in the BB *sugya* dealt with by RSdG (above) because RHG differs from RSdG in his interpretation of that *sugya*, believing that all the participating *amoraim*—including R. Simeon b. Laqis—follow the School of Hillel, leaving no reason to favor the School of Shamai. See RHG in RDG 79, p. 47.

[36]See also above n. 25 and RSHBM to BB 52b s.v. "*rayah bemai.*"

[37]We do not cite OG Ber., p. 126—end—as an example because it is highly doubtful that RHG encountered the same *sugya* structure (in Ber. 53b) as we do. See VL Ber., p. 284, n. 3.

[38]Omitting: "in the name of Rav" and substituting "ke" ("like") for "domeh le" ("like").

[39]*TEQUFAT* should have included this as an amoraic (!) example of p. 234 par. 35, rather than in p. 235, par. 37.

[40]In a responsum written jointly with RSG—which we published in ALEI SEFER (8, p. 15, ff.)--RHG changes his interpretation of BM 5a, and feels that the discussion does make sense according to the second tradition in R. Naḥman (ibid., 16-17). In all events, the principle and its formulation still hold true (see ibid., n. 68. See also OG BM 23 f.).

[41]The formula appearing at the foot of a deed. Anything added could then be detected as a forgery.

[42]That R. Yoḥanan's statement is known to *us* (the readers) only from this discussion, is a most common phenomenon (see e.g., OG Pes. 269), and irrelevant to our discussion.

[43]Lit. "reliance." An assurance that one will pay or forfeit something in case of the non-fulfillment of a certain condition, which, however, he is confident that he will fulfill.

[44]"Rav" is RHG's reading in *MQM* Ch. 17. Our printed editions have: Rabah, and the Mss. have: Rava.

[45]To the receiver, or about the field. See the variants to p. 210 line 380 in the Sobel-Dimitrovsky edition (ed. J. N. Epstein).

[46]He should now make another cut in this same loose windpipe. If the cuts resemble each other the animal is *terefah.*

[47]See e.g., RSBA Ḥullin 54a s.v. R. Nahman.

[48]In a different responsum RHG states: We do not accept the view of Rabina ... even though it is not grown [into the flesh] the wall shields it and covers it up. And this is the custom (HS 124a-b and Jüdischer Zeitschrift, 2, pp. 303-4). There RHG for some unknown reason is atypically and uncommonly relying on custom (as he intimates) and geonic tradition (cited by him in RDG, cit. sup.) rather than drawing his own conclusions based on the Talmudic discussion (cf. Tosafot Ḥullin 48a s.v. *amar* and see GNS, p. 539 and RNG, p. 260, n. 88). We hope to deal elsewhere with the rulings of RHG based on extra-Talmudic material.

Appendix

[1]In OG, Lewin normally includes such citations and headings.

[2]See Groner, ALEI SEFER 8, p. 21, n. 66.

[3]See RDG, pp. 347-49 and RLOW 133, n. 1. Cf. GEONICA, p. 287.

[4]Except for a change from plural to singular—since they were not copying the whole pamphlet. Note, however, that in RLOW the change to singular was not consistent (e.g., "*were* issued forth").

[5]See Abramson, WOLFSON JUBILEE VOLUME (Hebrew Section), p. 14, n. 23; Ginzberg, GEONICA, p. 135 and Assaf, *KRS* 21, p. 64.

[6]SINAI JUBILEE, p. 403 f. and SINAI 56, pp. 315-17. See also Lifschitz in MORIAH, loc. cit. and cf. *Moriah* 8-10, pp. 4-5.

[7]It is not part of the list to Baẓra found in Geonica, p. 71. See S. Abramson, WOLFSON JUBILEE VOLUME (Hebrew Section), p. 17, n. 1.

[8]The heading of the two responsa whose beginnings were preserved, "another question," shows that they were copied from a larger group. However, since they are numbered [6-] -8 in Assaf's Ms., they were probably copied from an abridgement of the original pamphlet (this copy may have been the abridgement). For identification of other responsa from the pamphlet, see Ginzberg's notes and Assaf's introduction.

[9]It follows that the group of subscripts in RDG which numbers 346 as "b" and 347 as "d" is probably original (see Lewin's introductory remarks). If so, since RDG 349 bears the subscript "tet" (9), it follows that in the original pamphlet there were four responsa between RDG 347 and RDG 349.

[10]No. 69 in MISIFRUT represents all the responsa on the Bar-Sika matter (from mid RDG 308 to the end of 309). RDG 302 and the beginning of RDG 308 are not represented in the list. I am unable to determine whether they were omitted accidentally, or if they were not in the original pamphlet, but were added later to the collection which comprised the RDG group.

[11]About the list and the questioner, see BEMERKAZIM, p. 79 f.

[12]For examples, see M. Margaliot, HAHILUQIM, p. 46.

[13]So, as a general rule, not applied when they incorporated other sources into their own works, with the term "gaon" appearing in those sources. There, identification is dependent upon the original source. We also excluded a few exceptional cases where we had reason to believe that "gaon"—even in the language of these three—did not refer to RHG.

[14]Qore Hadarot, ed. Cassel, 5a, cf. EJ 5, 891 f.

[15]49a-b. Ironically, the example he brings from RIF Sanhedrin 979 is one of those exceptions where "gaon" in RIF does not refer to RHG. R. Judah Almadari in his commentary to RIF (loc. cit.) identifies the Gaon as R. Zemah, RHG being, in fact, one of the other Rabbis ("Rabvuta") mentioned by RIF as opposing the view of the Gaon (RHG also seems to be one of the "Rabvuta" in RIF Sanhedrin 894 - cf. OG Sanhedrin 463).

[16]"Gedolim" Letter "gimel," final pamphlet, entry "Gaon."

[17]As we show p. 131. RH quotes a section in the name of RHG.

[18]GNK 5, p. 95 and see Epstein, loc. cit.

[19]Occasionally RH refers to RHG by the term Raboteinu Hageonim ("our Rabbis the Geonim"), v. RNG, p. 6, n. 9; OG Pessachim, 25, n. 11; DCA 192 in light of RIF, BB 683.

[20]In very exceptional cases, plain "gaon" in RH does not refer to RHG. In RH's commentary to Ketubot (OG Ketubot the commentaries, 17): "Gaon explained." ROSH, in his tosafot to the very same passage, writes: And RH explained in the name of Rav Aha Gaon. It would seem that ROSH knew, from tradition or some source that the reference was to R. Ahai, and this would be one of those rare exceptions. Strangely, R. Aha [Ahai of Sabha] was not really a gaon, a fact which could hardly have been lost on RH (though it might have escaped ROSH). Perhaps the deletion of R. Ahai's name in RH was a copyist's error, or maybe its addition in ROSH is the result of someone's guesswork, or a corruption of some other gaon's name.
Regarding plain "gaon" in the Geonic Novellae to Taanit, see p. 127.

[21]KELALEI HATALMUD BEDIVREI HARAMBAN, pp. 13-14.

[22]Commentary to RIF on Hullin, pp. 2-3; TMI 135; Eskol V. 3, p. 10.

[23]See the Talmudic commentaries to BT loc. cit.

[24]Hullin 215. See the text and the editor's notes.

[25] A not infrequent phenomenon. See e.g., our ensuing discussion of RDG 210.

[26] Hai's authorship (or joint authorship) of this responsum was assumed (without proof) by S. Assaf (*TEQUFAT*, p. 160 and n. 10 and p. 237 par. 43) and S. Abramson (*Bemerkazim*, p. 51 and n. 22).

[27] As already noticed and noted by B. M. Lewin, *METIBOTH*, p. 29.

GLOSSARY

Aggadah. Non legalistic parts of Talmudic and Rabbinic Literature

Àmidah. (pl. *Àmidot*). The central prayer of the daily services, recited standing three times a day—evening, morning, and afternoon. The daily *àmidah* contains nineteen benedictions (originally eighteen—hence the synonymous appellation: *shmoneh esreh* ["18"]). On the Sabbath, Festivals, and "New Moon" (first day of the lunar month) there is an additional *àmidah (Musaf)**, and on the Day of Atonement there are two additional *amidot (Musaf** and *Neilah*). The *Musaf àmidah* of the "New Moon" and all the Sabbath and Festival *àmidot* contain only seven benedictions, except for the *Musaf àmidah* of the New Year Festival which contains nine. When the prayer is recited in public by a *minyan* (quorum of ten adult Jews), the *àmidah* is repeated by the reader (except for the evening service).

Amoraim. (sing. *Amora*). Scholars of the academies of the amoraic period (c. 200-500 c.e.) who participated in the development and compilation of the *Gemara** (Babylonian and Palestinian Talmuds).

Asmakta. The condition under which one of the sides to an agreement binds himself to an unreasonable penalty or condition, or minute chance of gain. Such a condition is normally ruled invalid, under the presumption that it was not entered into with deliberate and serious intention.

Baraita (pl. *Beraitot*). Tanaic pericopae not included in THE MISHNAH (compiled by R. Judah Ha-Nasi, "The Prince").

Derashah. From *(DRŞ).* a) The expounding of scripture; b) scriptural interpretation or exposition, halakic (legal), or aggadic; c) a sermon. See *Midrash.*

Dinar ("*Zuz*"*). The most common and important monetary term in Rabbinic literature. In tanaic times it refers to the silver denarius. During the second half of the third century it comes to refer to the gold dinar (aureus, or, later, the solidus). See D. Sperber, ROMAN PALESTINE, MONEY AND PRICES, Ch. 2.

Edim Zomemin (Èdim: pl. of Èd, "witness"). False witnesses about whom others have testified that their testimony cannot possibly be the truth, because they were not at the supposed place of the event at the time it was meant to have occurred, i.e., the latter pair say nothing about the event itself. In such a case, the latter pair is believed, and the first (witness[es]) is declared a false witness. The punishment applied is: "Then shall ye do unto him as he had thought to have done unto his brother" (Deut. 19, 19).

Erub (pl. *Erubim*). Literally, "mixture," "amalgamation," or "combination." A term applied to various symbolic acts which facilitate the accomplishment of activities on the Sabbath and festivals, which the Rabbis had otherwise forbidden.

    a)   *Erub Tehumim:* The symbolic fusion of properties which extends the original 2,000 cubits, beyond the border of their town, to which the movements of townspeople are limited on the Sabbath, to a range of a further 2,000 cubits;

    b)   *Erub Hazeirot:* The symbolic fusion of private domains to permit carrying between them on the Sabbath;

    c)   An "*erub*" (consisting of poles with wire over them) erected around a given district permits carrying between private and public domain or within the latter;

    d)   *Erub Tabsilin:* To permit cooking for the Sabbath during a Festival immediately preceding it, bread and cooked food are put aside for the Sabbath before the Festival. See Danby, p. 793, EJ 6, 849.

Etrog ("Citron"). One of the four species taken and shaken on the Feast of Tabernacles. See Lev. 23, 40.

Gaon (pl. *Geonim*). The heads of the Babylonian Academies, Sura and Pumbedita from the end of the sixth century until the middle of the eleventh (see Introduction).

Gemara. a) The so-called "second constituent part of the Talmud," i.e., the collection of the discussions relative to The Mishnah at the hands of the *amoraim** (see H. Strack, *Introduction* . . . , p. 5). The term sometimes refers specifically to the anonymous material therein, particularly the edited *sugya**, and the views it expresses; b) verbal amoraic traditions or teachings, as opposed to *sebara**, reasoning and interpretative material.

Genizah. A storage place for religious objects fallen to disuse, and especially for worn out books, manuscripts, and, in the past, nearly every scrap of paper with Hebrew script. The Genizah of repute is that of the old synagogue in Fustat (ancient Cairo) explored by Solomon Schechter at the end of the nineteenth century, which yielded a wealth of literary treasures and historical documents. See EJ 16, 1333 f.

Get (Aramaic, Pl. *Gittin*, also name of tractate). Originally: Document or bill; later, specifically bill of divorce given by the husband (or his messenger) to the wife (or her's); eventually: whole divorce ceremony. The laws concerning the writing and giving of the *get* are very stringent. Among the requirements are prescribed script, scroll, witnesses, volition of husband, etc. See details in EJ under "divorce."

Habdalah. A short service recited at the termination of the Sabbath and Festivals. It consists of a long benediction whose text denotes the division between the sacred (Sabbath and Festivals) and the common (weekdays), preceded by Scriptural verses and the benedictions over wine, fire, and spices (the latter two only at the termination of Sabbath). A *habdalah* text (similar to that of the aforementioned benediction) is also inserted into the fourth benediction of the *Àmidah** in the evening service following the Sabbath and the Festivals.

Halaḳah. Jewish Law. The term is derived from *HLḲ*, "to go," i.e., the path of life one is meant to follow, the rule(s) by which one is guided.

   a)   The whole legal system of Judaism which covers every aspect of life; what is usually thought of traditionally as ritual topics (e.g., benedictions, prayer, Sabbath and Festivals, prohibited foodstuffs, illicit sexual relations, etc.); laws of personal status (e.g., marriage, divorce, relation between husband and wife, etc.); what is usually considered "civil" law (e.g., torts, rentals, purchase and sale, etc.); communal issues (e.g., appointment of officials, taxes, etc.); national issues (e.g., kings, wars, etc.). In short, the whole program of life for a Jew—for an individual, the community, and the nation.

   b)   The law in a particular issue or a specific point of law (e.g., *halaḳah k* . . . ," the law [on this point] is according to [scholar] X [who disputed Y]").

   c)   Legalistic portions of the Talmudic and Rabbinic literature.

   d)   Individual statements of law, or (in plural, "*halaḳot*") collection thereof.

Haliẓa. "Drawing off the shoe." The ceremony prescribed (in Deut. 25, 7-9) when a man refuses to perform levirate marriage, i.e., marry the widow of his brother who had died childless.

Hallel. A short service consisting of Psalms 113-118, usually preceded and followed by a benediction, recited after the morning prayer service on certain Festivals and Feast Days, and as part of the *seder** (and by some after the evening service as well) on Passover eve.

Ḥameẓ (Ḥametz). Leavened bread (antithesis of Mazah*), fermented dough, or any other matter containing fermented grain of the "five species." The "five species" are traditionally translated as wheat, barley, spelt, rye, and oats, but the latter two should probably be replaced in the translation by other species of wheat and barley (see EJ under "Five Species," 6, 1332). The consumption of ḥamez on Passover, its possession, or any benefit derived from it are prohibited. Ḥamez possessed by a Jew on Passover, remains prohibited even after Passover. All foods containing Ḥamez is likewise prohibited as are even some non-food products. The term "ḥamez" is sometimes used as a general term to designate all food not eaten on Passover. See also MISHNAH, Danby, p. 794 and EJ under Ḥamez, 7, 1235.

Havinenu. A shortened version of the Àmidah's* middle section which can be substituted for the full version under certain circumstances. It consists of one benediction, beginning with the word *"Havinenu,"* which is a synopsis of the usual thirteen. See BT Berakot 29a. The substitution is in fact rarely implemented.

Hazaqah. Literally: taking hold. A legal term denoting

   a) presumptive title or rights based on occupier's undisturbed possession or user's undisturbed use during a fixed legal period;

   b) a factual or legal presumption as to the existence of a particular fact or state of affairs;

   c) a mode of acquiring ownership; taking possession by means of a formal act of acquisition, e.g., digging, fencing.

See EJ 7, 1516 f.; Soncino edition of BT Baba Batra, The Glossary.

Kalah. The months (Adar and Elul) during which the Babylonian Academies conducted activities for the public at large. See the Introduction p. 3.

Ketanai. An amoraic term denoting that an amoraic dispute coincides with a tanaic dispute.

Ketubah (pl. *ketubot*). Originally the marriage contract containing the husband's obligations to his wife, and her compensation in case of divorce or his death. In later usage *ketubah* also represents the payments themselves and the conditions thereof. The payments usually consist of an obligatory portion (200 *zuz* for a virgin; 100 otherwise) and a voluntary additional increment as stipulated.

Kezayit. Like [the size of] an olive. Basic measure of volume for fulfilling legal eating requirements (e.g., *mazah**) or for violating prohibitions on forbidden food. Variously estimated as 28-50 cu. cm., or 19-30 grams.

Kor. Largest measurement of volume (estimated at between 248,832-430,000 cu. cm.) or area, i.e., ground for growing a kor (75,000 square cubits).

Kosher. Ritually permitted; particularly in regard to food or properly slaughtered animals.

Lulab. Palm branch. One of the four species taken and shaken on the Feast of Tabernacles. See Lev. 23, 40.

Maneh. 100 denarii (*zuzim*) during the tanaic and early amoraic times. From the third century onwards used in the sense of a single *denarius.* See D. Sperber, ROMAN PALESTINE, MONEY AND PRICES, Ch. 3.

Maror. The "bitter herb" (usually lettuce) eaten with *mazah** and the paschal offering on Passover Eve.

Mazah (Pl. *Mazot*). Flat and thin unleavened bread (antithesis of *Ḥamez**). There is a positive duty (commandment) of eating *mazah* on the first night of Passover. See EJ 11, 1155-58.

Midrash. From DRŠ. (See *Derashah**.)

a) examination, investigation, study, theory;

b) specifically: investigation, study, exposition, or interpretation of Scripture;

c) (pl. *Midrashim*) literary works which contain Scriptural interpretation of an aggadic or halaḳic character; anthology and compilation of homilies containing Biblical exegesis and sermons;

d) the outright title by which such literary works are known (The halaḳic *midrashim* are tanaic);

e) systematic verse-by-verse commentary of Scripture, teaching *halaḳot* and *aggadot* with their Scriptural basis.

Miggo. A legal rule or argument. If "A" could have made a statement acceptable to the court, and instead makes another statement, the one he actually makes is accepted as true, on the grounds that if he had intended to lie, a more advantageous plea had been open to him. (See EJ 13, 635, and M. Jastrow, DICTIONARY, Vol. 1, p. 216.)

Mimra. An amoraic statement.

Miqve. A pool or bath of water, immersion in which renders ritually clean (pure) a person or vessel which has become ritually unclean (impure). Since the destruction of the Temple its chief use is for the menstruant.

Mishnah (pl. *mishnayot*). Part of the oral law, or the body of ancient Jewish learning; particularly, traditional statements of law in categorical form. *Mishnah* signifies specifically:

a) the entire content of the traditional "law" as far as it had been developed by the end of the second post-Christian century.

b) the sum of the teachings of any one of the teachers active up to that date.

c) a single statement of law or ethics, or any saying.

d) any collection of such statements.

e) the MISHNAH (M) is the collection made by R. Judah ha-Nasi ("Rabbi") or the form in which it has come down to us.

(For the most part, this follows Strack, INTRODUCTION . . . p. 3. cf. Danby, "Introduction," p. 13 f. and EJ 12, p. 93 f.).

Modaà. Notification.

a) an affidavit by a person that what he is about to execute is being forced upon him, and that he intends—where and when the opportunity arises—to take legal action to annul the execution of that act;

b) a person's protest to the effect that he is not doing something (e.g., writing a document, presenting a gift, making a sale, etc.) of his own free will, and a call to people present to bear witness to that effect. Such a protest normally invalidates the document or action;

c) ascertainment by witnesses that a deed (document) about to be written, is being written under duress, or that an action about to be taken, is being taken under duress, and that the party has no real desire that the deed (or action) be valid.

Musaf. Additional. Originally designating the additional sacrifices brought in the Temple on Sabbath, Festivals, and "New Moon" (The first day of the lunar month). v.

Num. 28, 9 f.   Later designating the additonal amidah* prayer added to the service on those days on which the additional sacrifices had been offered.   The amidah of *musaf* contains seven benedictions (except for that of the New Year festival which contains nine).

Nebelah.   See *Terefah**.

Onaah.   Overreaching.   Selling or purchasing for more or less than an article's real worth.   Overreaching by a sixth requires compensation; more than one-sixth enables the injured party to void the transaction.

Posqim (sing.*poseq*).   Lawgivers (orally or written), codifiers, responders.

Prutah.   Coin.   The smallest Palestinian bronze denomination; hence considered a minimum value for torts, thefts, claims, marriage, etc.

Qiddus.   Sanctification.   A short service recited over wine on Sabbath and Festival eves. It consists of a Scriptural passage (Sabbath only) folowed by the benediction over wine, and then by a longer benediction whose text denotes the sanctification of the day.   A shorter *Qiddus*, recited on the Sabbath or Festival day, consists just of the benediction over wine, customarily preceded by some verses from Scripture.

Qusya (or *Qasya*).   A difficulty.

Rigla (Sabbath).   The Sabbath (in the month of [Mar] Heshvan) when the portion *Lek Leka* (Gen. 12 f.) was read (hence the third after *Simhat Torah**).   The heads of both Babylonian academies would gather at the Academy of Sura, honoring the Exilarch, who would preside over the gathering (v. IGRSG, p. 91).   This would, in fact, mark the opening of the new academic year, after the Elul *Kalah** and the holiday season.

Ris(h)onim.   The medieval Rabbis, savants, Talmudic commentators, *posqim**, responders, dating from the end of the geonic era to 14-15 c.

Saborai (pl. *saboraim*, adj. saboraic).   One of the group of scholars who lived between the amoraic and geonic period, and put the finishing touches on the Babylonian Talmud.   See also *sebara**.

Safsar.   Agent, go between.   Commonly a speculating trader, determining a fixed price for the original seller, hoping to receive a much higher price from the purchaser.

Satnez (Shatnez).   Mingled stuff, diverse sorts.   The junction of wool and linen in wearing apparel prohibited by Deut. 22, 11.   Exceptionally permitted—according to the Oral Law—when the requirement of *Zizit** is to be fulfilled and also in priestly vestments.

Seah.   A measurement of volume, one thirtieth of a *kor** (estimated at 8,294—14,333 cu. cm.) for dry objects or for liquids, or of area, an area in which a *seah* of seed is sown (50 cubits sq.).

Sebara.   Reasoning, or interpretative material in the Talmud (*Gemara,** a) as opposed to *Gemara**, b).   See also *Saborai**.

Seder.   The Passover eve festive ceremony, consisting of inter alia, drinking four cups of wine, eating *mazah**, *maror**, and the festive meal, and reciting the *Hagadah* which includes the narrative of the exodus from Egypt, and the *Hallel.**

Sefer Torah.   The parchment scroll containing the Pentateuch, written in a special manner, in prescribed script, with prescribed ink, for reading in the public prayer service on Sabbath, Festivals, feast days, the New Moon, and every Monday and Thursday.

Sekak.   See *Sukkah**.

Shas (Sas).   Acronym of *S(h)ishah Sidrei,* "The six orders (of MISHNAH*)", referring, in common usage to the Babylonian Talmud.

Ṣ(h)eḥitah.   Ritual slaughter of the permitted animals and fowl making them kosher*—permitted for eating. The slaughtering is performed with a sharp knife at the throat, cutting through the windpipe and gullet.

Ṣ(h)mitah. The sabbatical year in which debts are to be remitted (Deut. 15, 1-11) and the land is to lie fallow (Ex. 23, 10-11; Lev. 25, 1-7).   Only work necessary to avoid permanent damage to the field is permitted. Produce which grows of itself during the sabbatical year is "ownerless", all having equal right to it. The latter is tithe—free and free of the Heave—offering (Trumah).   None may trade with it or remove it from the Land of Israel. It may be eaten or utilized in its usual fashion, so long as similar produce is still available in the field. Afterwards the gathered produce of that same species must be eaten forthwith or destroyed.

Ṣ(h)ofar. Ram's horn blown in the New Year festival. See Lev. 23, 24 and Num. 29, 1. Particulars of the shofar and its blowing are discussed in MRH 3, 2-7; 4, 2; 4, 5 f. and BTRH 26a f. See also EJ 14, 1442 f.

Simḥat Torah. The last day of the Feast of Tabernacles. In Israel: the eighth day (22 Tishrei) coinciding with Ṣ(h)emini Àzeret (see Num. 29, 35). In the Diaspora: the ninth day (23 Tishrei), an independent Festival. On this day the annual cycle of reading the Pentateuch from the Sefer Torah* in public is completed and immediately begun again. The day is marked by great festive rejoicing with the Sefer Torah*, see EJ 14, 1571.

Sugya (pl. sugyot). The basic (literary) unit of amoraic* literature. Hence, also: study, lesson, subject, discussion. Also practice (common practice) and usage, and sometimes the entire group of anonymous participants in an amoraic discussion.

Sukkah (pl. sukkot).   Booths in which it is obligatory to dwell during the Feast of Tabernacles (v. Lev. 23: 42). The booth must have at least two complete and one partial wall (sides) and must be covered (roofed) by something cut from that which grew from the soil, and which is not susceptible to ritual impurity. This roofing is called sekak. Material left in place not for the purpose of (for the sake of) the sukkah, is also not valid as sekak. These qualifications apply only to the roofing but not to the sides (walls). The sukkah must be at least ten handbreadths high but not more than twenty cubits high. Its area must be at least seven handbreadths square.   During the seven days of the Tabernacles Holiday the sukkah should be regarded as one's principle abode, particularly for eating and sleeping. v. M Sukkah, Ch. 1 and EJ 15, p. 492 f.

Sukkot. Feast of Tabernacles.

Talmud. The Mishnah* and Gemara* combined. The collection of Jewish learning until the fifth century. "Talmud" is often used synonymously with Gemara*.

Tanaim (sing. tana, adj. tanaic). Scholars (mainly Palestinian) of the (academies of the) tanaic period (c. 30-200 C.E.), who are mentioned in the Mishnah* and other literature of the period and/or participated in its development and compilation.

Tefilah. a) Prayer, in the wider sense; b) in the narrow, technical sense, the Àmidah*.

Terefah. From TRF, "torn" (by wild beasts). Originally the flesh of clean (permitted) beasts which had been mauled or killed by beasts of prey and so rendered prohibited as food (see Ex. 22, 30). More common in Rabbinic literature as:

a)   the flesh of a beast expected to die within 12 months of illness, defect, or injury, thus already becoming forbidden food;

b)   the flesh of an animal slaughtered unskillfully (see Ṣ(h)eḥitah) although attempted in valid fashion is thus rendered prohibited food, as distinct from nebelah, "carrion" ("animal carcass"); a clean (permitted) beast that has suffered a natural or violent death, or was slaughtered not in a regular or valid fashion, thus also becoming prohibited food;

c)   in popular usage: all prohibited food.

Tisha be Ab. The ninth day of the Hebrew month of Ab (the eleventh month of the year according to common reckoning). A fast day and day of mourning commemorating the destruction of the Temple(s).

Torah. A term which, even in Rabbinic Literature, has both wide and narrow connotations (see A.J. Heschel, *TORAH MIN HA SHAMAYIM be ASPAKLARIYAH SHEL HA-DOROT*, V. 2, 1962). Among the narrow meanings: Pentateuch, and *Sefer Torah**. In wider meanings: Scripture (The Corpus of written Law) and/or the Corpus of oral law, or the whole Corpus of Jewish law, or the body of laws referring to a specific subject.

Torah in its wider connotations refers to knowledge in general, or to teaching, instruction, views, ideas, doctrine, or system, particularly those of a specific individual or group.

Tyubta. Refutation (often based on earlier sources).

Yeshivah (pl. *Yeshivot*). Academy for the study of Torah*, particularly "Oral Law".

Zizit. Fringes, usually of wool (or cotton) worn on the four corners of a four-cornered garment (usually especially fabricated) to fulfill the commandment in Num. 15, 38-39.

Zuz. See *Dinar.*

REGISTER OF NAMES AND PLACES

I.   Persons

    1.   *Tanaim* and *amoraim*

    2.   Post-Talmudic figures including *saboraim, geonim, rišonim* and *posqim*

II. Places

I. Persons

A selectively annotated list of persons mentioned in the work:

1. *Tanaim* and *amoraim* who figure most prominently in the Talmudic pericopae which
    were either cited in the geonic responsa discussed in the work, or were referred to
    by us as sources for those geonic responsa and rulings. The list includes some of the
    most central figures of the Talmudic period and literature, and emphasizes those
    tanaim and *amoraim* who played a major role in establishing or formulating Talmudic
    principles of adjudication, or were themselves the subjects of principles discussed in
    the work. Since most of these persons have been treated in the standard reference
    works, we have limited ourselves to a brief biographical sketch, stressing the aspects
    most relevant to this work.

R. ABA. A third generation (3-4 century°) Babylonian *amora*, disciple of R. Judah* and
R. Huna* who immigrated to Palestine but continued visiting Babylonia, thus
transmitting Babylonian teachings and traditions to Palestine and vice versa. Referred
to in the Babylonian Talmud as "our Rabbi(s) (or teachers[s]) in the Land of Israel
(Palestine)." Aba was a common name in the period and was the proper name of Rabah*,
Rav*, and Rava*.

ABA SAUL. Mid second-century *tana* (3-4 generation) whose terminology often differed
from that commonly used, e.g., "Aba Saul used to call the *stuqi* stock ("one whose father
is not known") [by the name] *beduqi* ("requiring examination") (M. Qid, 4, 2)." Some of
his tradition also differed from that of the mainstream. It is widely held that Aba Saul
compiled a mishnah (b)* used by Judah ha-Nasi* in his own mishnah (e)*.

ABAYE. (c. 278-338). Real name Naḥmani (?) b. Keilil. Major Babylonian amora, head of
the Pumbedita academy (c. 333-338), orphaned at birth and raised by a foster mother and
his uncle, Rabah*. His discussions with his colleague, Rava*, constitute a major element
of the Babylonian Talmud, which indeed is sometimes nicknamed *"havayot* (term unclear)

---

*Starred terms appear as independent entries in the Register and Glossary

° Dates are C.E.

of Abaye and Rava." Perhaps they were also its first editors. A principle of adjudication found in the Talmud determines that only in six instances does Abaye's view prevail in (his numerous) disagreements with Rava (Qid. 52a, s.n.). He himself formulated and classified rules and principles out of masses of Talmudic material, e.g., he sometimes ruled by instructing, "go outside and see what the people do."

R. AQIBA (or AKIVA). (Flourished c. 75-135). Central figure of the tanaic era, and late "Jabneh circle." Teacher par-excellence of generations of *tanaim* in his Bne-Braq academy. Among his numerous disciples were most of the outstanding mid-late second century *tanaim*, e.g., Jose,* Judah,* Meir,* Simeon b. Johai—who established the Torah academies of the North (Galilee) after the Bar Kochba uprising (132-135, in which many of his students participated), and the subsequent persecutions. According to R. Yohanan (BT. San. 86a), the anonymous mishnah* (e), *Tosefta*, *Sifra*, and *Sifrei* pericopae are all according to R. Aqiba. This probably means that Aqiba's arrangement, organization, and classification ("editing") of the oral law which had developed up to his time (perhaps the first such significant arrangement) served as the literary basis for the mishnah and *Tosefta*, and that the versions of *Sifra* and *Sifrei* known to Yohanan, followed, for the most part, R. Aqiba's "school" of Halakic *Midrashim* * (which differed in methodology and terminology from the school of R. Ishmael). According to a Talmudic principle (Erubin 46b. s.n.) the law follows R. Aqiba in all his disputes with any of his colleagues. For a complete study of Aqiba, see, L. Finkelstein, *Akiba*.

R. AŞI (ASHI) (c. 335-427/8). Head of the Sura academy from c. 371/2, he gathered around him hundreds of students and scores of distinguished colleagues, reestablishing Sura as one of the major centers of learning. During his long tenure he went through the cycle of the Talmudic tractates more than once. He was one of the major editors (if not *the* major editor) of the Babylonian Talmud and was one of the last to add original source material to it.

BAR QAPARA or KAPPARA. A Palestinian scholar in the transition between *tanaim* and *amoraim* (beginning of the third century), who compiled a collection of *beraitot*.

R. ELAZAR (b. Pedat). Second generation *amora* of Babylonian birth who emigrated to Palestine and succeeded R. Yohanan* as head of the Tiberias academy. Called "The master of the Land of Israel" (BT Yoma 9b. s.n.), Talmudic tradition asserts that the term, "they sent from there" (i.e., Palestine) refers to Elazar.

R. ELAZAR HAMODAI. Third generation (end of first, beginning of second century) *tana*.

Raban GAMALIEL (II). *Nasi* ("President") of the *Sanhedrin* at Jabneh after the destruction of the Second Temple (in 70 C.E.). Relentless fighter for the spiritual preservation and unity of the nation through adherence to the Oral Law. Champion of the central authority of the *Nasi* and *Sanhedrin* at Jabneh, particularly regarding standardization and institutionalization of prayer, calendar, and ritual custom, and clear authoritative rulings in case of disputes, disallowing the *practice* of the minority view.

HILLEL. (Flourished end of first century BCE beginning of first century C.E.). The most prominent sage of the latter part of the second temple period. He served as *nasi* ("president", pl. *nesiim*) in the last *zug* (pair. pl. *zugot*) who had been the keepers of the Oral Law tradition and heads of its institutions (e.g., *Sanhedrin*) since the beginning of the second century B.C.E. He was the founder of the dynasty of *nesiim* who ruled for some 400 years, and included—among others—Gamaliel*, Simeon b. Gamaliel*, and Judah ha-Nasi*. He established the "School [House] of Hillel," the leading group of scholars in the early tanaic period, according to whom the law has been decided (particularly in their disputes with the "School ["House"] of Shamai*") since Jabneh. A native of Babylonia, famous for his humility, Hillel instituted a number of legal innovations (*taqanot*) which were already widely accepted in his own lifetime.

R. ḤISDA. (c. 217-309). Second-third generation Babylonian *amora*. Together with R. Huna* styled "the pious men of Babylonia" or "elders of Sura*." His scholarship excelled in depth and thoughtfulness.

R. ḤIYYA. The scholar in the transition period between *tanaim* and *amoraim* closest to Judah ha-Nasi*. He enjoyed limited tanaic status. Together with his disciple Oshaiah he compiled the most authoritative and accurate collection of *beraitot*, much of which was incorporated into the Babylonian Talmud. A Babylonian by birth—and a patriot of his birthplace (he was the uncle and one of the teachers of Rav*)—he excelled in spreading the teaching of the Torah.

R. HUNA. Babylonian *amora* in the second half of the third century. Together with R. Hisda* styled "The pious men of Babylonia" or "elders of Sura." The outstanding disciple of Rav*—and the anonymous transmitter of traditions in the name of "The School of Rav"—he headed the Sura academy for over forty years after the death of Rav and Samuel* and saw it blossom, with a regular student body of many hundreds. He established that the principle of adjudication which determines that in disputes with Samuel the law follows Rav in all non-monetary (civil) affairs, holds, no matter whether Rav's view is the lenient or stringent one.

R. ISAAC (Napaha). Third century Palestinian *amora*, student of R. Yohanan, and one of Palestine's legal authorities after Yohanan's death, he travelled to Babylonia, where he transmitted Palestinian teachings, and vice versa.

R. JOHANAN (see Yohanan).

R. JOSE. Mid second-century *tana*. One of the leaders of the generation which reestablished the Torah academies in the north (Galilee) after the Bar-Kochba uprising (132-35 C.E.) and subsequent persecutions. According to a Talmudic principle of adjudication, the law follows Jose in disagreements with any of his colleagues. He probably compiled his own mishnah (b)* in his Sephoris academy, based on that of his mentor, R. Aqiba,* which served as one of the sources for the mishnah (e)* of R. Judah ha-Nasi*.

R. JOSHUA (b. Hananya). Prominent second generation *tana*, at first in Jerusalem, and, after the Temple's destruction (in 70 C.E.) in the Jabneh circle where he was one of the leading figures in both academic and communal affairs. He felt that a ruling of the majority should be binding on all.

R. JUDAH (b. Ezekiel) (d. 299). Babylonian *amora*, student of Rav* and Samuel*, founder of the Pumbedita* academy.

R. JUDAH (b. Ilai). Mid second-century *tana*. One of the foremost spokesmen of the group which reestablished the Torah* academies in the north (Galilee) after the Bar-

Kochba uprising (132-35) and subsequent persecutions. R. Judah compiled his own mishnah (b)* which was used by Judah ha-Nasi* in the compilation of his own. *Amoraim* dispute the meaning of the terminology of R. Judah's formulations as incorporated into our (i.e., "Rabbi's") Mishnah* (e). Early Talmudic principles of adjudication determine that the law follows R. Judah in disputes with his colleagues R. Meir* and R. Simeon b. Johai, and in all matters of *erubin**.

R. JUDAH Ha-NASI ("The prince"). Flourished at the end of the second century. Known most commonly in Talmudic literature as "Rabbi" (occasionally: "our holy Rabbi"). *Nasi* ("president," "patriarch") of the people and the land of Israel from the dynasty founded by Hillel.* Spiritual, legal, and ethical head of the Jewish community; its leader in all religious, secular, and administrative affairs, both internal and external. Venerated by countemporaries-colleagues, aristocrats and the "common folk"—and all ensuing generations. Compiler of our Mishnah (e),* which he based chiefly on the mishnah (b)* of R. Meir* but also on those of R. Meir's colleagues (e.g., R. Judah*) at whose academies he studied, and ultimately on that of R. Aqiba.* His academy in Beit Shearim was home to almost all the great scholars of this day. Among his students were the outstanding figures of the transition era and the early *amoraim* (e.g., R. Ḥiyya*, Bar Qapara*, Rav*, R. Yoḥanan*). According to a Talmudic principle of adjudication the law follows "Rabbi" in his disputes with any of his colleagues (but not in those with his father, Simeon b. Gamaliel II).

MAR BAR RAV AṢ(H)I (d. 468). Babylonian *amora*, son of R. Aṣi*, he followed his father's footsteps by heading the Sura* academy (from 455) and playing a role in the redaction of the Babylonian Talmud. Extensively cited by the *Gemara**, his rulings are authoritative in all cases but two (according to a Rabbinic principle of adjudication).

MAR ZUTRA. Sixth generation Babylonian *amora*, head of the Pumbedita* academy (411-14), disciple of R. Papa*, contemporary and friend of R. Aṣi*, transmitter of many early amoraic teachings (cf. EJ 16, 1244).

R. MEIR. Mid second century *tana*. Leading intellect of the group that reestablished the *Torah** academies in the north (Galilee) after the persecutions which followed the Bar-Kochba revolt (132-35). His mishnah* (b), which itself was based on that of R. Aqiba*, served as the main source of the Mishnah (e)* of R. Judah ha-Nasi*. According to Talmudic tradition the bulk of the anonymous material in our Mishnah (e)* came from R. Meir's. Though he was highly esteemed by his colleagues and the holder of prominent positions in the academy, the rulings, according to Talmudic principles of adjudication, go against R. Meir in his disputes with R. Jose* and R. Judah*.

R. NAHMAN. (b. Jacob, d. c. 320). Oft cited Babylonian amora from the court of Samuel, related through marriage to the exilarch, judge, and authority in monetary (civil) law, in which—according to an amoraic principle of adjudication—the law follows him in his disputes with any of his colleagues (cf. EJ 12,773).

R. PAPA (c. 300-375). Fifth generation Babylonian amora, student of Abaye* and Rava*. After their death he founded the academy at Naresh and headed it for nineteen years. His legal opinions often reconcile other conflicting opinions. Many of his rulings are deductions or conclusions based on the rulings of others, or have incorporated previously conflicting opinions.

RABAH (Aba b. Nahmani). Third generation Babylonian amora, disciple of Huna*, and Judah*, succeeding the latter as head of the Pumbedita* academy for the twenty-two years until his death (c. 322), leading it to its peak (in amoraic times), with hundreds of regular students and thousands in attendance during kalah months. He was known for his skillful dialectics, and devoted much time to interpreting mishnaic texts and reconciling apparently contradictory tanaic texts through elucidation and clarification.

RABBI. See R. Judah ha-Nasi.

RABIN (R. Avin, Avin, Bon, or Bun). Father and son of the same name. The father was born in Babylonia (c. 300), emigrated to Palestine, and frequently returned to Babylonia, conveying the teachings of each land to the other. Hence the oft found Talmudic comment, "When Rabin came. . . ." The son was born in Palestine and was the friendly disputant of R. Mana II, the head of the Sephoris academy.

RABINA (R. Avina). Talmudic tradition pairs Rabina with R. Asi* as one of the last to add original source material to the Talmud (and most likely, as one of the Talmud's editors). It is not clear if the reference is to Rabina I*, R. Asi's elder contemporary or to

Rabina II* (the view of IGRSG).

RABINA I* student of Rava*, had frequent discussions with R. Asi, studied at his academy in Sura, and, no doubt, participated, with him, in the editing of the Gemara*.

RABINA II. (b. Huna. d. 499). Head of the Sura* academy (from 474). One of the last of the Babylonian *amoraim*, who marked the end of the amoraic period.

RABUN. v. *Rabin*.

RAMI b. HAMA. Fourth century Babylonian *amora*, student and son-in-law of Hisda*, colleague of Rava*.

RAV. (Aba b. Aivu, Aba "Arika." Rav, "the teacher," i.e., of the entire diaspora). Foremost Babylonian *amora*. Born in Babylonia in the latter half of the second century, he immigrated to Palestine and studied with his uncle R. Hiyya*, and, eventually, at the academy of Judah ha-Nasi. He finally returned to Babylonia permanently (219) and soon thereafter founded the Sura* academy, which attracted over a thousand permanent students.   He was recognized by his contemporaries as Jewry's leading religious authority. The Babylonian Talmud confers upon him "tanaic status." He can be credited with disseminating the study of Torah* in Babylonia, and establishing it as the Torah center of the amoraic period, and, together with Samuel,* in laying the foundations for the institutions which led to the Babylonian Talmud.   Their discussions and their interpretations of tanaic material form the basic core of BT's material. They were accorded the honorific title, "our Rabbis in Babylonia" and "our Rabbis in the diaspora." A Talmudic principle of adjudication establishes that the law follows Rav in all non-monetary (civil) matters.

RAVA. (R. Aba b. Joseph b. Hama. d. 352). Student of Nahman,* and R. Joseph. Close colleague of Abaye* (for their joint activities see entry Abaye*). After the latter was chosen head of the Pumbedita* academy, Rava founded his own in his home town, Mehoza—emphasizing logical reasoning—which flourished. After Abaye's death, Rava became the titular head of the Pumbedita academy, but, in fact, his own in Mehoza became the principal academy for the remainder of Rava's lifetime.

RE(I)S(H) LAQIS(H). (R. Simeon b. Laqis). Second generation Palestinian *amora*, one of the mainstays of the Tiberias academy and of Palestinian amoraic learning. According to a principle of adjudication in the Babylonian Talmud, the law follows Reis Laqis in three cases (in disputes with his close colleague, R. Yoḥanan,* i.e., as a rule, the latter has the upper hand).

RSBG. See Raban Simeon b. Gamaliel.

SAMUEL. First generation Babylonian *amora* (d. 254), scion of an old, eminent (academically, economically, and socially) Babylonian family, head of the Nehardea academy and court, and keeper of their traditions, colleague of Rav* (for their joint activities, see the entry, Rav). Authority in monetary (civil) matters. According to a Talmudic principle of adjudication, the law follows Samuel in all his disputes (with Rav) on such matters. He was also an eminent physician and astronomer.

SHAMAI. Partner of Hillel* (see his entry) as last of the *zugot* (leaders of the *Sanhedrin*). Founder of the "School (House) of Shamai" (traditionally considered to have a more "stringent" line), which, since the days of Jabneh, was preempted on ideology and legal rulings by the School of Hillel except for a few cases in which the Hillel line gave in to that of Shammai.

RABAN SIMEON b. GAMALIEL II (RSBG). Flourished mid second-century. Son of Gamaliel II*, father of Judah ha-Nasi*. After the post-Bar-Kochba persecutions he settled in Usha in the Galilee where he took his place as *nasi* ("president;" "head") of its "*Sanhedrin.*" Cited often in the Mishnah (e)* and *beraitot**. According to R. Yoḥanan*: Whenever RSBG taught in our Mishnah (e)*, the law follows him, except in three cases.

R. SIMEON b. LAQIS. See Reis Laqis.

R. YOHANAN (Ben Napaha. c. 180-c. 279). Student in his youth of R. Judah ha-Nasi*. The most prominent Palestinian *amora*. Founder and head of the Tiberias academy which attracted the finest students of the generation. His teachings, rulings, expositions, analysis, and explanation of the MISHNAH (e)*, and *beraitot** (alone and together with Reis Laqis), not only comprise a major part of the Palestinian Talmud, but fill the Babylonian Talmud too. The latter's principles of adjudication give R. Yoḥanan the upper

hand, not only in his disputes with Reis Laqis, but in those with Rav* and Samuel* too
(and in effect afford him quasi-tanaic status). Yoḥanan himself was one of those who
laid the foundation for the genre of principles of adjudication by introducing such classic
rules as: "Wherever RSGB* taught in our Mishnah the law follows him, except . . . ; In
disputes between R. Judah* and R. Meir* the law follows R. Judah; between R. Judah and
R. Jose*, R. Jose;" "The law follows an anonymous mishnah," etc. He also became the
first prominent source critic of the MISHNAH by determining that the bulk of anonymous
MISHNAH (e)* pericopae stems from R. Meir*, that of *Tosefta* from R. Neḥemia, that of
Sifra from R. Judah,* those of *Sifrei* from R. Simeon (b. Joḥai), and they are all
according to R. Aqiba* (see his entry).

R. YOSE. See R. Jose.

R. ZBID. Fifth generation Babylonian *amora.* Disciple of Abaye* and Rava*. Head of
the Pumedita* academy (377-385).

2.   Post-Talmudic Figures

Post-Talmudic persons (*saboraim, geonim, rishonim,* and *posqim*) discussed in the
body of the work, mentioned in the geonic pericopae which permeate this study, or
cited by us as sources for geonic material. Since this is a study of the geonic period,
and much of the geonic material is known only from the works of the *rishonim,* and
whereas there is a natural affinity between the two periods and the two groups of
scholars (the *rishonim* being a continuation of the *geonim* in all spheres of their
activity) we deemed it proper to include partial biographies not only of the central
figures of the geonic period, but also of some of the most prominent *rishonim* (and
later *posqim*), and particularly of those *rishonim* with a special relationship to the
geonim and the geonic era, e.g., students and disciples of the *geonim* (and student's
students), correspondents of the *geonim,* those whose works lean heavily on geonic
material and tradition or cite extensively from them, and first and foremost: those
rishonim whose works are the major sources for our knowledge of geonic history and
literary activity. We have listed the post-Talmudic persons in alphabetical order
according to their *common acronyms* whenever applicable (and that is how we
usually cited them in the body of the work).

AHA(I) of S(h)abha (680-752 or 762). Prominent scholar of the Pumbedita* academy. Left Babylonia for Palestine (c. 749) after not having been appointed Gaon. Author of the *SHEELTOT*, the first post-Talmudic book to be attributed to its author. It is a collection of material—including legal rulings—suitable for Babylonian *derashot* (c)* and perhaps emanating from them in part.

AMRAM b. Sheshna Gaon. Gaon of Sura* (853-871). Author (together with his "number two" man in the academy, Zemah b. Solomon) of the first "Order of Prayers and Blessings" (actually a responsum to Spain). The work in Rabbinic language (Hebrew and Amaraic), much-cited by *rishonim*, became widespread and the basic text of its genre. It has been published in a number of editions. Many other of his responsa are dispersed in the responsa collections and in medieval works.

BARUCH of Greece. R. Baruch b. Samuel (c. 1070-1130). Probably born in Spain and lived in southern Italy. Talmudic commentator who used RIF* and RH* as well as the German school of commentary, and, in turn, was cited by medieval scholars from Germany, Spain, and Italy alike.

BHM. Zerahia b. Israel ha-Levi (Gerondi). Known as Baal ha Maor (the author of the Luminary) on account of his major work by that name. It comprises glosses to the *HALAKOT* of RIF.* The disputant of RABD*, he was born in Spain, but flourished in twelfth century Provence, and was very Provençal in his work.

(Ha)GRA. "Gaon Rabbi Eliyahu." Elijah b. Solomon Zalman. "The Vilna Gaon" (1720-1797). One of the greatest spiritual and intellectual figures of modern Jewry. Molder of Lithuanian Jewish culture (especially of its Torah academies). An intellectual hermit but an active polemical leader through his influence on disciples. He opposed *haskalah* and the Hassidic movement, and emphasized learning and *halakah*. Author of an important commentary to the *SHULHAN ARUK* of R. Joseph Qaro* (made up of terse notes), and commentaries (usually notes and/or glosses) to many books of Scripture and the oral law, many of them extant in better or poorer versions, e.g., Mishnah order *Zeraim*, tanaic Midrashim, Talmud, *TOSEFTA*.

HAI b. Sherira. See the chapter on his life and literary heritage.

HANAN of Asqiya. Generally recognized as the first of the *Geonim* Pumbedita* (589). But cf. Introduction p. 6.

HIDA. Hayim Joseph David Azulai (1724-1806). Kabbalist and one of the accepted legal authorities of Oriental Jewry. Emissary of the Palestinian communities, which facilitated his career as biographer; one of the fathers of Hebrew bibliography, and collector, investigator, and recorder of manuscripts and early printed books.

ISAAC b. Reuben al-Bargeloni (born 1043). Scholar, poet, and translator (cf. EJ 1,528) of RHG's MQM, and attributed author (or translator?) of Saarei Sebuot, printed after the RIF to BT Sebuot.

JACOB b. Asher. (c. 1270-1340). Son of ROSH*. Known as *Baal Ha Turim* ("author of the *TUR*") on account of his major work, a four-part legal compendium embracing all relevant matters of law and custom (Joseph Qaro* authored his *SHULHAN ARUK* by abridging his own commentary to the *TUR*). R. Jacob was born in Germany but raised in Spain, and his *TUR* is the fruit of the scholarship and literary achievements of both cultural spheres.

JACOB b. Nissim (d. 1006/7). Head of Kairouan* academy. African representative of the Babylonian academies and holder of (honorific?) titles from them. Correspondent of RSG and RHG (IGRSG was sent to him) for about twenty years until his death.

R. JEROHAM b. Mesulam. See R. Yeruham.

R. JOSEPH (Jose). One of the earliers *saboraim*, at the end of the amoraic era. He headed the Pumbedita academy for some forty years.

R. JOSEPH QARO (or Karo, or Caro, 1488-1575). Author of the *SHULHAN ARUK* (SUA); the authoritative Jewish legal code *par excellence*, the author's digest of his own Beit Yosef (BY), a super commentary on Jacob b. Asher's *TUR* in which Qaro, with his encyclopedic knowledge, cited all relevant sources—from Talmudic to his own generation—to each legal issue raised by the *TUR*, arranged them into groupings, and drew legal conclusions. The *SHULHAN ARUK* follows the *Tur's* division and order. He also authored *KESEF MISHNAH*, a commentary on Maimonides' MISHNEH TORAH. His responsa were collected under the title *Avqat Roķel*. Born in Spain (or Portugal), Qaro lived in Turkey, and eventually in Safed where he became one of the central figures of its kabbalistic circles, its religious court, and academies.

JUDAH b. Barzilai al-Bargeloni.   Late eleventh-early twelfth century, Rabbi of Barcelona. Author of a sizeable code encompassing—at least—Sabbath and Festivals, marriage and personal law, and "civil" law. Only the Sabbath part of *HA ÌTTIM* and *HASCHETAROTH* on legal documents have been published. The rest has been lost. The esteem in which his work was held for hundreds of years, and its magnitude, can be seen from: the *ESKOL* which is a condensation of the (complete) *ITTIM*; gleanings from *SEFER HADIN* (the work on "civil law") published by S. Assaf (see Bibliography IA 16G), and the many extracts found in other works, e.g., ha–*ORAH* (or *OREH*) of the RASHI* school, and *TEMIM DEIM* of Rabad*. His works are based mainly on the code and responsa of RIF, and on geonic responsa (with a subtle tendency to nudge the latter back to the forefront after their having been displaced by the former in Spain). Some collections of geonic responsa were actually gleaned from his works (see Bibliography IA 4, 7). His commentary on the *Book of Yeṣira* also includes much geonic material, including parts of RSdG's commentary on the same book.

MAHRAM. Meir b. Baruch of Rothenburg (c. 1215-1293). Teacher, scholar, tosafist, Mishnah commentator (orders of Zeraim ["Seeds"] and Toharot ["Purities"]), codifier, responder, poet, supreme arbiter in ritual, legal, and community matters in Germany. Born in Worms, student of the great Tosafists of Germany and France. One of the greatest responders of German Jewry, he received questions from as far away as Spain, to resolve civil and community disputes, decide matters of ritual law, and serve as "court of appeals." Through his many students, some of whom later occupied important Rabbinical posts, and some of whom composed major legal works, his "school" exercised lasting influence on the *halaķah* of European Jewry. In 1286 he was imprisoned for his part in a Jewish exodus from Germany, and died in prison.

MESHARSHAYA, Gaon. See Moses Gaon.

MHRM. See MAHRAM.

MOSES ([Mesharshaya] Kahana b. Jacob) Gaon. Gaon of Sura (c. 825-836). Many of his responsa have been preserved in collections, in *SRA*, in *rishonim*, and in questions to and responsa of later *geonim*.

NAHMANIDES (RAMBAN or RMBN). R. Moses b. Nahman (1194-1270). Spanish Rabbi and scholar. One of the leading Talmudic authors in the middle ages, philosopher, kabbalist, biblical exegete, poet and physician. Born in Gerona, later head of its academy, he nurtured not only from Spanish sources, but from French (tosafist) and Provençal as well, synthesizing them into a very distinctive system which he transmitted to his numerous disciples. His "school" became the prominent one in Spain and, with the expulsions, in North Africa, and endured for hundreds of years. His main literary works are novellae on the Talmud and a commentary to Pentateuch. He also composed legal monographs and glosses and defenses of earlier halakic works (e.g., RIF). In all his Talmudic and halakic works he leans heavily on citations and traditions from the *geonim*, and on the textual readings of the Babylonian academies. In c. 1266 he escaped from Spain—after successfully debating an apostate—and emigrated to Palestine.

NATRONAI (b. Hilai) Gaon (of Sura* 853-58). Author of a relatively large number of extant responsa, including a famous one to Spain (with which he had particularly strong ties) about the obligation of reciting a hundred benedictions a day, which was later incorporated (together with other responsa of his) into SRA.

NISSIM b. Jacob. See RNG.

RABAD or RABD. Abraham b. David of Posquières. Outstanding Provençal (born in Narbonne) twelfth century Talmudic authority, Rabbi, personality, and teacher. Most famous historically for this critical annotations and glosses to Maimonides' MISHNEH TORAH (and RIF's* laws and BHM*). However, to the generations immediately succeeding him he was the great Talmudic commentator. He also composed halakic monographs, commentaries to the Mishnah and tanaic *Midrashim*, and authored responsa. He frequently cites *geonim* and geonic works. Considered by kabbalists to have been one of their spiritual ancestors. For a full study see, I. Twersky, RABAD OF POSQUIERES, and H. Soloveitchik, in *Studies in the History of Jewish Society*, presented to J. Katz, English section.

RABIAH (Eliezer b. Joel ha-Levi. c. 1140-c. 1225). Eminent Rabbinic scholar of the German tosafist school (grandson of RABN*). His major work is commonly known as THE BOOK OF RABIAH (also known as *AVI HAEZRI* and *AVIASAF*, as is the author sometimes called). It is a voluminous legal code structured like that of RIF, following the order of the Talmud and dealing with relevant material. Once the text of the complete manuscripts of his book became known to scholars, it became clear that all the great codifiers of the German tosafist school (e.g., ROSH*, *Or Zarua*, Mordecai) relied heavily on him. See V. Aptowitzer, *INTRODUCTIO AD SEFER RABIAH*, and his edition of the first parts of the text.

RABN (or RABAN. Eliezer b. Nathan of Mainz. c. 1090-c. 1170). Grandfather of RABIAH*. His major work commonly known as the *Book of RABN* (or *EVEN HA-EZER*) is the first complete extant work of German Jewry, about whom it contains a mine of historical information. The work contains responsa, extracts, and legal rulings following Talmudic tractates. He cites RH often and accurately.

RADBAZ. David (Ben Solomon) Ibn (Abi) Zimra (c. 1480-1573/4). Spanish born. Religious and legal authority and teacher of Egyptian Jewry for fifty years, before retiring to Palestine and spending his last years in Safed. One of the great responders of his (and any) age, he also composed a treatise on the methodology of the Talmud (*Kelalai ha Gemara*) and a commentary to part of Maimonides' *Mishneh Torah*.

RAH. R. Aaron (b. Joseph) Ha Levi (of Barcelona. c. 1235-c. 1300). Rabbi in Saragosa. Descendant of BHM*, student of Nahmanides*, colleague of RASHBA*, teacher of RITBA*, author of novellae to the Talmud, responsa, and critical comments to the works of others (RIF, RASHBA). *Sefer HaHinuk* is sometimes attributed to him (with no firm basis).

RAH. See RH.

RAMBAN. See Nahmanides.

RAS(H)BA (or RS(H)BA. Solomon b. Abraham Ad(e)ret. 1235-c. 1310). Rabbi of Barcelona and head of its court and Torah academy. One of the foremost scholars and figures of Spanish Jewry. Student of Jonah of Geronda and Nahmanides*. Responder *par* *excellence* of Spanish Jewry (and one of the most outstanding ever) to questions from all over the world. The eight published volumes, and others in Ms., paint a picture of Jewish life and life in general in Christian Spain in the second half of the thirteenth century and the beginning of the fourteenth (See I. Epstein, THE "RESPONSA" OF RABBI SOLOMON BEN ADRETH OF BARCELONA, and its second edition [1968] under the name STUDIES IN THE COMMUNAL LIFE OF THE JEWS OF SPAIN). Author of novellae to the Talmud, which are some of the finest representatives of the "Nahmanides school" (in method and use of sources. See Nahmanides), legal monographs, and a commentary to the Talmudic *Agadah**.

RAS(H)BAM. See RSHBM.

RASHI (Solomon b. Isaac[?]. c. 1040-1105). Born in Troy, France which he left only for study and consultation at the German academies. Commentator *par excellence* of the Bible and Talmud. Teacher and religious authority of French and German Jewry, upon whom the works of the "Rashi school" and, later, the Tosafists were founded. His running commentary to the Talmud leads the student through the *sugya*, pausing only where Rashi anticipates that the student might have difficulty understanding a word, concept, idea or argument. Within a relatively short period after its composition it became the norm to study *Gemara* with Rashi. It became the basis for all further literary activity in the field. To this day it remains an undivided part of the study of Talmud. Similarly, his commentary to the Bible, particularly to the Pentateuch, has been studied by generations together with the sacred text. The Bible commentary is not limited to simple literal explanations of the passage. Of the massive available bibliography, outstanding is E. M. Lipscheutz, "RASHI," in (J. L. Maimon, ed.) *SEFER RASHI*, 1956 (also published independently).

RDVZ. See RADBAZ.

RH. Hananel b. Hushiel of Kairouan*. Flourished first half of the eleventh century (d. 1056?). *Poseq** and commentator. Among the first *rishonim*. Like his father, he was accorded the title, *reis bei rabanan* ("chief among the Rabbis") by the Babylonian academies, with whom he had close ties. Author of one of the first commentaries on the Talmud, his style was to summarize the *sugya* and formulate the laws to be learned from it. He emphasized correct readings. The commentary gained wide circulation soon after its appearance, and was used extensively by RIF*. RH made extensive use of geonic literature in his commentary, relying particularly on the commentaries of RSG and RHG (especially the latter to whom he refers as just plain "the Gaon") to various tractates, which he incorporated into his own commentary, sometimes verbatim.

RIBAI of Rub. One of the last *saboraim* in Pumbedita*, see introduction p. 6.

RIF. Isaac b. Jacob Al Fasi (of Fez) 1013-1103. Head of the academy in Lucena, Spain (from 1089). His major work, his code ("*HALAKOT*"), is an extract or epitome of all the legal material of the Talmud which is still practiced and operative. He closely follows the Talmud's order, ascertains the ruling, and provides a comprehensive compendium for ready reference. Among his sources are all the works of the geonic literature. He made extensive use of the commentary of RH*, and consequently of RH's sources (see his entry). He, too, refers to RHG as "the Gaon." The work was a major success and served as a basis for much of the later literary output in the field (especially in "Tosafist" Germany). In Spain it was widely studied in place of the Talmud. Leading scholars wrote glosses to and/or defenses of it (e.g., BHM*, RABD*, RAH*, Nahmanides). Hundreds of RIF's responsa are extant (many in their original Judeo-Arabic). His importance as a *poseq* survived through the ages.

RIH (Judah b. Samuel ha-Hasid. d. 1217). Prominent in ethics and theology. Main teacher of the Hasidei Askenaz movement upon whose teachings their works in *halakah* and theology are based. Principal author of *SEFER HASIDIM* and of a commentary on Pentateuch in the spirit of the movement.

RITBA. Yom Tov b. Abraham A(or I)sbili (of Seville). Leading thirteenth-fourteenth century Spanish Rabbi and religious leader. Student of RAH* and RASHBA*. His novellae on the Talmud are an outstanding representative of the development of the "Nahmanides school."

RMBN. See Nahmanides.

RNG. R. Nissim (b. Jacob b. Nissim*) "Gaon" of Kairouan*. (d. 1062). Head of a prominent academy in Kairouan, he maintained a very close relationship with the

Pumbedita* academy and was accorded the title *reiṣ bei rabanan* ("chief among the Rabbis") after the passing of RH. Disciple of Hai Gaon through abundant correspondence, RNG (and his circle) was the questioner and receiver of many of Hai's responsa. Much of his halakic tradition stems from Hai with whose writings RNG was very familiar. Hai's literary output was a major source of RNG's works, and much of it was incorporated into them, especially into his *MAFTEAḤ, MEGILAT SETARIM,* and Talmudic commentaries. RNG, in turn, was a major channel for the dissemination of the teachings of the later *geonim.* Prof. S. Abramson composed a monumental study of RNG and his works (in which he reconstructed much of RNG's work from Genizah* fragments) by the name of *R. Nissim Gaon Libelli Quinque,* Hierosolymis, MCMLXV (also "RNG").

ROṢ(H). R. Asher b. Jehiel. (Germany c. 1250-Toledo, Spain, 1327). Tosafist (author of extant *Tosafot* on many tractates) of the German school, disciple of MAHRAM*. Fled Germany in 1303. Welcomed by RASHBA* to Spain where he became head of the Toledo court and academy (the first such emigration of so eminent a Talmudist). His major work—known as the Laws of (or just plain) ROṢ (or Aṣeri)—is a legal code following the order of the Talmud, structured on RIF*, but very much in the spirit of, and using the material of, the Franco-German "Tosafist school." He was an eminent teacher and major responder in both countries. His responsa reflect the spirit and life of them both. An index to his responsa (*MAFTEAH,* ed. M. Alon) was published in Jerusalem, 1965. A major study of ROṢ was published by A. Freimann in JJLG 12-13.

RṢ(H)BA. See RAṢ(H)BA.

RSBH. See Samuel b. Ḥofni.

RSdG. See Saàdya Gaon.

RSG Ṣ(h)erira Gaon (b. Ḥaninah Gaon b. Judah Gaon. c. 906-d. 1006). Father of Hai Gaon. Gaon* of Pumbedita* 968-1004 (when he "abdicated" in favor of Hai, and remained "Gaon Emeritus" until his death). The Gaon chiefly responsible for raising the Pumbedita academy from its lowly position, at the beginning of his ascending the Gaonate, to its central position as the major seat of learning and authority in the Jewish world by the time he transferred power to Hai, despite some turbulent times (with the

Arab government) during this period. He expended much energy in reestablishing connections with far flung Jewish communities and sending out the requests to regain contributions and contributors (beseeching, influencing, and pressuring) in order to strengthen the Academy, and reestablish its position of authority. His most special relationship was with Jacob b. Nissim* of Kairouan and his circle. Nevertheless he found ample time to lead and instruct in the rejuvenated academy, and to author many responsa. His most famous responsum is his epistle to R. Jacob b. Nissim (IGRSG) on the composition of the Mishnah, beraitot and the Talmud, the history of the tradition and transmission of the Oral Law, and the history of the academies—their heads and institutions—down to his own day. He also wrote commentaries on (tractates, chapters, sugyot, passages, and words of) the Talmud (probably in response to specific requests). He resolved the dispute with the Sura* academy by marrying his son, Hai, to the daughter of Sura's head, R. Samuel b. Hofni*. Much of his literary, communal, and academy activity was with the help and participation of his son, Hai.

RSHBM. Samuel b. Meir. Flourished in twelfth century France. Grandson and student of RASHI*. Most famous for his commentary to Pentateuch. One of the first tosafists (the Franco-German Talmudic school following RASHI). His commentary to most of BTBB and to part of BT Pesahim is printed in the standard volumes where RASHI is incomplete.

SAADYA (b. Joseph) Gaon. (RSdG). Born Pithom (Fuyum), Egypt (882), died Babylonia (942). Functionary of the Babylonian Academies from 922. Appointed Gaon (the only non-Iraqi [Babylonian] ever to become Gaon) of Sura* in 928 in order to save the academy from the danger of closing when it had reached a low ebb, deposed in 932 by the Exilarch, after a lengthy and bitter dispute; reinstated in 937 and succeeded in reestablishing Sura as a major seat of learning and authority. One of the greatest and most versatile figures in Jewish history. A many faceted personality who excelled in each of his numerous undertakings—literary and public (except, perhaps, for "human relations"). Polemicist par excellence. Real-life and literary arch-opponent of Karaism and all other heresies and schisms from traditional Rabbinic Judaism. Champion of Babylonian supremacy in the Jewish world; of denying the right of Palestine (in the person of the Jerusalem academy head, Aaron b. Meir) to tamper with or change the established calendar or determine festivals; and of rallying the assistance (financial and other) of the outlying communities around the Babylonian academies (especially his own) and their authority. Prolific author of Talmudic legal literature. The first Jewish author to compose monographs on a single legal topic; the first to write complete legal works in Arabic; the first to write detailed introductions to his legal works. Extant—in the main—is his most important and influential treatise on prayers, *"Siddur,"* which includes the texts of many prayers and liturgical poems. His published treatise on "Inheritance" is in abridged form. There exist fragments of and/or citations from his works on "Testimony" and "Contracts," "Laws of Pledges," "Laws of Incest," on *"Terefot*,"* on the commandments, etc. He possessed encyclopedic knowledge of all the Rabbinic material which preceded him, which he put to full use in his monographs, responsa (many of which exist; they too, written for the most part, in Arabic) and rulings. His legal writings excelled in arrangement, organization, and order. The topics are broken down into categories, and ultimately into details which are explained with clarity and facility. His works were well known to all succeeding *geonim* who were deeply influenced by them (whether evoking agreement or refutation). Saàdya translated the Bible (into Arabic) and wrote a detailed commentary to a good part of it. He is perhaps most famous as the author (in Arabic) of the earliest medieval Jewish philosophic work (of rationalistic Mutazilite bend) to have remained intact (BELIEFS AND OPINIONS), which had far reaching influence and is a basis of Jewish philosophy. Author of many grammatical works, he is called "the first Hebrew grammarian." He was also a prolific poet and liturgist and was a historian. His son, Dosa, was Gaon of Sura (after R. Samuel b. Hofni*) from 1013 (Saadya may also have had a son called Sheerit, and other children). Of the massive bibliography available, especially noteworthy is H. Malter, SAADIA GAON HIS LIFE AND WORKS, Philadelphia, 1942, and the anniversary volumes that appeared c. 1942.

SAMUEL b. Hofni (RSBH). d. 1013. Father-in-law of Hai Gaon. Gaon of Sura* after Zemah b. Isaac, who was the first Gaon of Sura after it reopened during the tenure of Serira* as Gaon of Pumbedita*. Samuel b. Hofni was very much a follower of Saàdya* (albeit on a modest scale). Philosopher, anti-Karaite polemicist, commentator on Pentateuch, and prolific author of Biblical and Talmudic commentaries and of legal monographs (many composed as responsa; all modelled after Saàdya). None of his monographs have survived whole, in their original Arabic. Many were known to *rishonim* by the title "Gates of RSBH" *(Abwab* ["gates" or "chapters"] pl. of *bab)* because they were meticulously divided into chapters, each chapter dealing with a different aspect of the topic. In fact, he was somewhat more systematic even than Saàdya, but not as rich in sources (although he tends to mention his predecessors more often than Saàdya does). Two of his better known gates, published in an abridged Hebrew form, on "Benedictions" and Meat Inspection, were, in fact, probably sections of larger works. Among his monographs of which fragments (and/or citations) exist, are treatises on: Divorce, Prayer, Acquisition, Admissions, Abutters' Rights, Witnesses and Testimony, Guarantors, Zizit*, Manners of the Judges, Maintenance, Conditions, Partnership, Puberty, Rentals, and Debt Collection. He also authored the first systematic, all-encompassing (148 chapters) introduction to the Talmud and its methodology, including terminology, persons, rulings, etc. His works seem to have been well known to Hai Gaon. His son, Israel, also served as Gaon of Sura, from 1017 until his death in 1033.

SAR S(H)ALOM (b. Boaz). Gaon of Sura* (838-848). Authored many responsa known to later *geonim* and *rishonim.* They were collected and published, with an introduction, by Raphael Weinberg, Jerusalem, 1975, under the title: *TESUVOT RAV SAR S(H)ALOM GAON.*

SEMAH. See Zemah.

S(H)ERIRA Gaon. See RSG.

SIM(E)ON Qayara (BHG). Named by Hai Gaon as the author of *HALACHOTH GEDOLOTH* (HG), who used the *Halakot* of Yehudai Gaon* *(HALACHOT PESUQOT),* an unquestionably accurate and authoritative determination. Like *HALACHOT PESUQOT** before him (which served him as a major source) and the LAWS of RIF* after him (for which he served as a major source) *HALACHOTH GEDOLOTH* is an abridgement (extract or epitome) of the Babylonian Talmud (mainly the relevant legal material) following, as a rule, the order and language of the Talmud, more detailed and with more additions than *HALACHOT PESUQOT* but less than RIF. He gives the ruling as the summary of the *sugya* sometimes relying on the rulings of the academies, and on other *geonic* and early sources. The work became very widespread and has come down to us in a number of versions (some containing later additions). Nothing is really known about the author or his name. He seems to have been affiliated with the Babylonian academies, although he was never a Gaon.

YEHUDAI (b. Nahman) Gaon. Flourished in the middle of the eighth century. Most prominent and authoritative of the early *geonim*. Eminent scholar of the Pumbedita* academy. Appointed Gaon of Sura* at an advanced age although blind, in order to enhance Sura's declining prestige. He served for three and a half years. Author of the first post-Talmudic legal code called by the *Geonim* the *Halakot* of R. Yehudai, but identified (by Hai and others) with what we commonly call *HALACHOT PESUQOT* (HP, or in its Hebrew translation *HILKOT REÚ*). The work, in Babylonian Aramaic of the *geonim*, is a concise extract of the Babylonian Talmud, following—for the most part—its language and order, but extracting only the relevant legal material (not the whole discussion). The book was probably arranged by Yehudai's disciples. According to Hai it was used by Simeon Qayara* in his *HALACHOTH GEDOLOTH*, and obviously served him as a major source, as it was for the whole genre of legal codes which were Talmudic extracts (e.g., RIF*). Yehudai was a fighter for the supremacy of the Babylonian custom and tradition. There exists a large number of his brief responsa and/or rulings.

R. YERUHAM (or Jeroham. b. Mesulam). Flourished first part of the fourteenth century. Born in Provence, expelled 1306. Student of ROSH* in Toledo. Author of two legal codes, arranged topically:

> a. *Sefer Meisarim* on "civil law" and *TOLDOT ADAM AND EVE*, on ritual and personal law, arranged according to the life of a person from birth to death (the works, especially the latter are commonly called, simply, R. Yeruham). The originality is in the order rather than the subject matter, which mostly comprises the teachings of his predecessors. The codes are cited often by succeeding generations but were superseded by Jacob b. Asher's *Tur*

ZEMAH (or Semah b. Paltoi) Gaon. Gaon of Pumbedita* (872–c. 890). Great-great-grandfather of Hai Gaon. Reputed author of the first Talmudic dictionary.

II. Places

A selected list of places mentioned in the work.

BAGHDAD. Capital of Iraq (Babylonia). On the Tigris River. Capital of the Abbasid Dynasty (Caliphate) from its foundation (762) as a result of which it eventually became the seat of the Jewish Exilarch. The Pumbedita* academy moved there under the gaonate of Hai b. David (890-98). It is widely held that the Sura* academy shortly followed.

FEZ. City in north-central Morocco. Inhabited by Jews almost from its founding (789). A center of Jewish activity from the ninth century. In 987 a section of the community was deported to Aṣir. The community maintained a regular correspondence with the Babylonian academies in the tenth and eleventh centuries. RIF* spent most of his productive years there.

GABES (or Qabes or Qabis). Maritime town in Tunisia. Was an important commercial center. During the geonic period many of its Jews became wealthy merchants, others—e.g., Ibn Jama family—indulged in academic and intellectual pursuits, established an important academy, and maintained contacts with the Babylonian academies, and later with the important Spanish centers.

KAIROUAN. (Qayrawan). Tunisian coastal town south of Tunis. Leading Jewish cultural and economic center in North Africa during the middle ages. Many scholars from Baghdad* and elsewhere settled there. In the tenth and eleventh centuries there were two major academies in the city. Among their heads were Hananel b. Ḥusiel (RḤ*), Jacob b. Nissim*, Nissim b. Jacob (RNG*), all of whom had close connections with the geonim Ṣerira* and Hai, corresponded with them, sent them questions and received responsa, served as representatives or functionaries of the Babylonian academies, and/or incorporated geonic works into their own literary output.

MAGHREB. North Africa, Morroco, Algeria, and Tunisia of today. Home of Jewish communities from about 300 B.C.E. till the present day, and of important ones since the ninth century and all through the geonic era.

PUMBEDITA. A large commercial city in Babylonia (Iraq) on the Euphrates River.

Important Jewish community and religious center from mid-third century, when the amora, Judah b. Ezekiel* established an academy and court there. The academy, together with that of Sura, became one of the two leading academies for Torah study, for much of the following eight hundred years. It flourished for some hundred years after R. Judah, and then became subordinate of Sura. It made a comeback during the geonic era, especially after the ninth century. At the end of the ninth century, under the Gaonate of Hai b. David it was transferred to Baghdad, the seat of the Caliphate, but retained its name, customs, institutions, and traditions. During the Gaonate of Serira* and Hai it reached a new peak of bloom and authority.

Qab(e) (i)s. See Gabès.

SINAI, Mt. Mountain in the Sinai desert where, according to tradition, the Torah* was revealed to the Children of Israel, after their exodus from Egypt, on their way to the Land of Israel.

SURA. An agricultural city in Babylonia (Iraq) on the Euphrates River. The amora, Rav*, established it as a Jewish religious and Torah* center by founding the academy there (throughout its history referred to also as the academy of Mata Mahasya), which, together with that of Pumbedita*, became one of the two leading academies for Torah study, for much of the following eight hundred years. Rav's disciple, R. Huna*, maintained the standard of the academy, but after his death (end of the third century) its importance diminished until the days of R. Asi* (c. 335-427/8). After R. Asi's death it again gradually diminished in importance until geonic times, when it regained its status in the eighth and ninth centuries. In the beginning of the tenth century it again came upon difficult times. The Gaonate of Saàdya* provided a respite, but after his death it closed down. Although it reopened (during Serira's tenure in Pumbedita), it was overshadowed by Pumbedita* under Serira* and Hai. It is commonly held that the academy followed Pumbedita to Baghdad* early in the tenth century.

TLEMCEN. City in northwest Algeria whose Jewish community corresponded with the geonim in the tenth and eleventh centuries. After an abortive revolution (971-2) some of Tlemcen's Jews were expelled to Asir.

BIBLIOGRAPHY

I. Sources

A. *Chronological list of geonic responsa collections*

An annotated bibliography of the printed collections of Geonic Responsa, arranged in chronological order (of first editions).*

1. *KURZE GEONÄISCHE ENTSCHEIDUNGEN* (KGE), *erschienen zum ersten Male in Constantinople,* 1516. *Verbesserte Ausgabe, mit Einleitung, Commentar und Index versehen, von Dr. Joel Müller, Krakau,* 1893. The Hebrew title (of the Müller edition) is: *HALAḲOT PESUQOT MIN HA GEONIM.* The first edition is extremely rare.

The collection consists of 196 paragraphs, most of them superscribed with the name of the supposed author (the exceptions are 91, 107, and 194). In the Muller edition they are numbered, but in the first edition they were not; the name—in larger letters—serves as the divider between sections. Most of the assigned authors are *geonim;* but some nine are not, having been added to the collection by an early editor or copyist.

The paragraphs are not responsa in their original forms, but are, rather, abridged versions of responsa, or adaptations of the essential legal rulings which they contain (described best by the titles. The Hebrew title—*HALAḲOT PESUQOT*—is, in fact, the opening description of both parts of the collection. See below). Many of these brief rulings are not from responsa at all, but are extracts from other works.

Some paragraphs contain more than one sub-topic. Most likely they were gleaned from two or more responsa or other works, and were combined—by some later editor or copyist—into one paragraph revolving around a central topic. In many of these cases it was a number of rulings of the same Gaon which were combined into a single paragraph. In other cases, rulings of different *geonim* were joined into a single paragraph—because of the affinity between the topics of the rulings. When this happened, usually the name of only one of the *geonim* appeared at the head of the paragraph. This makes attempting to identify the author of the rulings an arduous and hazardous task (see, also, *Ha Ḥiluqim,* introduction, pp. 46-47). This practice of

---

*When citing or quoting from a source throughout the work, we use the last critical or "edited" edition.

combining related rulings of different *geonim* into a single paragraph probably explains the phenomenon (in paragraphs 131 and 157) of two names appearing in the superscription of a single paragraph (though it might be a case of the editor's, or copyist's, uncertainty or, even two conflicting traditions).

The paragraphs are generally grouped according to topic. The collection itself is divided into two sections. The first section (following the Müller edition 1-122) is arranged according to the books of Maimonides' MISHNEH TORAH. The heading of the section reads: "Legal rulings of the *geonim* and matters of prohibition and permission according to the Book of Seeds and according to the Book of Knowledge and according to the Book of Holiness [in the detailed "table of contents" as in the collection itself, there follows: Book of Adoration] and according to the Book of Cleanness and according to the Book of Asseverations [Distinction]," i.e., books 7, 1, 5, [2], 10, 4, 6. A very strange order indeed, though, verily, the common order of the Orders of the Mishnah begins with "seeds." Matters of prohibition and permission are grouped in KGE 91-95 with the appropriate heading.

The second section (Müller 123f.) is headed: "Legal rulings of the *geonim* and matters of prohibition and permission according to the [Mishnah] Order 'Set Feasts'," i.e., the equivalent of Book 3 of MISHNEH TORAH. Noticeably absent, then, are all matters of what we would call civil law (e.g., torts, acquisition, civil laws, judges, found in MT books 11-14 [of those names], damages, found in Talmud [Mishnah] Order of that name, and cases stemming from the marriage contract [deed] *ketubah* [the laws found in the tractate of that name]).

Most of the "responsa" found in KGE are also found in other collections of geonic responsa. KGE is related to ṢT and ṢZ, (see Hildesheimer *Komposition*, p. 46 f. and his tables pp. 78-85). See also Einleitung Ch. 2, and *HE ḤALUTZ* 8, 135 f.

2.   QUESTIONS AND RESPONSA OF THE *GEONIM*, consisting of 400 responsa of the early *geonim* in clear and simple language, first published in Constantinople in the year [5]335 (1575), again in Prague, c. [5]350 (1590), for the third time in Mantua in the year [5]357 (1597), and later for the fourth time in Vilna [5]644 (1884) . . . printed anew with major additions, 30 geonic responsa deleted by the censor in the Vilna edition . . . with glosses, comments, references, corrections, and omissions [and detailed indices] . . . by . . . T. Moskovitz, Jerusalem [5]720 (1960). (Often referred to as *Haqzarot* ["the brief

ones"] because of their form, or as *Hamudpasot* ["the printed ones"] because they were the first—and for over 200 years the only—geonic collection printed independently).

Not all the "geonic responsa" are actually geonic nor responsa. Post geonic authorities are cited (e.g., RIF in 284, *Tosafot* and *Posqim* in 288), and the last 50 are, in fact, rulings of the SUA, disguised as responsa. The responsa are not attributed to specific responders. Many are found in other responsa collections (some in less abridged form). See *Einleitung*, Ch. 3.

3. *SAAREI ZEDEQ (SZ)*, . . . Geonic responsa . . . published by . . . Nissim b. Hayim Modai . . . [5]552 (1792)] . . . in Salonika. Reprinted (different pagination) in Jerusalem 5726 (1966).

The manuscript (and consequently the printed work) is divided into sections *(heleq)* and chapters *(saàr)* [hence the name given to the collection], beginning with section three and ending abruptly after the second responsa in section four, chapter nine. According to the table of contents appearing before section four, it was meant to contain 10 chapters. The collection consists of 533 responsa.

The arrangment is topical, with each section and chapter carrying a heading. Section three, "The laws of *àrayot* [i.e., personal status] and other matters." The chapters on personal status are: levirate marriage, divorce, and marriage. The "other matters" are: mourning, circumcision, slaves, foodstuffs of gentiles, and proselytes. Section four, "Monetary ["civil"] laws and the like." Its chapters: torts, fines, pledges and securities, inheritance, gifts, *ketubah*, oaths, purchase and sales, court procedures, partnerships, rentals, loans, deposits and guardians and abbutters rights. The tenth chapter was meant to be: "Sundry items."

The names of the responders appear on some of the responsa and they include most of the important Babylonian *geonim*, and a number of the early Spanish authorities, and others. Some of the responsa carry superscriptions noting that they have been translated from the original Arabic.

The manuscript was discovered in Egypt by Hayim Modai of Safed, forty-three years prior to the printing of the book, as he notes in his *haskamah* ("printed consent"). Both his *haskamah*, which is actually an introduction to the book, and his addition of important notes and references to some of the responsa, lead us to speculate that he was the main editor of the book, though his son Nissim, the publisher, contributed a lengthy introduction and notes of a more technical nature. Their excitement at the discovery and publishing are understandable, since this was the first time a collection of lengthy geonic responsa was published. They may be excused for thinking—in that day and age—that "their responsa" were in their original form.

The manuscript of ṢZ is related to the Halberstam Ms. described in detail in *Einleitung* in the chapter dealing with ṢZ (Ch. 4. p. 13, and the notes throughout the chapter), and Hildesheimer (p. 11 f. and the table p. 18 f.) and to some degree to the Vienna Ms. *(Einleitung*, loc. cit.; Hildesheimer, 25 f.). Many corrections and supplements to ṢZ can be made from them, and scholarly conclusions about ṢZ can be drawn with their aid. Much of this has been done in the two works cited.

4. *SHAARE TESHUBAH* (ṢT), first published in Salonika, [5]562 (1802) *(NEHAROT DAMESEQ)* from a Ms. belonging to R. Moses Mordecai Meyuhas (1738-1805. Chief Rabbi of Jerusalem), again in Leipzig, 1858, with introductory notes and comments taken from a work of R. David Luria (this edition was faithfully photographed in New York, 1946, with a foreward, annotations, and references by R. Wolf Leiter). Rabbi Israel Moses Ḥazan composed an extensive commentary on ṢT (including comments to each responsum individually) by the name of *IYEY HAYAM*, which, in addition to his significant comments, includes citations and parallels from related mss., collections, and medieval sources. Unfortunately, the commentary was published only to the first 193 responsa (Leghorn, 1869).

The collection consists of 352 paragraphs (numbered to 353 in the ed. pr. because of a "counting" error). Not all are geonic, and many are not responsa at all. Some 26 paragraphs can be attributed to RIF and another dozen or so to other non-geonic authorities. S. Albeck included a study of this collection, inter alia, in his article, "*Meḥoqeqei Yehudah*," in the *FESTSCHRIFT ZU ISRAEL LEWY'S SIEBZIGSTERN GEBURTSTAG*, Breslau, 1911, Hebrew section, p. 104 f. He suggested (p. 128) that paragraphs 334 f. are compilations of the editor (a suggestion generally accepted). The "kabbalistic passages" in many of the other paragraphs are also suspect (despite the clever interpolation) as every scholar who has dealt with the collection has noticed (Luria's work, cit. sup., is an attempt to defend the "originality" of those passages).

Ḥazan was the first to propose (in *SEÉRIT HA NAḤALAH*, p. 13) that the geonic responsa (and other authentic material) in ṢT were copied from the works of R. Judah b.

Barzilai al-Bargeloni. The theme was developed in great detail by S. Albeck (op. cit., p. 119 f.). If it is indeed true (and it seems to be at least partly so), then the predominence of matters of daily ritual in the ṢT collection would suggest that the material was from al-Bargeloni's first volume, *Ha-Ittim*, which deals with these matters.

The ṢT collection was printed from a Ms. related to the Vivante-Almanzi-Gaster "family" of responsa mss. Since the "Lyck" collection (below, No. 7) was also printed from this family (Vivante?) there are many parallels between Lyck and ṢT (see Albeck, loc. cit., Hildesheimer, p. 34 f. and the tables on pp. 39-42, 57, and J. Tavory, "Sources of the Geonic Responsa collection *'Sha'arei-Teshuvah'*," ALEI SEFER 3, p. 5 f.). There are also many parallels to KGE (as can be seen from the tables in Hildesheimer, p. 80 f. and Albeck p. 122 f.). The al-Bargeloni connection seems to be a major factor in the relationships between the collections, although later scholars have diminished the al-Bargeloni factor to a major (rather than "the sole") source (see Tavory op. cit., p. 6, n. 12). The Almanzi-Vivante-Gaster connection to ṢT had also better be downgraded just a bit, since in reality none of the mss. contain a majority of the ṢT geonic responsa as we readily see from the tables cited.

Many of the responsa have superscriptions of authorship. They are generally reliable with two reservations: 1. They apply only to the responsum immediately following the superscription. 2. References such as *lo* or *we'od lo* ("to him" or "to him too") do not necessarily refer to the author immediately preceding in ṢT but might refer to the author immediately preceding in the original Ms. from which the ṢT Ms. has been copied. Since not every responsum was copied from that original Ms., such superscriptions can be, and often are, misleading.

5. *DIE RECHTSGUTACHTEN DER GEONIM* (DRG), Nach einer Handschrift [Berlin, Kaiser Ms. or qu. 685] herausgegeben von David Cassel, mit einer Einleitung von S.L. Rapoport, Berlin, 1848. (Hebrew: *TEṢUVOT GEONIM QADMONIM*).

The Hebrew introduction by Rapoport (which is in addition to the editor's German introduction) is a very significant study. Even more important is the review by J. N. Epstein in JJLG 9, pp. 214-305, which is in reality a monumental study of the collection, its manuscript, parallel mss., variants, responders, etc. (a review also appeared in Heḥalutz 8, 135 f.).

The collection consists of 153 sections, not all proper responsa. Some are attributed to specific authors, geonic and non-geonic. Rapoport points out that the collection is arranged not topically (which would have been a sure sign of late arrangement) but according to responders. He believed that some of these groups of responsa of the same responder, were (at least in part [from]) original pamphlets of responsa (on "original pamphlets" see appendix "Pamphlets"). There is no solid foundation for this belief (cf. e.g., Epstein, loc. cit., 220-25; RNG, introduction, pp. 30-31). There is likewise no basis for Rapoport's assumption that the collection is the one copied by Joseph B. Samuel Bonfils (Tov Elem). In fact, the collection does not appear to be an original collection, nor to be composed of original pamphlets. (See also, *Einleitung*, Ch. 6).

6. *ḤEMDAH GENUZAH* (HGN), Jerusalem, 5623 (1863), 166 responsa of *geonim* and early Spanish authorities, printed from a Jerusalem Ms. by two brothers-in-law, Z. W. Wolfinsohn and S. Z. Schneerson.

The collection is divided into groups, most of which carry the name of the responder as a heading. The attributions seem to be a moderately reliable tradition, particularly applicable to the first responsum (or first few responsa) in the group. Regarding the Ms. from which the collection was printed, and others akin to it, and what can be learned from them about responsa collections, see, most recently, S. Z. Havlin, "Concerning one manuscript that was split in two," ALEI SEFER 1 and 2.

7. *Geonic Responsa* (Lyck) copied from a Ms. collection, edited and annotated by Rabbi Jacob Musafia, Lyck, 5624 (1864).

In his introduction the editor informs us that the book was printed from a Ms. which included—inter alia—geonic responsa in two sections, 124 paragraphs in the first section and one hundred and ten in the second section, and that not all the paragraphs are geonic responsa, but include gleanings from later medieval works. Two years after "the Lyck" publication, the editors published (also in Lyck) additional comments and corrections to the book by S. Buber and S. Z. H. Halberstam. They both noted that the majority of the responsa printed in Lyck had already been printed in ST. A simple conclusion must therefore be that the Ms. of Lyck must have been identical with or akin to one of the mss. of the ṢT family (see also *Einleitung* Ch. VIII). Therefore, much of what we said regarding the ṢT family applies here too. Our references there are also relevant here (e.g., Hildesheimer). See in particular J. Tavory, op. cit., p. 13 f. regarding the relationship between Lyck and the Vivante Ms.

8. *Gaonaische Gutachten* . . . Nach einer Handschrift in Hebron herausgegeben von Rabbiner N. Coronel aus Jerusalem . . . Wien, 5631.

The Ms. was from the collection of R. Judah Bibas, who was a world traveller. The collection contains one hundred and seventeen paragraphs, many of which are not geonic responsa. Even those that are, appear in a far from original form. See, also, *Einleitung*, Ch. IX.

9. *HALACHISCHE SCHRIFTEN DER GEONIM* (HSG), . . . herausgegeben von C. M. Horowitz, Frankfurt a.M., 1881. (Hebrew: *TORATAN SEL RISONIM*).

Legal and liturgical works of *geonim* and other early authorities, published from mss. in two sections. Section one contains a collection of twenty-six "geonic responsa" (pp. 45-53), eighteen of which seem to be proper geonic responsa, all but one with superscriptions identifying the responder (although not every identification is accurate). The second section is largely made up of geonic responsa—or supposed geonic responsa—from various mss. Here too, most (though not all) are authentic, but not all the identifying superscriptions are accurate; some are not in their proper place, thereby making the attributions even more misleading. A review appeared in *HEHALUTZ* 12, pp. 94-104.

10. *RESPONSEN DER GEONIM* (RDG) . . . *Nebst Ammerkungen und Einleitung von Dr. A. Harkavy*, Berlin, 1887.

This collection, published as the fourth part of *STUDIEN UND MITTHEILUNGEN AUS DER KAISERLICHEN OEFFENTLICHEN BIBLIOTHEK ZU ST. PETERSBURG* (with extensive notes and comments), represented a major breakthrough in the publication of geonic responsa, and a milestone in their study. It remains to this day the most important collection of geonic responsa ever published. They were taken from mss. in the Firkovitch collection, described in detail in the editor's preface, which means that they probably stem from the Cairo *Genizah* or some other ancient eastern source. Although we cannot accept the editor's assumption that the responsa were copied from the archives of the Babylonian Academies, there can nevertheless be little doubt that they have been well preserved, with the principal part of the responsum in most cases, varying but little from its original form.

The collection—printed from four mss.—contains five hundred and fifty nine responsa and/or questions, over one hundred and seventy in the original Arabic (including responsa of RIF). The responsa in Ms. 4 are almost all original Arabic responsa of Saàdya Gaon. There are a number of factors which attest to the authenticity of the collection as copied by Harkavy, particularly the first, or main, manuscript (from which a majority of the responsa were copied). We refer to its authenticity as an "early" and reliable replica of the original responsa, i.e., from an "early" collection in contrast with collections published before RDG and the *Genizah*. These factors are: its orthography; the responsum appearing in full, as a rule, including a discussion of the relevant Talmudic passages; the large number of Judeo-Arabic (Arabic dialect in Hebrew script) responsa [the editor provided Hebrew translations]; a good many questions not only appear, but were left intact not abridged nor abruptly terminated by "etc."; the name(s) and/or locale of the questioners often appears at the head of a group of questions; the date of the responses to a group of questions sometimes appears at the group's close as does a notation of the number of questions responded to in that group; all or parts of many of the salutations of the questioners attached to the first of a group of questions have been preserved; so have some of the preambles of the responders to the first responsum of a group and many of their closing greetings attached to the last responsum of a group; the lack of any attempt at a topical arrangement; many of the groups, in fact, comprise parts, most, or (in a rare case or two) perhaps all of original pamphlets of responsa (see appendix "Pamphlets"). Many of these characteristics were already noted by the editor (or reviewers cited below).

On the other hand, unfortunately even in this superb collection, many of the questions and introductions were unable to escape the editor's (or copyist's) abridgement. Moreover, Harkavy even then realized that the multiple numbering system found on the responsa, represented various stages of recopying from earlier collections, and the combining of collections. The multiple numbers are valuable in enhancing our knowledge or original pamphlets and groups, by teaching us that there were responsa which at one time formed part of the group and no longer do, or that responsa which are now part of a group, were not always so. Hence, it cannot be that this collection was actually copied from the archives of the academies (see, also, the reviews cited below), for, in fact, the groups—for the most part—are not exact replicas of original pamphlets (see appendix "Pamphlets" and our article in ALEI SEFER 2). Since the publication of *Genizah* material in later collections (see, e.g., below, and the text we published in ALEI SEFER 8) we have a clearer picture of what early copies of responsa and collections looked like. Despite these reservations, the Harkavy Collection remains to this day a most outstanding major collection of large masses of responsa, closely resembling their original form, and a major source of at least parts of original pamphlets and groups.

A detailed review was published by Schor in HEHALUTZ 13, pp. 47-93 and by J. Müller in *Einleitung*, Ch. XI. The collection was photographed and published with additional comments in New York, 1959, and in Jerusalem, 5727 with an index to the Talmudic literature.

A supplement to the collection, containing eight responsa or fragments thereof from yet another Ms. was published by Harkavy under the title "Old and New" part 2, pamphlet 4, in *HA PELES* 2, 5662, pp. [71-] 77 (and also A. E. Harkavy, *HADASIM GAM YESANIM*, Jerusalem, 5730, pp. 349-55). Another group of eight responsa (from the Antonin Ms. 333) was published by Harkavy under the same title, (*HADASIM GAM YESANIM*, part 2, pamphlet 10, in Hakedem 2, 1908, p. 82 f. Jerusalem ed. cit. sup., 426-34).

11.   *RESPONSEN DER LEHRER DES OSTENS UND WESTENS* (RLOW), nach Handschriften herausgegeben und erklart von Dr. Joel Müller, Berlin, 1888.

Most of the responsa were originally published by Müller in *BEIT HATALMUD* 4-5. The full collection contains a topical index. Its 235 responsa and legal decisions of *geonim* and European Rabbis—many carrying the attributed author's name in superscription—were gleaned from four different mss.:

A.   1-130.   A Ms. from the Halberstam collection related to the mss. from which KGE and SZ were published (see above). The Ms. contains responsa of *geonim* and European authorities. It begins with long responsa, continues with shorter ones, and ends with short legal rulings. That is precisely the order in which the editor has published them in this section, choosing only those which had not been published in one of the earlier related collections

B.   131-138.   From a Vienna Kaiser Ms. (XII. 125 [120]) whose missing first part became the De Rossi Ms. from which group C was published. This Ms. is related to the Ms. from which SZ was published. See S. Assaf cited below, collection 16.

C.   139-151. From a Parma Ms. De Rossi Ms. or qu. 685 (3525). This was at one
time the first part of the Ms. from which group B was published. See our
reference above.

D.   152-155. From the same Ms. as group A.

E.   226-235. Were gleaned from the Ms. from which DRG was published. These
paragraphs were not published in DRG (see above).

As a general rule, what we wrote about the collections related by way of the
mss. is true of RLOW as well. See also, *Einleitung*, Ch. XII.

12.   *KOHELET SHLOMO*, responsa of *geonim* and other early authorities with notes
and references by S. A. Wertheimer, Jerusalem, 5659. Sections 21-40 had been published
previously by the editor in his *GINZEI YERUSHULAYIM*, Jerusalem 5656, part 1, pp. 1-
10.

The collection consists of seventy two responsa collected from Genizah mss.
The Arabic responsa are given in Hebrew translation; the Arabic original being published
en petite at the end of the volume. The mss. are not of the same quality as those in
RDG. There do not seem to be any original pamphlets in the collection. On pp. 69-73
are lists of geonic responsa (corrected by Mann, in Tarbiz 6, p. 240 and Lewin, in GNK 3,
p. 81) which are always very valuable (see appendix "Pamphlets" and our article in ALEI
SEFER 2). An important review was published by Poznanski in MGWJ 44, pp. 142-44.

13.   GEONICA [vol.] 2, "Genizah Studies" (Geonica) by Louis Ginzberg. Hebrew
title: RESPONSA OF THE GEONIM FROM THE CAIRO GENIZAH, with corrections and
comments. New York, 5669, (Volume one is entitled: THE GEONIM AND THEIR
HALAKIC WRITINGS, New York, 1909).

The volume contains geonic responsa (many preserved in almost their original
forms), fragments of responsa (some of the responsa and fragments comprise parts of
original pamphlets or of early arrangements of groups of responsa), responsa lists,
Talmudic commentaries, and fragments of larger works of the geonic period. There are
forty seven sections in all, each with an English introduction. Corrections based on the
mss. were published by Lewin in GNK 1, pp. 93-104. A detailed review was published by
Poznanski in JQR, NS, 3, pp. 397-425.

14.   *GAONI RESPONSUMOK* ... kiadta, fordittota, es magyareizatokkal ellata Kis
Ch. Henrik, Budapest, 1912. Printed from two Genizah fragments from the D. Kaufmann

collection.

There are three main groups of responsa in this collection. The first one (in Arabic) contains responsa of RIF. The second (in Hebrew) contains part of a pamphlet of RHG's responsa. The third (in Arabic) is part of a group authored by Saàdya Gaon. Poznanski added a review of this collection as a postscript to his review of GEONICA, JQR, NS 3, pp. 426-27.

15a. *GENIZA FRAGMENTE DER BIBLIOTHEK DAVID KAUFMANN* . . . Herausgegeben von Dr. Max Weiz, Budapest, 1924.

Fragments 6-9 (pp. 24-33) of this collection are fragmented or abridged responsa, published with comments.

15b. *Festschrift zum 50 Jahrigen Bestehen der Franz-Josef-Landsrabbiner Schule in Budapest*, Budapest, 1927.

On pp. 77-97 Weiz published a companion collection to a., consisting mostly of exegetical responsa. The two sections were published together in a photographic edition, Jerusalem, [5]729.

16. *Geonic Responsa* (MH) . . . published by S. Assaf, Jerusalem, [5]687. Originally section 1 of *Madaèi Hayahadut*, book 2.

The responsa are taken from a number of non-Genizah mss., described in detail in the editor's introduction:

A.   1-23. Ms. Parma, De Rossi 65 (3525) from which Müller published 139-151 of RLOW. The Ms. is the "missing first part" of the Ms. from which Müller published 131-138 in RLOW. These responsa are, for the most part, full length and whole.

B.   24-44. From an Oxford Ms. (658) of SBHL vol. II, which was initially published in installments by Ḥasidah. The installments were photographed together in Jerusalem [5]729.

C.   45-51. Originally published in KRS I, pp. 117-126, from a Jerusalem, National Library, Ms.

D.   52-58. Originally published in *JESCHURUN*, 12, Berlin, 1925, pp. 45-54 from Cambridge Univ. Library Ms. Add. 474.

E.   59-62. Gleaned from the Eskol (Paris Ms. used for variants in the Albeck ed., Jerusalem, 5695-98).

F.   63. From the Genizah*.

G.   The rest of the responsa are taken from "Gleanings from *SEFER HADIN* of R. Judah b. Barzilai al-Bargeloni," published as the second section of this collection from a British Museum Ms. Add. 21.181 (Margaliouth catalogue, 2, no. 565).

17.   GEONIC RESPONSA (Marmorstein) from [Genizah] mss., with an introduction and notes by A. Marmorstein, Deva, [5]688.   Published as a supplement to *OZAR HACHAIM*.

Some are lengthy. Some are fragmented. Not all are geonic. There are also a number of responsa lists. This small collection abounds in copyist's and printer's errors. A critical review was published in KRS 5, pp. 335-36 by S. Assaf.

re *OZAR HACHAIM:* In vol. 3, 5687, pp. 97-102. E. Hildesheimer published a few responsa from manuscript.

18.   GAONIC RESPONSA (GRA), from Geniza mss. edited with prefatory and other notes by Simcha Assaf, Jerusalem, 1928.

The collection contains two hundred and seventy-seven geonic responsa or fragments, including parts of original pamphlets, most in an early form typical of good Genizah mss.   Many of the responsa are from the earlier *geonim*, a relatively rare phenomenon among the Genizah collections. The bulk are from the Antonin collection and other Leningrad collections.

19.   GENIZAH STUDIES in memory of Doctor Solomon Schechter, 2, Geonic and Early Karaitic Halakah (GNS), by Louis Ginzberg, New York, 1929.

The volume contains an English preface and Hebrew introduction. Most of the first eighteen sections (and some seventeen in all) contain geonic responsa.   Three sections (43-45) are devoted to important responsa lists. Again, as is common in Genizah material, many of the responsa have been preserved in a very good (early) form. Detailed reviews were published by S. Assaf in KRS 6, pp. 328-34, by B. M. Lewin in JQR 22, pp. 35-41, and by J. Mann in THE AMERICAN JOURNAL OF SEMITIC LANGUAGES AND LITERATURES, v. 46: 4, July 1930, pp. 263-83.

20.   GAONICA (Misifrut) Gaonic Responsa and Fragments of Halachic Literature from the Genizah and other Sources, edited . . . with an introduction and notes by Simha Assaf . . . Jerusalem, 1933. Hebrew title, *MISIFRUT HAGEONIM*.

Eight of its thirty-one sections contain geonic responsa (9-16, pp. 101-159), some from large collections of geonic responsa, which had been compiled from various early collections. Others clearly meet the criteria of early copies, close to the original: names of questioners; salutations; Judeo-Arabic originals, etc. A detailed review by S. Lieberman appeared in Tarbiz, 5, pp. 395-400.

21.   *RESPONSA GEONICA* (RGA) ex Fragmentis Cantabrigiensibus Collegit Edidit annotavit S. Assaf . . . Jerusalem, 1942.

The collection contains a wealth of important material even though—as the editor notes in his introduction—many of the fragments were in a poor state. Not all the responsa are geonic, nor is all the geonic material responsa. The bulk, however, does consist of geonic responsa, containing all these elements of early Genizah material: orthography; full responsa and questions; early collections and even parts of original pamphlets; names of responders (especially later *geonim*) and of questioners and their abodes; greetings, introductions and closing remarks; Judeo-Arabic originals, etc. The collection also contains lists of geonic responsa.

22.   *OTZAR HA GEONIM* (OG), Thesaurus of the Gaonic Responsa and Commentaries, following the order of the Talmudic Tractates, by Dr. B. M. Lewin, vol. 1-13 (The last—BM—incomplete), Haifa-Jerusalem, 1928-44.

This major work differs from the collections discussed previously, in that, for the most part, it is a compilation assembled from previously printed material, rearranged. Nevertheless, so significant is this masterpiece's contribution, as to justify its presence among "the sources." Lewin assembled geonic responsa and citations from all the known collections, from the published works of post-geonic authorities and from many mss. containing geonic and Rabbinic material. He arranged them according to the Tractates of the Talmud i.e., any geonic material relating to the Talmudic passage, be it exegetical material, comments on the text, or a responsum discussing a legal point relevant to the text, are all arranged according to that Talmudic pericope.

Each volume is divided into two major parts, responsa and commentaries. This division is a bit artificial since many responsa are commentaries to or explanations of the Talmudic text, and many of the so-called commentaries are, in fact, segments of responsa or other works (not necessarily commentaries per se). But this is a minor inconvenience. The major parts are divided into subsections. The subsections are arranged under citations of the relevant Talmudic pericopae. Each *original unit* (responsum, commentary, or portion of a larger commentary) is given a consecutive number (i.e., section). In the larger volumes the commentaries begin anew with "one" ("aleph"). In the smaller ones, their numbers run on. Some volumes have additional parts containing commentaries of RḤ and other early post-geonic authorities, who often cite or rely on geonic tradition.

Lewin excelled in the arrangement and organization of his material. He possessed an uncanny knack of reproducing the original unit effectively and authentically from among the various fragments and citations, giving each unit its own section. His keen eye caught and recognized different traditions of the same responsum or commentary, and he printed them in parallel columns within the same section (rather than giving them consecutive numbers). He divided different citations or fragments, all stemming from the same source, into *different* paragraphs (or sentences) under the same subsection, thereby reconstructing that original source. He juxtaposed divergent geonic opinion into consecutive sections, in an order that emphasized most forcefully that the latter view was held in specific contrast to the earlier one. When a medieval scholar cites or refers to a text which Lewin has printed in a more complete version—from a collection, Ms., or other medieval author—reference to that scholar is duly recorded in the notes.

This arrangement makes the work very easy to use advantageously, since one finds all material related to any particular Talmudic passage (and consequently to any narrow topic mentioned in the tractate) in close proximity and logically juxtaposed. The detailed indices of subjects, authors, book titles, customs, rulings, and sundry topics, found in each volume, further facilitate OG's use.

Since OG, being a later work, is commonly found in most libraries, because it is so easy to use and to locate the desired material in it, and whereas it almost always contains most of the important parallels (citations or versions) of the geonic pericopae, we have cited OG extensively throughout this work and give references according to it, on almost every occasion that the pericope we were alluding to was, in fact, to be found in OG. We cited according to the consecutive numeration of the subsections. If we did not specify otherwise, the first part of the volume—the responsa—is always meant. When we were referring to the commentaries (in the volumes that begin anew from 1 ["aleph"]), or to a supplementary part (medieval non-geonic commentaries) we said so explicitly.

The wealth of citations from OG throughout this work attest to the enormous debt we (and all those engaged in the study of the *geonim* and their works) owe to Lewin. In gracious payment, Prof. S. Abramson devoted Ch. IX of *Inyanot* to OG.

22a. OG SANHEDRIN, responsa and commentaries edited by H. T. Toibes, Jerusalem, 1966.

Toibes attempted to follow the same pattern as Lewin but eliminated the artificial division between "responsa" and "commentaries." Unfortunately he lacked Lewin's instinctive feel for the material, and the volume is a discredit to the author and to the publishing house. There are numerous errors and omissions. Countless sections are actually variant versions of the same source. Many entries cannot be considered geonic by any stretch of the imagination. Often the editor does not draw simple conclusions from material that he himself cited in the book, and so on. This volume just serves to intensify our sorrow that Lewin did not complete his work.

22b. *GINZE KEDEM* (GNK), "A Geonitic Scientific Periodical," by Dr. B. M. Lewin, 6 volumes, Haifa-Jerusalem, 1922-44.

This periodical should be mentioned here, right after OG, because of the large quantity of geonic (mostly of the later *geonim*) and early Rabbinic material which was published in its six volumes. The material includes responsa, groups of responsa and parts of original pamphlets, responsa lists, fragments of legal monographs, commentaries, poetry, etc. Most of it was copied from Genizah mss. Much of it was also published in OG. The main contributor was Lewin himself, but he was joined by all his major contemporaries among the scholars of the period. Detailed reviews—with additions and corrections—of the volumes were published in various forums, e.g., REJ 76, p. 99 f. (GNK 1, by A. Marmorstein), DVIR 1, pp. 310-12 and 2, pp. 322-34 (GNK 1 and 2 by J. N. Epstein), KRS 2, p. 182 f. (GNK 3, by S. Assaf), and S. H. Kook, *IYUNIM UMEHQARIM*, vol. 2, pp. 336-40 (GNK 4).

B. *Alphabetical list of responsa collections* ("Tesubot" or "Seélot utesubot")

Responsa collections (other than the printed geonic collections), arranged alphabetically according to the name (or acronym, when common) of the responder, or the collections (when applicable) or of the title in Latin letters (where one exists).

ABRAHAM B. ISAAC, ed. Y. Kafah, Jerusalem, 5722.

ABRAHAM MAIMUNI, *RESPONSA* ... A. H. Freimann ... S. D. Goiten, Jerusalem, 1937.

ALMANZI MANUSCRIPT OF GEONIC RESPONSA. V. A 4 and 7.

R. MEIR'S VON ROTHENBURG ... *RESPONSEN* ... von ... M. Bloch, Berlin, 1891.

R. MOSES AL ASQAR, *Sabbioneta*, 1553, Jerusalem, 1959.

R. MOSES B. MAIMON *RESPONSA* ... J. Blau, Hierosolymis, MCMLVII (1947).

RAN, Rome 5305, Koenigsberg 5622.

TESHUVOT SHE'ELOT LEHARASHBA, [facsimile of] First ed., Rome ca. 1470, Jerusalem, 1976.

RDBZ, Venice 5509, Sudylkow, 1836.

RESPONSA ET DECISIONS ... ed. ... E. Kupfer, Jerusalem 5733.

RIBAS, Vilna, 5639.

RITBA, ed. Y. Kafah, Jerusalem, 5719.

ROSH, Venice, 5312, Jerusalem, 5731.

RESPONSA OF THE SAGES OF PROVENCE, published by A. Schreiber, Jerusalem, 5727.

TESUBOT MAIMONIYOT, in the standard editions of MISHNEH TORAH.

C.   Other works (listed alphabetically by title)

ARUCH COMPLETUM ... *auctore Nathane filio Jechielis* ... edit A. Kohut, 8 v., Vienna-New York, 1878-1892.

ARUGAT HABOSEM, auctore R. ABRAHAM B. R. AZRIEL ... ed ... E. E. Urbach, 4 vol., Jerusalem, 1939-1963.

BAÁLEY HANEFES, RABD, ed. Y. Kafah, Jerusalem, 5725.

THE BABYLONIAN TALMUD (BT) ... Translated into English with notes, glossary, and indices under the editorship of I. Epstein, London, Soncino Press, 1935-48. The translation is based on the text of the Romm edition, Vilna. At our discretion we revised the translation, elaborated on it or supplemented it by interpolations. Our references are by tractate and pages. The page references are to the standard editions, which normally contain parallel references (s.n.) in Masoret Hasas. The standard abbreviations are used for the names of the tractates.

BABYLONIAN TALMUD, tractates *Baba Qama, Baba Mezià,* and *Baba Batra,* with a Hebrew translation, commentary, variants and references, ed. J. N. Epstein, Jerusalem, 1952-58.

BABYLONIAN TALMUD, THE TREATISE TA'ANIT, critically edited ... by H. Malter, New York, 1930.

BAYIT HADAS v. Tur.

BEIT JOSEPH v. Tur.

BETH HABEHIRA ON THE TALMUDICAL TREATISE SHABBATH by R. Menahem Hameiri, edited . . . by I. S. Lange, Jerusalem, 1965.

THE BOOK OF TRADITION by Abraham Ibn Daud, a critical edition with a translation and notes by G. Cohen, Philadelphia, 1967.

CAFTOR WA-PHERACH, (CP), *par Estori ha-Parchi, adjecit H. Edelmann*, Berolini 1852, A. M. Luncz, Jerusalem, 1897.

DARKEI MOSHE. v. *TURIM.*

A DIGEST OF COMMENTARIES ON THE TRACTATES *BĀBHĀ KAMMĀ BĀBHĀ Me̱ṢĪ'Ā* and *BĀBHĀ BHĀTHe̱RĀ* (DCA) . . . compiled by Zachariah Ben Judah Aghmāti . . . edited . . . by J. Leveen, London, 1961.

AN ELEVENTH CENTURY INTRODUCTION TO THE HEBREW BIBLE . . . edited . . . by E. N. Adler, Oxford, 1897.

EPISTLE OF SERIRA. See *IGERETH.*

ESKOL, Abraham b. Isaac, ed. Auerbach, 3 vol., Halberstadt 5628-29, ed. S. and H. Albeck, 2 vol., Jerusalem 5695-98 (references to vol. [part] 1-2, are to the Albeck edition and to vol. [part] 3, to the Auerbach).

THE ETZ HAYYIM. R. Jacob ben Jehuda Hazan of London, edited . . . by I. Brodie, 3 vol., Jerusalem, 1962-67.

EVEN HAEZER, RABN (RABN), ed. S. Z. Ehrenreich, Samboya, 5686.

FRAGMENTS OF THE GEONIC COMMENTARY TO TRACTATE SHABBATH, pub. E. Hurvitz, HADOROM, 46, pp. 123-227 and 49, pp. 67-118.

DER GAONÄISCHE KOMMENTAR ZUR MISCHNAORDNUNG TEHAROTH (DGK), ed. J. N. Epstein, Berlin, 1921.

GIDULEI TERUMAH. See *TERUMOT.*

HAGAHOT HARAMAK, R. Moshe Hakohen, ed. J. Kohn, Jerusalem, 5730.

HAGAHOT MAIMONIOT (HGHM), in all standard editions of *Mishneh Torah.*

HAHILUQIM, ed. M. Margalioth, Jerusalem, 5698.

HALACHOTH GEDOLOTH. R. Ṣim(e)on Qayara (BHG), Venice, 5308, ed. A. S. Troib, Warsaw, 5635, (HG), nach dem Texte der Handschrift der Vaticana, Herausgegeben . . . von J. Hildesheimer, Berlin, 1888 (HGB).
Sefer Halakhot Gedolot . . . ed. E. Hildesheimer, 2 vol., Hierosolymis, 1971-80.

HALACHOTH KEZUBOTH, edited . . . by Mordecai Margulies, Jerusalem, 1942.

HALACHOT PESUQOT auctore R. Jehudai Gaon . . . ed. . . . . S. Sasoon, Jerusalem, 1950.

HALACHOT OF R. YITZHAK ALFASI (RIF), facsimile ed. of Ed. Constantinople 1509, Jerusalem, 1973, and in standard editions of Babylonian Talmud.

HALIKOT OLAM, R. Yeṣuàh Halevi (with *KELALEI HAGEMARA* of R. Joseph Qaro, et al.), Warsaw, 1883.

HAMAKRIA, R. Isaiah di Trani, with commentary by N. H. Lifṣiz, Lublin 5657. Our references are to sections according to the Munkacs edition, 5660 (just text).

HAMAOR (BHM), to the RIF, in the standard editions.

HASAGOT HARABAD (RABAD), to MISHNEH TORAH in the standard editions, and to RIF and HAMAOR in the standard editions.

HASAGOT HARAMAK, R. Moshe Hakohen, ed. S. Atlas, Jerusalem, 5729.

HIDUSEI HA ["*NOVELLAE OF*"] RAMBAN, to various tractates, 2 vol., ed., I. Z. Melzer, Jerusalem, 5688, 3 vol., ed. M. Hersler, Jerusalem, 1970-76, *HIDDUSHE HA'RAMBAN* on Hullin, ed. S. Reichman, New York, 1955.

HIDUSEI HA RAN, to various tractates, a photo offset edition of various editions, New York, 5706; ditto, New York, 1965.

HIDUSEI HA RASHBA, to various tractates, a photographic edition in 3 volumes, Jerusalem, 5723.

HIDUSEI HA RITBA, to various tractates, a critical edition, Mossad Harav Kook, Jerusalem, vol., 1974—and in standard editions. *HIDDUSHE HA'RITBA* ... on the tractate Sabbath ... ed. .... S. Reichman, Monsey, 1966.

HILKHOT HANNAGID, R. Shmuel *Hannagid*, ed. M. Margalioth, Jerusalem, 1962.

HILKOT SEHITAH, ,R. Samuel b. Jama (HS), Oxford ms. 793 (fragments in the article by Steinschneider listed in the "studies" section).

IGERETH [LETTER ("EPISTLE") OF] RAV SHERIRA GAON, (IGRSG or Epistle), ed. A. Hyman, London, 5671, B. M. Lewin, Haifa, 5681.

ITTUR, Isaac b. Aba Mari, Venice, 5368; vol. 2, Sepher Jttur, ed. S. Sehnblum, Lemberg, 1860. Vol. 1-3, ed. M. Jonah, Vilna-Warsaw, 5634-45.

IYEY HAYAM. See IA4 (Bibliography).

KATUV SHAM, RABD, ed. B. Bergman, Jerusalem 1957; ed. M. Z. Hasidah (offprint from installments in *HASGULAH*), Jerusalem, no date.

KELALEI HAGEMARA. See *HALIKOT OLAM.*

KESEF MISHNEH. See MISHNEH TORAH.

KORE HADOROT, R. David Conforte, ed. D. Cassel, Berolini, 1846.

LEB SAMEAH, A. Aligeri, Constantinople, 5412.

LEXICON HEBRAICUM ("*MAHBERET HEARUK*"), Salomonis b. Abrahami Parchon ... ed. S. G. Stern, Posonii, MDCCCXLIV.

LIBER JUCHASSIN, A. Zacuti, ed. H. Filipowski, London-Edinburg, 1857.

MAASEH HA- GEONIM, Berlin, 1909.

MAGID MISHNEH (MM), In standard editions of MISHNEH TORAH.

MASEKET SOFRIM, ed. M. Higer, New York, 5697.

MEISARIM, R. Yeruham b. Mesulam, Venice, 5313.

MEKACH UMEMKAR (MQM), R. Hai Gaon, Venice, 5362, Wien 5560.

MEKILTA, ed. and translated by J. Lauterbach, Philadelphia, 1933.

METHIBOTH, by B. M. Lewin, Jerusalem, 1933.

MIGDAL ÒZ. In the standard editions of MISHNEH TORAH, see its entry.

MILḤAMOT HASEM. RMBN, in standard editions of RIF.

THE MISHNAH (M) translated . . . by H. Danby, London, 1950 (reprinted from the 1933 edition). We used the Danby edition because it is commonly and readily available, in one volume. We have revised the translation at our discretion, with particular attention to the work of the editor of this series, Prof. J. Neusner, noted in "studies" (Bibliography II). References are to Tractate, chapter, and *Mishnah.*

MISHNEH TORAH (MT or "Yad Haḥazaqah"), Maimonides, Rome ca. 5340, and the standard editions which include Hasagot Harabad ("Rabad's critical glosses"), Magid Mishneh of Don Vidal de Tolasa (MM), Hagahot Maimoniot (HGHM) by R. Meir Hacohen, Migdal Òz by R. Sem Tov b. Gaon, Kesef Mishneh by R. Joseph Qaro, Teṣubot Maimoniyot, etc.

MISPETEI ṢABUÒT (MPS), R. Hai Gaon, Venice, 5362, Jerusalem, no date.

NEMUQEI JOSEPH, R. Joseph b. Ḥaliba, commentary to RIF on some tractates, in the standard editions.

ORCHOTH CHAJIM (ORH), von R. Aharon Hakohen aus Lunel. Part I, Florence 5510, Jerusalem 5716. *Zweiter Teil* . . . von M. Schlesinger, Berlin, 1902.

ÒR ZARUÀ (OZ), R. Isaac b. Moses of Vienna, Sections 1-2, Zhitomir 5622, sections 3-4, Jerusalem, 5647.

OTZAR HILLUF MINHAGIM (OHM), by B. M. Lewin, Jerusalem, 5702.

PEQUDAT HALEWYIM, Mainz, 5634.

PERUS BASAFAH HAÀRABIT LEÈHAD MIḤAḲMEI YAHADUT TEIMAN, a commentary to RIF, tractate Ḥullin, ed. Y. ḲAFAḤ, Jerusalem, 5720.

PERUS RABENU NISSIM, to RIF (RAN to RIF), on some tractates, in the standard editions of RIF.

PERUṢ RAṢI (RASHI), Rashis' commentary to the Talmud, in all standard editions.

PISKEI HARIAZ, Vol. 1., Tractate Berakhot and Shabbat, Jerusalem, 1961.

PISQEI RAV MORDECAI, (Mordecai), with all standard editions of RIF.

RABENU AṢER, HALAKOT OF ROSH, (ROSH), in the standard editions of the Babylonian Talmud.

RABENU ḤANANEL (RḤ), commentary to some tractates of the Babylonian Talmud, in the standard editions.

RADICUM LIBER, R. Davidis Kimchi, ed. J. H. R. Biesenthal, *et.* F. Liebrecht, Berolini, 1847.

RASHI. See *Peruṣ Raṣi.*

REṢUYOT LEPARṢIYOT HATORAH, R. Hai Gaon, ed. Y. Ḥasidah, Jerusalem, 5737.

DIE RUNDREISE DES R. PETACHJAH AUS REGENSBURG, ed. L. Grünhut, Jerusalem, 1904.

SEDER R. AMRAM GAON (SRA), part 1 by D. Hedegärd, Lund, 1951, part 2 by T. Kronholm, Lund 1974. Pagination according to ed. D. Goldschmidt, Jerusalem, 1971.

SEDER TANNAIM WE-AMORAIM (STA), ed, A. Marx, Breslau, 5671, von K Kahan, Frankfurt, 1935.

SEFER DERASHOT AL HA-TORAH, R. Joshua b. Shueib, Jerusalem, 1969 (facsimile of Cracow, 1573).

SEFER HAMANHIG R. Abraham b. Nathan of Lunel, Jerusalem, 1978 (2 Vol.).

SEFER HAMENUHAH, R. Manoah of Narbonne, Jerusalem, 1970.

SEFER HAMISVOTH, Maimonides, glosses by Nahmanides, standard editions: critical text by Ch. Heller, Jerusalem-New York, 1946.

SEFER HANNER, Zekharya Agamati, ed. M. Ben-Shem, Jerusalem, 1958.

SEFER HA-QABBALAH, See: BOOK OF TRADITION.

SEFER HASTAROT, R. HAI GAON, ed. S. Assaf, Jerusalem, 5690.

SEFER RABIAH (RABIAH), von Rabbi Elieser ben Rabbi Joël ha-Levi, ed. V. Aptowitzer, Berlin-Jerusalem, 1913-38. On Tractates *Abodah Zarah* and *Hullin*, ed. D. Dablizky, Bnei Braq. 5736.

SEPHER ha-ITTIM (Itim), Judah b. Barzilai al-Bargeloni, Berlin (Cracow), 1902.

SEPHER ha-PARDES, attributed to RASHI, ed. H. L. Ehrenreich, Budapest, 5684.

SEPHER HASCHETAROTH, von R. Jehuda ben Barsilai *aus* Barcelona, von S. J. Halberstam, Berlin, 1898.

SEPHER HASCHORASCHIM, von Abulwalid Merwan ibn Ganâh, . . . von W. Bacher, Berlin, 1896.

SEPHER HAYASHAR by Rabbenu Tam, ed. S. Schlesinger, Jerusalem, 1959.

SHEELTOT de RAB AHAI GAON, ed., S. K. Mirsky, Jerusalem, 1959-77 (5 vol.).

SHIBOLEI HALEKET, R. Zidkeiah b. R. Abraham Harofe (SBHL), Venice 5306, part 2, ed. M. Hasidah, Jerusalem 5729 (photo of installments from *HASEGULAH* 5694-97), *Completum* ed. S. K. Mirsky, Brooklyn, 1966. References according to paragraphs in S. Buber, ed., Vilna 5647.

SIDDUR R. SAADJA GAON (SRSG), ed. I. Davidson, S. Assaf, B. I. Joel, Jerusalem, 1941.

SIFRAN SEL RISONIM, ed. S. Assaf, Jerusalem, 5695.

SIYATA Di SEMAYA, Jerusalem, 5730.

SAAREI SIMHAH (SS), R. Isaac b. Ghayyat, ed. I. Bamberger, Fuerth, 5621.

SILTEI HAGIBORIM, commentary to RIF, in standard editions.

SIRAT YISRAEL, Moses ibn Ezra, ed. B. Halper, Leipzig, 5684.

SITAH MEQUBEZET (STMQ), ed. R. B. Askenazy, to various tractates.   Standard editions.

S(H)ULHAN ARUK (SUA or SA), R. Joseph Qaro (The Code of Jewish Law par excellence). In four sections: 1. *Orah Hayim* (OH), on the daily commandments, prayers and benedictions, Sabbath and the festivals, etc. 2. *Yoreh Deah* (YOD) on prohibitions, dietary laws, usury, mourning, etc. 3. *Even Haèzer* (EHE) on personal law, marriage, divorce, dowry, etc. 4. *Hosen Mispat* (HOSM or HOM), on torts, civil and criminal law, judiciary process, etc. Published in the standard editions with the glosses of R. Moses Isserles (Poland d. 1572) and with various commentaries, e.g., *Siftei Kohen* (SAK), *Turei Zahav* (TAZ), *Biur Hagra* (BGR), *Sefer Meirat Áynayim* (SMA), *Magen Avraham* (MGA), etc. v. EJ 14:1475-76.

TAJNIS, Judah b. Balàm, ed. P. Kokovtsov, St. Petersburg, 1916. See, S. Abramson, in Bibliography, Section II.

TALMIDEI R. JONAH, (TRY), commentary to RIF, tractate Berakot, in standard editions.

TEMIM DEIM (TMI), ed. I. Malẓan, Warsaw, 5657.

TERUMOT, R. Samuel Hasardy, with *Gidulei Terumah* by A. Figo, Venice, 5403.

TOLDOT ADAM WEHAVAH ("Adam and Eve"), (R. YERUHAM), R. Yeruham (Jeroham) b. Mesulam, Venice, 5313.

TORAT HAÁDAM, NAHMANIDES, Venice, 5355.

TOSAFOT, in the standard editions of THE BABYLONIAN TALMUD.

TOSAFOT OF R. JUDAH, to TRACTATE *BERAKOT*, ed. N. Zaks, 2 vol., Jerusalem, 5729-32.

TOSAFOT, of R. PEREZ, to TRACTATE *BABA QAMA*, Leghorn, 5579.

TOSEFTA, with *Tosefta Ki-fshutah*, on orders: *Zeraim, Moed*, and *Nashim*, by S. Lieberman, New York, 1955-1973, 12 vol. *TOSEFTA*, ed. M. Zuckermandel, Pazevalk, 5641.

TRACTATE *ABODAH ZARAH* (AZA), Ms. Jewish Theological Seminary, New York, 1957.

TUREI ZAHAV, see *Sulhan Àruk*.

TURIM ("The Four Turim"), R. Jacob b. Aser, the standard editions with the standard commentaries, e.g., *Beit Joseph* (BY) by Joseph Qaro, *Darkei Moshe* by M. Isserles, *Bayit Hadas* by J. Sirkes. Pagination according to the Jerusalem facsimile (5717-5720) of the 5642 Warsaw edition.

WEHIZHIR, ed. I. M. Freiman, Leipzig, Warsaw, 5633-40. 2 vol.

YAD MALAKI Malaki b. Jacob Hakohen, Berlin, 5617.

II. Studies

Abramson, S., "A Fragment of the Arabic Original of *'HAMMIQAH VEHAMIMKAR'* of R. Hai Gaon," J. N. EPSTEIN JUBILEE VOLUME, Jerusalem, 1950, pp. 296-315.

_____, *BEMERKAZIM UBITFUZOT BITQUFAT HAGEONIM*, (BEMERKAZIM), Jerusalem, 1965.

_____, "B. M. Lewin, OTZAR ha-GEONIM. Vol. XII" (review), KIRJATH SEPHER XXI, 1944-45, pp. 238-42.

_____, *INYANOT BESIFRUT HAGEONIM* (INYANOT), Jerusalem, 1974.

_____, *"Inyanot Besifrut Hageonim,"* SINAI 54, 5724, pp. 20-32, 56, 5725, pp. 303-317.

_____, *KELALEI HATALMUD BEDIVREI HARAMBAN* (KELALEI), Jerusalem, 1971.

_____, "Maftehot Litsuvot Geonim," HARRY AUSTRYN WOLFSON JUBILEE VOLUME, Jerusalem, 1965, Hebrew Section, pp. 1-23.

_____, "Milon Hamishnah LeRav Saàdya Gaon," LESONENU 19 ("Qovez Meyuhad"), 5714, pp. 49-50.

_____, "Min Hapereq Hahamisi Sel MAVO HATALMUD LeRav Samuel b. Hofni," SINAI 88, pp. 193-218.

_____, "Min KITAB AL HAWI LeRav Hai Gaon, LESONENU 41, 5737, pp. 108-16.

_____, "Mitorat Rav Elhanan," SINAI 60 (5727), pp. 149-59.

_____, "Mitesuvot Hageonim," SINAI JUBILEE BOOK, Jerusalem, 5713, pp. 403-417.

_____, "On the ÀRUK of R. Natan," LESONENU, Vol. 36, pp. 122-49, Vol. 37, pp. 26-42.

_____, "Perus Qadmon Lemaseket Baba Batra," SINAI 25 (5709), pp. 259-71.

_____, "Perus Rabenu Hananel Lebaba Batra Pereq 2," SINAI Year 12 (5708), pp. 57-86.

_____, "R. Joseph Rosh ha Seder," KIRJATH SEPHER XXVI, 1949-50, pp. 72-95.

_____, R. NISSIM GAON LIBELLI QUINQUE (RNG), Hierosolymis, MCMLXV.

_____, "SEFER HaMASHKON Attributed to Rav Hai Gaon," TALPIOTH V, New York, January 1952, pp. 773-80.

_____, "SEFER HATAJNIS ('Hazimud') of R. Judah b. Balam," HENOCH YALON JUBILEE VOLUME, Jerusalem, 1963, pp. 51-149.

_____, TALMUD BABLI (Babylonian Talmud), TRACTATE BABA BATRA (BBA), translated and explained (ed. J. N. Epstein), Jerusalem, 1958.

_____, "Varia on Gaonic Literature," TARBIZ XVIII, 1947, pp. 202-06, XIX, 1948, pp. 192-97.

Allony, N., "Two Autograph Book Lists of R. Joseph Rosh-haseder," KIRJATH SEPHER XXXVIII, 1962-3, pp. 531-57.

Aptowitzer, V., INTRODUCTIO ad SEFER RABIAH, Jerusalem, 1938.

_____, "Responses Wrongly Attributed to R. Hai," TARBIZ 1, No. 4, July 1930, pp. 63-105.

As(s)af, S., "Àl Haqesarim Sel Yehudei Teiman Im Hamerkazim BeBabel UvErez Yisrael," FIRST WORLD CONGRESS OF JEWISH STUDIES, Vol. 1, Jerusalem, 5712, pp. 390-95.

_____, "Ancient Book Lists," KIRJATH SEPHER XVIII, 1941-42, pp. 272-81.

_____, "Codex of Commentaries on the Talmud and Alfasi," KIRJATH SEPHER XXIII, 1946-47, pp. 233-38.

_____, "Leheqer Sefarav Hahalakyim Sel Rav Hai Gaon," HAZOFEH 7, 5683, pp. 277-87.

_____, "Maftehot Litesubot Hageonim Hamuvaot BeSEFER Ha 'ITTUR' LeR. Isaac b. R. Aba Mari," HAZOFEH 6, 5682, pp. 289-309.

_____, "Mann, TEXTS AND STUDIES" (Review), TARBIZ 3, 1932, pp. 340-53.

_____, "Mehoraot Hageonim," AZKARAH (Rabbi A. I. Kook memorial volume). Jerusalem, 5698, Department 4, pp. 47-56.

_____, "PERUŞ RABENU HANANEL LEMASEKET ZEBAHIM, ed. I. Ben-Menahem" (Review), KIRJATH SEPHER XIX 1942-43, pp. 229-31.

_____, "PERUŞ ŞIŞAH SIDREI MISHNAH LERABEINU NATAN Áv HAYESHIVAH," KIRJATH SEPHER X 1933-4, pp. 381-88, 525-45.

_____, "SEFER HAHOB of R. Hai Gaon," TARBIZ XVII, 1945, pp. 28-31.

_____, "Seridim MiSEFER HADAYANIN LeRav Hai Gaon Z"L." HAZOFEH 9 5685, pp. 76-79.

_____, "S. Löwinger, 'Gaonic Interpretation of the Tractates Gittin and Qiddushin'," (Review), KIRJATH SEPHER XXIX 1953-54, pp. 64-65.

_____, TEQUFAT HAGEONIM WESIFRUTAH (TEQUFAT), Jerusalem, 5615.

Asulai, C. J. D., LITERARISCHES LEXICON, vol. 1, Krakau, 1905, vol. 2 SZEM HAGDOLIM HASZOLEM, Pyotrkow-Tryb, 1930.

Brody, H., "Religious and Laudatory Poems of R. Hayya Gaon," STUDIES OF THE RESEARCH INSTITUTE FOR HEBREW POETRY, Vol. III (Berlin, 1936), pp. 3-63.

Derenbourg, H. et Derenbourg, J., OPUSCULES ET TRAITES D'ABOU'L-WALID MERWAN IBN DJANAH [Rabbi Jonah] DE CORDOBA, Paris, 1880.

Efrat, I., "Rav Hai Gaon," HASCHILOAH XXX Odessa, 1914, pp. 50-55, 116-24, 425-38, 555-61.

ENCYCLOPEDIA JUDAICA (EJ), 16 volumes, Jerusalem, 1972.

ENCYCLOPEDIA TALMUDICA (ET), English version, vol. II, Jerusalem, 1974, p. 21, entry: "Eyn Halakah k'Thalmid bi Mkom ha Rab." Hebrew version, entries: "Halakah Kebatrai," "Halakah Kedivrei Hamakrià," Halakah Kistam Mishnah."

Epstein, A., MIQADMONIYOT HAYEHUDIM, Jerusalem, 5717.

Epstein, J. N., A GRAMMAR OF BABYLONIA ARAMAIC, Jerusalem, 1960.

_____, "DIE RECHTSGUTACHTEN DER GEONIM, ed. Cassel nach Cod. Berlin und Ms. Michael," JJLG 9, pp. 214-304.

_____, DER GAONÄISCHE KOMMENTAR ZUR ORDNUNG TOHOROTH (GKT), Einleitung, Berlin, 1915, (Text ed. Berlin, 1924).

_____, "Gaonic Halachoth," TARBIZ 10, 1938-39, pp. 119-34.

_____, "GINZE KEDEM, Volume 2" (Review), DEBIR 2, 5684.

_____, "Le Commentaire de Scherira sur BABA BATRA." REJ 64, pp. 210-14.

_____, "Lepeiruş Rav Hai Gaon Librakot," HAZOFEH 7, 5683, pp. 95-96.

_____, "Notes on Post-Talmudic-Aramaic Lexicography," JQR, NS 12, pp. 299-390.

_____, "On the Commentary of R. Sherira and R. Hai Gaon to BABA-BATHRA," TARBIZ, 5:1, 1933, pp. 45-49.

_____, "Remainders of She'ilthoth (I)," TARBIZ 6:4, 1935, pp. 460-97.

_____, "Taṣlum *PEIRUṢ HAGEONIM LETOHOROTH*," TARBIZ 16, 1944-5, pp. 71-134.

Feldblum, M. S., *DIKDUKE SOPHERIM*, Tractate Gittin, New York, 1966.

Fishman, J. L., " 'Haminhag' Besifrut Hageonim," *SEFER HAYOBEL LEDR. B. M. LEWIN*," Jerusalem, 5700, pp. 132-59.

_____, Editor, SINAI, Year 1, Vol. 2, 5698, (Qobeẓ Rav Hai Gaon), pp. 461-712.

Fleischer, E., "*Nosafot Lemoraṣto Hapaytanit Ṣel* Rav Hai Gaon," SINAI 67, 5730, pp. 180-98.

Ginzberg, L., *GEONICA*, New York, 1909.

Goitein, S. D. F., "A Colophon to R. Hai Gaon's Commentary to *Hagigah*," KIRJATH SEPHER 21, 1955-56, pp. 368-70.

Goodblatt, D., RABBINIC INSTRUCTION IN SASSANIAN BABYLONIA, Leiden, 1975.

Gotheil, R., "Tit-Bits from the Genizah," JEWISH STUDIES IN MEMORY OF ISRAEL ABRAHAMS," New York, 1927.

Groner, T., "Responsa by R. Sherira Gaon to Kairouan," ALEI SEFER 8, 1980, pp. 5-22.

_____, "The Original Form of Five *'Kuntresim'* of Geonic Responsa," ALEI SEFER 2, 1976, pp. 5-16.

Harkavy, A. E., "Hai, Rav," *OẒAR YISRAEL*, New York, 1910.

_____, *ḤADAṢIM GAM YEṢANIM*, Jerusalem, 5730.

_____, *STUDIEN U. MITTEILUNGEN*, 1, St. Petersburg, 1879.

Hildesheimer, E. E., *"Die Komposition der Sammlungen von Responsen der Gaonen"* (*Sonderabdruck aus: JUDISCHE STUDIEN*, Dr. Josef Wohlgemuth *Gewidmet*, pp. 172-272), Frankfurt am Main, 1928.

_____, *"Mystik und Agada im Urteile der Gaonen* R. Scherira *und* R. Hai" (*Sonderabdruck aus: "ZEITSCHRIFT FÜR JACOB ROSENHEIM"*, pp. 259-86), Frankfurt am Main, 1931.

Hirschberg, H. Z., A HISTORY OF THE JEWS IN NORTH AFRICA, 2 vol., Jerusalem, 1965.

Hyman, A., *TOLDOTH TANNAIM VE'AMORAIM* (TTA or TTV), 3 vol., London, 5670-71.

Jastrow, M., A DICTIONARY OF THE TARGUMIM, THE TALMUD BABLI AND YERUSHALMI, AND THE MIDRASHIC LITERATURE, Many editions.

Kahana, D., *"Zur Geschichte der Gaonen,"* HAKEDEM 3 1909, *(Hebr. abt.)*, pp. 115-128.

Kaplan, J., THE REDACTION OF THE BABYLONIAN TALMUD, New York, 1933.

Kasher, M. M., *HAGADAH SHELEMAH*, Third edition, Jerusalem, 1967.

_____, and Mandelbaum, J. B., *SAREI HA-ELEF*, First edition, New York, 1959, "New-Edition," 2 vol., Jerusalem, 1978.

Kook, S. H., *IYYUNIM UMEHQARIM*, 2 vol., Jerusalem, 5719-1963.

Lewin, B. M., *"MITEQUFAT HAGEONIM, RAV SERIRA GAON,"* Jaffa, 5677.

_____, *PROLEGOMENA ZU EINER NEUEN AUSGABE VOM SENDSCHREIBEN DES* RABBI SCHERIRA GAON, Frankfurt a. M. 1911.

Lieberman, S., *TOSEFET RISONIM* (TOSR), 4 vol., Jerusalem, 5697-99.

_____, *TOSEFTA KI-FSHUTAH*, See Bib. I.C. *TOSEFTA*.

Löw, I., *ARAMAEISCHE PFLANZENNAMEN*, Leipzig, 1881.

Malter, H., SAADIA GAON HIS LIFE AND WORKS, Philadelphia, 1942.

Mandelbaum, J. B. see Kasher

Mann, J., "Gaonic Studies," HEBREW UNION COLLEGE JUBILEE VOLUME (1875-1925), Cincinnati, 1925, pp. 223-62.

_____, TEXTS AND STUDIES IN JEWISH HISTORY AND LITERATURE, Vol. 1 (T & S), Cincinnati, 1931.

_____, THE JEWS IN EGYPT AND IN PALESTINE UNDER THE FATIMID CALIPHS (The Jews), 2 vol., London, 1969[2].

_____, THE RESPONSA OF THE BABYLONIAN GEONIM AS A SOURCE OF JEWISH HISTORY (Responsa), Tel Aviv, 1970.

Marmorstein, A., "Hai Gaon et les usages des Deux Ecoles," *REJ* 73, 97-100.

Morag, S., "On the Form and Etymology of Hai Gaon's Name," TARBIZ 31, pp. 188-90.

Müller, J., *EINLEITUNG IN DIE RESPONSEN DER BABYLONISCHEN GEONEN* (Einleitung), Berlin, 1891.

Neubauer, A., CATALOGUE OF THE HEBREW MANUSCRIPTS in the Bodleian library and in the college libraries of Oxford, Oxford, 1886-1906.

_____, MEDIEVAL JEWISH CHRONICLES AND CHRONOLOGICAL NOTES, 2 vol., Oxford, 1887-95.

Neusner, J., A HISTORY OF THE MISHNAIC LAW OF HOLY THINGS, Leiden, 1978-79.

_____, A HISTORY OF THE MISHNAIC LAW OF PURITIES, Leiden, 1974-77.

_____, FROM POLITICS TO PIETY, New York, 1979.[2]

Poznanski, S., "Ginzberg's 'GEONICA'," JQR NS 3, pp. 397-425.

Price, J., THE YEMENITE MS. OF MEGILLA, Toronto, 1916.

Rabbinovicz, R., *VARIAE LECTIONES* (VL), Munich-Mainz-Nurenburg, 1867-97.

Rapoport, S. L., "Toldot Rabenu Hai Gaon Weqorot Sefarav," BIKUREI HAITTIM, year 5590, pp. 79-95.

Sassoon, D. S., *OHEL DAWID*, London, 1932.

Schecter, S., SAADYANA, Cambridge, 1903.

Scholem, G., *CATALOGUS CODICUM CABBALISTICORUM HEBRAICORUM*, Hierosolymis, MCMXXX.

Soloveitchik H., "Pawnbroking: A study in *Ribbit* and of the *Halakah* in Exile" (Reprinted from PROCEEDINGS OF THE AMERICAN ACADEMY FOR JEWISH RESEARCH, Vols. 38-9, pp. 203-268), New York, 1972.

Sperber, D., "Patronage in Amoraic Palestine (c. 220-400): Causes and Effects," JOURNAL OF THE ECONOMIC AND SOCIAL HISTORY OF THE ORIENT, 14, part 3, 1971, pp. 227-52.

_____, ROMAN PALESTINE 200-400 MONEY AND PRICES, Ramat Gan, 1974.

Steinschneider, M., *DIE ARABISCHE LITERATUR DER JUDEN*, Frankfurt a. M., 1902.

_____, *"Schlachregeln in Arabische Sprache," JÜDISCHE ZEITSCHRIFT für WISSENSCHAFT und LEBEN* 1 (1862), pp. 232-43, 304-18, 2 (1863), pp. 76-80, 297-310, 3 (1864/5), pp. 305-6, 4 (1866), pp. 155-60.

Strack, H., INTRODUCTION TO THE TALMUD AND MIDRASH, Cleveland-New York-Philadelphia, 1963.[6/3]

Tavory, J., "Sources of the Geonic Responsa collection 'SHAÀREI-TESHUVAH'," ALEI SEFER 3, pp. 5-19.

Tchernowitz, C., *TOLEDOTH HA-POSKIM*, 3 vol., New York, 1946-47.

Tykocinski, H., THE GAONIC ORDINANCES, Jerusalem, 1959.

Weil, G., "Teṣuvato Ṣel Rav Hai Gaon [c]al Haqez Haqazuv Lahayim," *SEFER ASSAF*, Jerusalem, 5713.

Weiss, J. H., *ZUR GESCHICHTE DER JUDISCHEN TRADITION*, Wilna, 1910.[5]

Zucker, M., "Fragments of the *KITĀB TAḤṢĪL AL-SHARĀT ĀL-SAMĀI'YAH*," *TARBIZ* 41, 1971-72, pp. 373-410.

INDEX OF SOURCES AND STUDIES[*]

---

[*]Thanks to Ms. Yael Levine for her aid in indexing.

Der Gaonishe Kommentar zur Ordnung
Tohoroth,
    introduction p. 25/172

REJ   64 p. 210-212/132
       p. 210 f/133

Tarbiz   5 pp. 45-49/133

Fleischer E.
    Sinai 67, p. 180-198/14

Goitein S.D., Kirjath Sefer 31
    p. 68-70/133

Goodblatt David, Rabbinic Instruction in
Sasanian Babylonia, Leiden 1975/5

Groner Tsvi, Alei Sefer, 2/4.
    p. 5 f/119
    p. 7 f/119
    8 p. 15 f/139
    p. 16/139
    p. 17/139
    p. 21 n. 66/139
    p. 21 n. 68/139
    p. 21 n. 79/3
    Rav Hai Gaon His Halachic
    Methodology/137

Grunhut (editor), Rundreise Des R.
Petachyah
    p. 41, n. 71/133

Harkavy, Studien U. Mitteilungen
    1 p. 45 f/11, 132

Hasidah Y. Reshuyot Leparshiot Hatorah
    introduction p. 5/14

Hazan Israel Moshe, IYEY HAYAM to
Shaare Teshuvah
    65/131

Heschel A.J., Torah Min Ha Shamayim
Be Aspaklariyah Shel Ha Dorot
    Vol. 2/148

Hida, Szem Hagdolim
    124

Hildesheimer, "Komposition"
    p. 88/131
    p. 90/131

Hurvitz E. Hadarom
    46/133
    49/133

Hyman A., Toldoth Tannaim
VeAmoraim i
    89, b/139

Jastrow, M.,Dictionary Vol. 1
    p. 216/145

Judischer Zeitschrift
    2, p. 303-04/139

Kaplan Julius, The Redaction of the
Babylonian Talmud
    21, 22, 25/5

Kasher M., Hagadah Shelemah
    p. 94 and n. 36/133

Lewin B.M., Iggereth Rav Sherira Gaon
    supplements to/14

Metiboth
    p. 29/141

Otzar Ha Geonim, Jom Tow
    references to 39-49/135

Rav Serira, Mitqufat Hageonim
    32f/121-22

Lieberman Saul, Tosefet Risonim, iii,
    178/49

Lifschitz, J. Moriah 7a (5737)
    p. 3/120, 139
    8, pp. 4-5/139

Malter, Taanit
    p. 43, 1.7 f/71

Saadia
    p. 278/xi

Malachi b. Jacob Hacohen, Jad Malachi,
"Principles of the RIF"/124

Mann Jacob, The Jews in Egypt and in
Palestine under the Fatimid
    Caliphs, Volume 1 p. 40/132
    p. 67/132
    p. 107/132
    p. 115/132
    p. 119/132

The Responsa of the Babylonian Geonim
as a Source of Jewish History/14
    p. [3] f/11
    p. [7] f/132
    p. [13] f/11
    p. [17] /32
    p. [18]/132
    p. [54]/132
    p. [150]/132

Mann Jacob, Texts and Studies in Jewish
History and Literature
    Vol 1
    p. 68/133

BROWN JUDAIC STUDIES SERIES